AF556127

TAXMANN'S

INTERPRETATION OF TAXING STATUTES

TAXMANN®'S

Interpretation of Taxing Statutes

Dr. K. N. Chaturvedi
(LLM, Ph.D.)
Advocate, Supreme Court of India
Former Secretary, Legislative Department
Ministry of Law & Justice
Government of India

2nd Edition

Price : ₹ 895

Published by :
Taxmann Publications (P.) Ltd.

Sales & Marketing :
59/32, New Rohtak Road, New Delhi-110 005 India
Phone : +91-11-45562222
Website : www.taxmann.com
E-mail : sales@taxmann.com

Regd. Office :
21/35, West Punjabi Bagh, New Delhi-110 026 India

Printed at :
Tan Prints (India) Pvt. Ltd.
44 Km. Mile Stone, National Highway, Rohtak Road
Village Rohad, Distt. Jhajjar (Haryana) India
E-mail : sales@tanprints.com

About the Author

Dr. K.N. Chaturvedi served in academics and the Government of India for 35 years and has been in the legal profession for 15 years. His expertise is more prominent in Legislative drafting and legal interpretation. He handled complex legal issues of drafting in the government and challenging matters of legal interpretation as an advisor. Dr. Chaturvedi advised on complex tax issues.

He obtained a Master of Laws from the University of Allahabad and a Ph.D. from the Kurukshetra University with the topic "Taxation of Charitable Trust: Perspective and Proposals for Reform in Indian Law".

Chaturvedi worked as a reader in Taxation Law in the postgraduate department of Law at the University of Pune from 1984 to 1988. In 1988 he joined the Indian legal service and supervised the drafting of the finance bills from 1995- 2007. He served as Member Secretary of the Law Commission of India (October 2003 to March 2006) and thereafter Secretary Legislative Department, Ministry of Law and Justice, Government of India from April 2006 to December 2007.

Dr. Chaturvedi's first book titled "Income Tax Law: A Critical Analysis" was published by the Law Book Company, Allahabad. Dr. Chaturvedi's most recent book is titled "Modern Statutory Interpretation: Legislative Process and Principles of Statutory Interpretation" published in 2022 by the Eastern Law House, Kolkata.

Dr. Chaturvedi can be reached by email at chaturvedi.kn@gmail.com.

Preface to the Second Edition

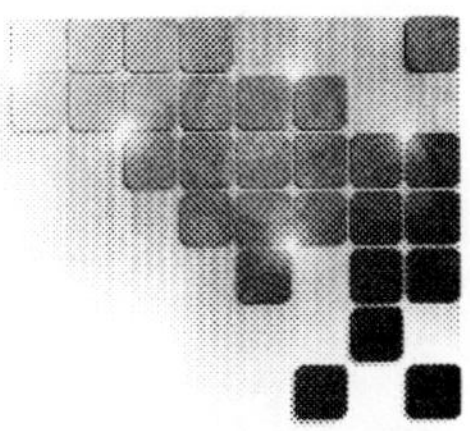

Since the publication of the book "Interpretation of Taxing Statutes" in 2008, there have been developments, both in India and abroad, in tax policies and approaches to tax interpretation. The GST regime implemented in 2017 is now firmly settled in India. The GST regime is unique as it is about One-Nation-One -Tax and One-Market.

In the field of direct taxes, the introduction of GAAR and MLI aligns the Indian tax laws with global developments. In recent years, the Supreme Court of India has given judgments on many important areas of the Income-tax Act,1961. These judicial decisions have been discussed in various chapters of the book. Some of them are fees vs. tax, exemptions from tax, and deductions. Supreme Court discussed the social purpose of law in Apex Laboratories. Further, the Supreme Court adopted strict construction in tax exemption cases.

The scheme of the book is the same as in the year 2008. The changes made in the second edition are as under—

(*a*) New chapters on Tax exemptions and DTAA have been added.

(*b*) In chapter Four, recent judgments on classification under the Customs Tariff Act have been added.

(*c*) The last chapter of the book is on simplification and Rationalisation of the Direct Taxes.

Recently, the Provisional Collection of Taxes Act, 2023 has been enacted. This Act replaces the Provisional Collection of Taxes Act, 1931.

It is hoped that the book will be useful to tax practitioners, lawyers, judges, academicians, and policymakers.

March 2024 **K.N. Chaturvedi**

Preface to the First Edition

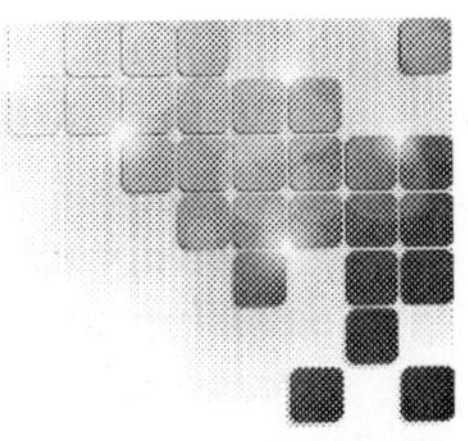

We live in an age of legislation, and most new law is statutory law. Law is doing of a purposive activity which aims at continuous striving to solve the basic problems of social living. The work of a judge is the interpretation of text produced by a democratic institution. No approach to interpretation is self-justifying and there is no good general theory of how to interpret texts. Debates over interpretation are institutional - raise issues about who should make what sorts of decisions and about minimizing the discretion of the various institutions. Any approach requires a justification and depends on judgments and commitments that are independent of texts themselves.

Finding fault with the products of the drafters art is often seen in the judicial pronouncements. Two illustrations from the House of Lords are Mirvahedy and Inco Europe v. First Choice. *In* Mirvahedy *the question for the Court was whether strict liability applied when a horse ran out of its field and unto main road and damaged a car. The provision in issue was section 2 of the Animals Act, 1971. Lord Nicholls said :*

> *"Unfortunately, the language of section 2(2) of the Animals Act,1971 is itself opaque. The draftsman zeal for brevity has led to obscurity. Section 2(2) has attracted much judicial obloquy."*

In Roe *v.* Russell *[1928] 2 KB 117 at 130 Scrutton LJ lamented that he could not order costs to be paid by the draughtsmen of the Rent Restrictions Acts, and the members of the Legislature who passed them, whom he considered responsible for the obscurity of the legislation.*

The judiciary soon found that they could not interpret the Rent Acts in the same way as ordinary legislation. Sir Robert Megarry's great work on the Acts, first published in 1939, contains in its (1988) edition, at pages 14 to 18, an anthology of judicial comments on the peculiar difficulties of construction to which they have given rise. They include the observations that the Acts had "not been framed with any scientific accuracy of language". Sargant L.J. in Roe *v.* Russell *[1928] 2 K.B. 117, 138 said that it was essential "that, wherever possible, [they] should be construed in a broad, practical, commonsense manner so as to effect the intention of the Legislature"* McCardie J. in Read *v.* Goater *[1921] 1 K.B. 611, 615.*

In the Indian Chamber of Commerce *(1976) 1 SCC 324, while determining the meaning of the expression "charitable purpose" under section 2(15) of the Income-tax Act, 1961. Justice Krishna Iyer observed:*

> *". . .we appreciate the involved language we use, but when legislative draftsmanship declines to be simple, interpretative complexity becomes a judicial necessity."*

Should the laws be written in plain English?

Fransis Bennion, an authority on statutory interpretation in his forward to the Irish Statute Book : A Guide to Irish Legislation by Brian Hunt (First Law Limited, Dublin 2007) has remarked:

> *"Some reformers think all would be well if the mass of current laws were replaced by something to similar effect written in plain English, so that every ordinary citizen could understand it. That persistent notion is fallacious (and here I can put down one certain pointer amid all the confusion). Ordinary citizens should be discouraged from trying to understand raw legislation. Why? Because it may cause them harm to attempt it. They may think they understand a vital law and act on that belief. Their belief is likely to be mistaken, and that might lead them into harm.*
>
> *The citizen needs, and the state must provide, adequate information, in lay terms, about what the law enacts. The citizen must not be encouraged to go direct to an Act of Parliament for information because, as I have said, no Act is complete in itself. It must be read in context, and the context for every Act is the whole of the law. An individual Act is the single part that must fit into the mechanism of the Swiss watch and assist its efficient working. It is the legal experts who know about that - or should do."*

In the Newsletter of CALC (October 2003), commenting upon the consistent pattern of criticism by the House of Lords, the following response from a drafter is quoted:

"How nice to be a learned judge,
Who never writes a law.
He sits all dressed up every day
And feels quite free to pour
The greatest scorn upon the work
of those who drafts the Bill.
He thinks it fun to say that their
Mistakes causes all ills
That make the people go to law.
But he should never smirk
The drafter fault are just the things
That keep the courts at work."

The truth of the matter is that judicial interpretation is evolving. The three rules - literal rule, golden rule and mischief rule are no longer sole guiding factor in statutory interpretation. The plain meaning approach, words in total context approach and purposive approach are gaining acceptability. The 'interpretation' covers not merely the general approach to the problem but also the question of what materials (written or other) outside the statute itself may legitimately be used for the purpose of ascertaining the intent of the Legislature. It is believed that the great majority of legal disputes centre around the interpretation and operation of statutes.

In his 1983 Hamlyn lectures, the British Legal System Today, Lord Hailsham stated that nine-tenths of all cases heard by the Court of Appeal or the House of Lords either turn upon or involve the meaning of words contained in primary or secondary legislation.

In common law countries the desirability of a more flexible rule for the interpretation and construction of statutes and for a departure from what is at present largely a purely literal interpretation is quite evident.

The leading theories of interpretation may be broadly divided into four categories : intentional, purposive, textual and dynamic. The Anglo-American legal tradition emphasizes intentionalism. Intentionalists view statutory interpretation as an exercise in finding out the Legislature's intent. When a statute is applied to a particular set of facts, the judge should ask "How would the Legislature have wanted this case decided?" Statutory text seems to make a good starting point but it need not be the end point: legislative history (which includes committee reports, speeches, and the like) may also be consulted. Otherwise, the judge may interpret the statute in such manner so as to achieve the general intent it embodies, which is called "purposivism".

The "legal process method" of Professors Henry Hart and Albert Sacks, purposive interpretation is an endeavour to integrate the law coherently and harmoniously into the legal system as a whole. Textualists, on the other hand, are concerned not with the Legislature's actual or imagined intent, but with the "plain meaning" of the statutory text. Textualism is in the present times most prominently and forcefully advocated by Justice Antonin Scalia. The dynamic interpretation suggests that statutory interpretation should be a search for best answers.

In Chapter 5 of the book the different approaches of statutory interpretation in common law countries namely United Kingdom; Canada; Australia; United States of America and India have been discussed. It may be mentioned here that the highest Court in Australia is the High Court of Commonwealth of Australia.

Chapter 1 is devoted to the Tax System in India, both at federal level and State level. Chapter 2 deals with the Constitutional Scheme relating to taxation; Chapter 3 traces the law-making process particularly of taxing statutes and the use of law Commissions' Report; Select Committees' Reports, etc., as aid to statutory interpretation. Chapter 4 contains Structure of an Act and the relevance of various parts of the statute in statutory interpretation.

Chapter 6 analyses numbers of additional aids which the courts may take help in interpretating statutes. These are general presumptions; maxims and internal and extrinsic aids to interpretation. Chapter 7 on Tax Evasion, Tax Avoidance and Tax Mitigation is important both for the taxpayers and the policy makers. There is growing acceptance to the general anti-tax avoidance provisions as they are found in Canada and Australia. A more detailed study and a debate is needed for its adoption in India. An issue of utmost urgency is part of Chapter 8, that is, the need of updating the General Clauses Act, 1897. In the appendix the Interpretation Acts of, i.e., *the Interpretation Act, 1901 (Australia) as amended in 1984; the Interpretation Act, 1999 (New Zealand) and the Irish Interpretation Act, 2005 have been appended.*

The book is intended for tax practitioners, lawyers, judges, academicians and the policy-makers. It is hoped that the book will be useful to all concerned.

New Delhi

September 1, 2008 **K.N. Chaturvedi**

Chapter-heads

APPENDICES

Contents

3

VARIOUS STAGES OF LAW-MAKING AND THEIR RELEVANCE AS AN AID TO INTERPRETATION

4

STRUCTURE OF A TAXING STATUTE

5

TAX INTERPRETATION OF EXEMPTION PROVISIONS

PAGE

6
DTAA AND INTERNATIONAL TAXATION

7
DIFFERENT APPROACHES TO INTERPRETATION

8
TAX EVASION, TAX AVOIDANCE AND TAX MITIGATION

PAGE

9

AIDS TO INTERPRETATION

10

SIMPLIFICATION AND RATIONALISATION OF DIRECT TAXES

APPENDICES

List of Cases

A. Nag...

Aashirwad...

Abdul...

Abhiram...

Additional...
Cloth M...

Addy v...

ADIT...
com 24...

Abraham...

Admini...
1992 SC...

Agassi...

Airtours...
Majesty...

Ajmera...
2010 (8)...

Ajay Kr...

Alcan (NJ)...
(2009) 2...

All India...
7 SCC 5...

Aluminium...
1975 SC...

List of Cases

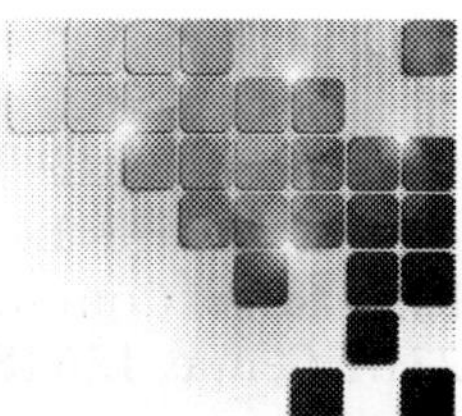

PAGE NOS.

A

B

C

PAGE NOS.

D

E

PAGE NOS.

J

K

L

M

PAGE NOS.

N

O

PAGE NOS.

P

PAGE NOS.

R

S

PAGE NOS.

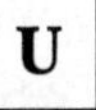

1 Tax system in India

1.1 The rule of law and good governance

Justice Krishna Iyer in Aluminium Corporation of India[1] observed that the rule of law is the cornerstone of democracy and how can there be a rule of law society, if the members, the bulk of whom are too poor to buy legal services, cannot decode legislator's law and therefore obey it? There is hardly any part of our national life or personal life that is not affected by one statute or other. The affairs of local authorities, nationalised industries, public corporations, and private commerce are regulated by legislation. The life of ordinary citizen is affected by various provisions of the statute book from cradle to grave. Incomprehensible law annoys the administrator and estranges the citizen at a time when quick justice and less sterile litigation are the desiderata. The command of law can claim the allegiance of the law by simplicity in legislation.

The above observations made by Justice Krishna Iyer in Aluminium Corporation of India Limited v. Union of India in the context of exemption notification issued under the Central Excise Act still hold good. In fact, in a taxing statute, it is often repeated that there must be simplicity or easy comprehensibility in drafting legislation including rules and notifications affecting the people.

1.2 The rule of law and good administration

Very recently, CJI Dr. D.Y. Chandrachud, in an epoch-making judgment observed that good administration requires public authorities to act in a predicable manner and honour the promises made or practices established unless there is a good reason not to do so. In a constitutional system rooted in the rule of law, the discretion available with public authorities is confined within clearly defined limits. The primary principle underpinning the concept of rule of law is consistency and predictability in decision-making.[2]

1.3 Statutory interpretation is a difficult task

The task of statutory interpretation is not a mechanical task. It is more than a mere reading of mathematical formulae because few words possess the

1. *Aluminium Corporation of India Limited* v. *Union of India* AIR 1975 SC 2279 at p 2284.
2. *Sivanandan C T* v. *High Court of Kerala* [Writ Petition (Civil) No. 229 of 2017 paras 38 and 42 (a Constitution Bench Decision of Five Judges dated 12 July, 2023)]/[2023 INSC 709].

precision of mathematical symbols. It is an attempt to discover the intention of the legislature from the language used by it and it must always be remembered that language is at best an imperfect instrument for the expression of human thought. As pointed out by Lord Denning it would be idle to expect every statutory provision to be drafted with divine prescience and perfect clarity[3]. With fiscal legislation or taxing statutes, the task of statutory interpretation becomes more difficult.

1.4 Complexity of taxation statute

Taxation is a statutory field. No tax can be levied and collected except according to the authority of law. There is fiscal legislation every year much of it prepared in great secrecy and under severe pressure of time, and it directly affects most people. This legislation is complicated and elaborate because of the intricate prepositions it has to express, and the variety of circumstances and conditions in which it falls to be applied, and the refined distinctions it embodies in order to attempt to cater expressly for them. Consequently, the body of tax statute used as a whole is voluminous and complex in structure as well as in concept and expression[4]. There is another reason for the fiscal legislation being complex and complicated. In fact, taxes are as complex as life. The moralist calls for just taxes, but taxes cannot (be based on morality) if we recall the scheme of special bearer bonds for mopping up black money. The administrator asks for simple taxes, but experience shows that they cannot simply be simple. The businessman demands practical taxes, but financial history proves that it is impracticable to make them practical.

A complex tax system is often viewed as a threat to a country's global competitiveness. The "tax complexity" arises from the difficulty of reading, understanding, and complying with the tax code (tax code complexity), and from the tax framework complexity. About the tax complexity of Canada, Susann Sturm[4a] states-

> "Canada has a higher level of tax code complexity and a lower level of tax framework complexity. A closer look at the dimensions of tax code and tax framework complexity reveals that in the Canadian tax code, the most complex laws are those on corporate reorganization, transfer pricing, and controlled foreign corporations, while in the tax framework, the most complex areas are tax audits, tax-law enactment, and tax guidance."

Individuals and businesses face compliance costs. The government bears enormous costs on enforcement and tax collection (administrative costs). There is an urgent need to collect data on the tax complexity which will help the policy makers in devising appropriate policies.

---

3. *K.P. Verghese* v. *ITO* AIR 1981 SC 1922, 1927.
4. The Preparation of Legislation Cmnd 6053 (May, 1975) p. 110.

4a. Susann Sturm. Income Tax Complexity Faced by Multinational Corporations: A Comparative Study of Canada, the United States, and Other Selected OECD Countries, Canadian Tax Journal Volume 69 Issue 3 (2021).

1.5 Tax systems in India

The tax system of British India reflected the characteristics of a traditional agricultural economy. Revenues of the central government were dominated by custom duties as domestic requirements for manufactured goods were met mostly from imports, chiefly from Britain and other Commonwealth countries. Import duties were levied on almost all items of import whereas major items subject to export duties were jute and tea in which India enjoyed a near monopoly in the world market. Various customs and tariff enactments were passed from time to time mainly, the Sea Customs Act, 1878 and the Tariff Act, 1934. After independence, the Sea Customs Act and other allied legislation were replaced by consolidating and amending legislation titled the Customs Act, 1962. Similarly, the Tariff Act, 1934 was repealed and re-enacted by the Customs Tariff Act, 1975[5].

Excise taxation dates back to 1894 when for the first time duty at the rate of 5% at valorum was imposed on cotton yarn of more than twenty counts. Excise at the rate of six annas per Imperial gallon was imposed on the motor spirit in 1917 and on kerosene at the rate of one anna per imperial gallon in 1922. In 1934, excise duties were imposed on Sugar, matches, and steel ingots. Duties were imposed on tyre in 1941 and on vegetable products and tobacco in 1943 and on coffee, tea, and betel nuts in 1944. Cigarettes came within the excise net in 1948 and mill-made cotton clothes in 1949. Before 1944, excise duties were levied under 16 separate enactments and the Central Excise and Salt Act, 1944 repealed old laws[5].

Under the Central Excises and Salt Act, 1944 (now in Central Excises Act, 1944) the tariff items were 11 in number and they were arranged in alphabetical order. In 1960, the number of tariff items increased to 30 and they were arranged in accordance with the sections of the standard international trade classification. The excise schedule increased to 137 tariff items in 1986 and including the sub-items their number was well over 355. The description of tariff commodities was based on the definition of the International Standard Institution, and the description and explanatory notes of the Customs Co-operation Council nomenclature.

The Central Excise Tariff Act, 1985 is based on an internationally accepted harmonized commodity description and coding system (HSN). The schedule of the Central Excise Tariff Act, 1985 describes the excisable commodities and the rate of duty leviable thereon. There are 91 chapters having 700 four-digit headings and 1400 six-digit headings.

The main features of the Act are—

(*a*) Central Excise Tariff has been made more detailed and comprehensive after taking into account all technical and legal aspects;

---

5. M.M. Sury, Fiscal Developments in India (1947 to 2007) India Tax Foundation at pp 93-94.

(*b*) It is based on the system of classification derived from the international convention of harmonised community description and Coding system (HSN) with such contractions or modifications as are necessary to fall within the scope of levy of central excise duty;

(*c*) Goods of same class have been grouped together to enable parity in treatment;

(*d*) It contains section/chapter notes giving detailed explanations as to the scope and ambit of the respective section/chapter;

(*e*) Special provision has been incorporated in their respective chapters in relation to the goods which pose problems in the matter of levy of excise duty;

(*f*) General residuary tariff item 68 has been dispensed with and instead residuary items have been provided separately for each class of goods under each chapter;

(*g*) Interpretative rules have also been provided to serve as a statutory guideline for interpreting the tariff schedule.

In M/s Ballarpur Industries Ltd.[6], it was observed that the Tribunal has not looked into the merits of the appeals at all on the facetious ground that the show cause notice did not contain any basis to doubt the classification of the goods and that while issuing the notice, the adjudicating authority had not examined the classification based on the report of the laboratory. The findings of the Tribunal are contrary to the record and cannot therefore be sustained.

Under the Central Excise Law MODVAT scheme was introduced which aimed at avoiding the cascading effect of duties on a product. In the year 2000, the MODVAT Rules were replaced by CENVAT Rules. MODVAT is basically duty-collecting procedure which aims at allowing relief to a manufacturer on the duty element borne by him with respect to inputs used by him.[7]

Section 174 of the CGST Act, 2017 now repeals the Central Excise Act, 1944 (except as respects goods included in entry 84 of the Union List of the Seventh Schedule to the Constitution), the Medicinal and Toilet Preparations (Excise Duties) Act, 1955, the Additional Duties of Excise (Goods of Special Importance) Act, 1957, the Additional Duties of Excise (Textiles and Textile Articles) Act, 1978, and the Central Excise Tariff Act, 1985.

Central Excise duty is continued to be levied on five Petroleum products as these products are out of GST at present, and will be brought under GST later. Tobacco products are subject to Central Excise and GST both.

The Customs Act, 1962 is an Act to consolidate and amend the law relating to Customs. The object of the Act is to regulate the import and export of goods, into and from the shores of India, or otherwise, and determine the customs duty

---

6. *Commissioner of Customs, Pune* v. *Ballarpur Industries Ltd.* [Civil Appeal Nos. 5644-5645 of 2021 decided on September 21, 2021] by a bench of three judges.

7. *Ichalkaranji Machine Centre (P.) Ltd.* v. *Collector of Central Excise* (2005) 1 SCC 465/[2004] 2004 taxmann.com 216 (SC).

payable. It also attempts to fill the lacunae of the previous customs legislations, viz., the Sea Customs Act and the Land Customs Act. It also aims to counter the difficulties that have emerged over the years due to the changing economic and financial conditions; amongst them, it proposes to tackle the increasing problems of smuggling both in and out of the country. The Act aims to sternly and expeditiously deal with smuggled goods, and curb the dents on the revenue thus caused. In order to deal with the menace of smuggling, the authorities are enabled to detect, conduct search and seizure, and if necessary, confiscate such smuggled goods, within the territory of India[8].

Dutiable goods are goods whose import is permitted by the Act or any other law in force. Duty is the tax leviable on the goods occasioned by their import into India or their export out of India. Other duties leviable are additional duty equal to excise duty, sales tax, etc., special additional duty, preferential area duty, protective duties, safeguard duties, countervailing duties, and anti-dumping duties .

Anti-dumping duty - Dumping is a well-known method of competition which is adopted by foreign companies. This is done by selling goods at a very low price for some time so that the domestic industries cannot compete and are thereby destroyed and after such destruction has taken place prices are again raised. Anti-dumping measures are permitted to ensure fair competition. The anti-dumping legislation is meant to protect domestic industries as a whole against the unfair practice of dumping. In *Reliance Industries* v. *Designated Authority*,[9] the Supreme Court observed that anti-dumping law is a salutary measure which prevents the destruction of our industry.[10] The purpose behind the imposition of the duty is to curb unfair trade practices resorted to by exporters of a particular country of flooding the domestic markets with goods at rates which are lower than the rate at which the exporters normally sell the same or like goods in their own countries so as to cause or be likely to cause injury to the domestic market[11]. In *Kumho Petrochemicals*[12] it was noticed that India as a signatory to GATT and the Marrakesh Agreement, the Anti-Dumping Rules (ADA) are to be assimilated into domestic laws.

Anti-dumping duty was introduced as section 9A of the Customs Tariff Act, 1975 by the Customs Tariff (Amendment) Act, 1982. Section 9A was substituted by the Customs Tariff (Amendment) Act, 1995 with effect from 1st January, 1995. In section 9A sub-section (8) was inserted by the Finance Act, 2000 that Act also inserted a new section 9AA. Sub-section (1) of section 9A was amended by the Finance Act, 2004. The provisions of the Customs Act would be applicable relating to the rate for determination of the rate of duty, non-levy, short levy, refunds, interest, appeals, offences, and penalties in respect of anti-dumping

8. *Commissioner of Customs* v. *M. Ambalal & Co.* (2011) 2 SCC 74.
9. (2006) 10 SCC 368.
10. See also, *Designate Authority* v. *Halder Topose* (2006) 6 SCC 626; *Sterlite Industries (India) Ltd.* v. *Designated Authority* (2006)10 SCC 386/[2003] 2003 taxmann.com 29 (SC).
11. *S&S Enterprise* v. *Designated Authority* (2005) 3 SCC 337/[2005] 2005 taxmann.com 750 (SC).
12. *Union of India* v. *Kumho Petrochemicals Company Ltd.* (2017) 8 SCC 307/[2017] 83 taxmann.com 149/63 GST 311 (SC).

duty. Section 9C of the Customs Tariff Act provides for an appeal to the Customs, Excise and Service Tax Appellate Tribunal (CESTAT) against an order "of determination or review thereof regarding the existence, degree and effect of any subsidy or dumping in relation to import of any article." Judicial review is to be exercised in a circumspect manner, especially where final findings are rendered by the DA[13]. In M/s the Andhra Petrochemicals Limited, the decision of the High Court was set aside[14].

1.6 Service tax

Tax Reforms Committee headed by Dr. Raja Chelliah suggested a levy of service tax. Service Tax is a VAT which in turn is a destination-based consumption tax. Just as excise duty is a tax on value addition of goods, Service Tax is on value addition by rendition of services. Broadly, services fall into two categories *i.e.*, property-based services and performance-based services.

The Supreme Court in the All-India Federation of Tax Practitioners case[15] held:-

> "Service tax is on performance-based services itself. It is on professional advice, tax planning, auditing, costing, etc. Parliament has legislative competence to levy service tax by way of the Finance Act, 1994. By the Finance (No. 2) Act, 1998 Chartered Accountants, Cost Accountants, and Architects were brought within the ambit of service tax. Parliament's legislative competence is derived from entry 97 of List 1. This position stands fortified by the Constitution (Eighty-eight Amendment) Act, 2003 which inserted article 268A and entry 92C in List I which clearly indicates that entry 60 of List II of the seventh schedule of the Constitution and entry 92C of List I operate in a different sphere." (See also *T.N. Kalyan Mandapam* (2004) 5 SCC 632).

An integrated structure of the service tax was built up by amending the Constitution and by enacting four Acts by the Parliament. The Constitution (One Hundred and First Amendment) Act, 2016 inserted new articles 246A, 269A, and 279A and amended some other articles of the Constitution. By the Constitution Amendment Act entries of the seventh schedule to the Constitution were also amended. In the Union list, entry 84 was substituted and in the State List entries 52 and 55 have been omitted, entries 54 and 62 have been substituted. The Parliament enacted the Central Goods and Services Tax Act, 2017, and the Integrated Goods and Services Tax Act, 2017. The States also enacted their Goods and Services Tax Acts, respectively for their States by notification. Thus, GST Law comprises of (*i*) Central Goods and Services Tax Act, 2017 including Central Goods and Services Tax (Extension to Jammu and Kashmir) Act, 2017, (*ii*) State Goods and Services Tax Act, 2017 as notified by respective States, (*iii*)

---

13. *Designated Authority* v. *Sandik International* (2018) 13 SCC 402; *Association of Synthetic Fibre Industries* v. *Apollo Tyres Ltd.* (2010) 13 SCC 733.
14. *Designated Authority* v. *Andhra Petrochemicals Limited* [Civil Appeal No(s). 3046-3048 of 2020 three bench decision dated September 1, 2020].
15. *All India Federation of Tax Practitioners* v. *Union of India* (2007) 7 SCC 527/[2008] 2008 taxmann.com 1072 (SC).

Union Territory Goods and Services Tax Act, 2017, (*iv*) Integrated Goods and Services Tax Act, 2017 including Integrated Goods and Services Tax (Extension to Jammu and Kashmir) Act, 2017 (*v*) Goods and Services Tax (Compensation to States) Act, 2017 and (*vi*) Rules, Notifications, Amendments and Circulars issued under the respective Acts.

Goods and Service Tax

The salient features of the GST are as follows: —

(*a*) subsuming of various Central indirect taxes and levies such as Central Excise Duty, Additional Excise Duties, Excise Duty levied under the Medicinal and Toilet Preparations (Excise Duties) Act, 1955, Service Tax, Additional Customs Duty commonly known as Countervailing Duty, Special Additional Duty of Customs, and Central Surcharges and Cesses so far as they relate to the supply of goods and services. "Supplies" would constitute both "sale" as well as "consignment" transactions;

(*b*) subsuming of State Value Added Tax/Sales Tax, Entertainment Tax (other than the tax levied by the local bodies), Central Sales Tax (levied by the Centre and collected by the States), Octroi and Entry tax, Purchase Tax, Luxury tax, Taxes on lottery, betting, and gambling; and State cesses and surcharges insofar as they relate to supply of goods and services;

(*c*) dispensing with the concept of 'declared goods of special importance' under the Constitution;

(*d*) levy of Integrated Goods and Services Tax on inter-state transactions of goods and services;

(*e*) levy of an additional tax on the supply of goods, not exceeding one per cent in the course of inter-State trade or commerce to be collected by the Government of India for a period of two years, and assigned to the States from where the supply originates;

(*f*) conferring concurrent power upon Parliament and the State Legislatures to make laws governing goods and services tax;

(*g*) coverage of all goods and services, except alcoholic liquor for human consumption, for the levy of goods and services tax. In the case of petroleum and petroleum products, it has been provided that these goods shall not be subject to the levy of Goods and Services Tax till a date notified on the recommendation of the Goods and Services Tax Council;

(*h*) compensation to the States for loss of revenue arising on account of implementation of the Goods and Services Tax for a period which may extend to five years;

(*i*) creation of a Goods and Services Tax Council to examine issues relating to goods and services tax and make recommendations to the Union and the States on parameters like rates, exemption list, and threshold limits.

The Council performs its functions under the Chairmanship of the Union Finance Minister and have the Union Minister of State in charge of Revenue or Finance as a member, along with the Minister in charge of Finance or Taxation or any other Minister nominated by each State Government. Every decision of the Council to be taken by a majority of not less than three-fourths of the weighted votes of the members present and voting in accordance with the following principles: — (A) the vote of the Central Government shall have a weightage of one-third of the total votes cast, and (B) the votes of all the State Governments taken together shall have a weightage of two-thirds of the total votes cast in that meeting.

GST is a tax on the supply of goods and services. The expression 'goods' has been given a meaning in the taxation laws different from its ordinary meaning under the Sales of Goods Act, 1930. **Under the Constitution**, the expression 'services' means anything other than goods. The term 'supply' includes both sales and consignments. While "sale" is for consideration, "consignments" are in the nature of branch transfers. The input tax credit is available for GST paid on both sales as well as consignments in the course of inter-State trade. Thus, GST is a consumption-based tax *i.e.*, tax is payable in the state where goods or services or both are finally consumed. The Central Goods and Services Tax is payable to the Central Government on the supply of goods and services within the state or union territory, as the case may be. The State Goods and Services Tax (SGST) is payable to the State Government on the supply of goods and services within the state. For the Union territories, the Union Territory Goods and Services Tax (UTGST) is payable to the Union Territory Government on the supply of goods and services within the Union territory. The Integrated Goods and Services Tax (IGST) is payable in the case of inter-State supply of goods and services, IGST is levied by the Government of India. On imports of goods or services in India, equivalent IGST is also levied on imports into India. IGST is apportioned between the Union and the States in the manner as may be provided by Parliament by law on the recommendations of the Goods and Services Tax Council. In addition to GST, a cess named GST Compensation Cess is levied on some goods *i.e.*, Tobacco products, Coal, Aerated water, Motor cars, etc. The rates of GST are changed as recommended by the GST Council depending on various factors such as economic conditions, revenue buoyancy, etc.

1.7 Income tax

The first Income Tax Act on a regular basis was introduced in 1886. Since then, it has remained in the statute book meeting the requirements of the state in times of peace and war. Now in a welfare state, the income tax law besides raising revenue for the government also aims at meeting socio-economic objectives. The present Income-tax Act, 1961 was enacted following the recommendations of the Law Commission of India in its 12th report. The provisions of the Income-tax Act have been the subject matter of conflicting interpretation by the taxpayer on the one hand and the revenue on the other. This has led to the mass of case law from the superior courts. On some occasions the Parliament has made amendments to the Act still there remain areas where the case law reigns supreme. Such areas are the distinction between revenue and capital that is whether the receipt is revenue or capital and whether the expenditure is capital or revenue in nature.

Broad features of the Act - Under the Income-tax Act there are three stages in the imposition of the tax.

Firstly, there is a declaration of liability on the basis of charge which determines the person in respect for whom the liability is to be determined.

Secondly, the stage of assessment. The assessment particularizes the exact sum which is payable. This also includes the relief by way of exemptions and deductions which are available to a taxpayer.

Thirdly, the stage of collection and recovery of the tax. The Act also contains incidental provisions to prevent tax avoidance and prevention of tax evasion.

As regards first, it is the taxpayer or an assessee who is either a resident or a non-resident. Tax liability is to be determined for each year separately and the basis on which the total income of such person is to be determined is known as the previous year. The period in which the assessment is to be made is known as the assessment year. The tax rates are to be prescribed in the Finance Act, which accompanies the budget each year.

The second stage is of assessment. A procedure of assessment commences with the filing of a return by the assessee. An assessment particularizes the exact sum payable or refundable. There are various types of assessment such as self-assessment, provisional assessment; regular assessment; best judgment assessment, and reassessment. An aggrieved person has remedies in the form of appeal and revision.

The third stage includes payment of advance tax, deduction of tax, and collection of tax. The Act also has elaborate procedures for the recovery of tax.

1.8 Other taxes

After independence following Acts were enacted:

(*a*) The Taxation Laws (Extension to Jammu and Kashmir) Act, 1954 and the Taxation Laws (Extension to Jammu and Kashmir) Act, 1972.

(*b*) Terminal Tax on Railway Passenger Act, 1956.

(*c*) Wealth Tax Act, 1957; Gift Tax Act, 1958; the Voluntary Surrender of Salary (Exemption from Income Tax) Act, 1961; the Compulsory Deposit Scheme Act, 1963; the Company's Profits Tax Act, 1964; the Interest Tax Act, 1974; the Hotel Receipt Tax Act, 1980; the Expenditure Tax Act, 1987.

(*d*) The Central Sales Tax Act, 1956.

(*e*) The Customs Act, 1962; the Customs Tariff Act, 1975; the Central Excise Tariff Act, 1985; the Additional Duties of Excise (Goods of Special Importance) Act, 1957; the Central Excise Conversion to Metric Units Act,

1960; the Customs Duty and Cesses Conversion to Metric Unit Act, 1960; the Salt Cess Act, 1953; the Produce Cess Act, 1966; the Tobacco Cess Act, 1975; the Iron Ore Cess Act, 1976; the Water Prevention of Pollution Cess Act, 1977; the Sugar Cess Act, 1982; the Jute Manufacturers Cess Act, 1983'.

(*f*) The Central Board of Revenue Act, 1963.

(*g*) The Taxation Laws Amendment and Miscellaneous Provisions Act, 1965.

(*h*) The Delhi Motor Vehicles Taxation Act, 1962.

1.9 State taxes

Direct taxes in states are land revenue; agricultural income tax and profession tax. States' power to impose land revenue flows from entry 45 in List II to the Seventh Schedule of the constitution. During the pre-independence period, land revenue formed the main source of revenue. In some States, land revenue has been abolished altogether (see, Sixty Years of Indian Economy, 1947-2007, New Century Publication).

Agricultural income is subject to tax by the state legislature under entry 46 of List II of the Seventh Schedule of the Constitution. Initially, States enacted laws to tax agricultural income but now many states have abolished the law. Based on the K.N. Raj Committee report the agricultural income is clubbed with non-agricultural income only for the rate purposes. Under the Income-tax Act, 1961 agricultural income is exempt from tax.

A tax on profession may be levied by the state under entry 60 of List II of the Seventh Schedule of the Constitution. It is levied as a fixed amount on every person on his income. This is distinct from tax on income. Clause 2 of article 276 of the Constitution fixes that the amount payable cannot exceed rupees two thousand five hundred per annum.

Indirect Taxes before GST: Entry 54 of List II of the Seventh Schedule of the Constitution empowered States to levy sales tax. It grew considerably in depth and coverage and forms the mainstay of a state's revenue. It was levied not only on consumer goods but also on raw materials and capital goods. In the classical concept of the 'sale' there had to be three essential components to constitute a transaction of sale before tax could be imposed, namely, (*a*) an agreement to transfer the title; (*b*) supported by consideration; (*c*) actual transfer of title in the goods. In the absence of any one of these elements, the Supreme Court in the *State of Madras* v. *Gannon Dunkerley*[16] held that in an indivisible contract, no sales tax could be imposed on the supply of materials used therein treating it as a sale, as the same did not involve any sale of goods. The Constitution Forty-sixth Amendment Act pursuant to the recommendation of the Law Commission of India in its 61st report introduced separate categories of deemed sale and the word 'goods' was not altered. The amendment introduced fiction by which six

---

16. (1959) SCR 329/[1958] 9 STC 353 (SC).

instances of transactions were treated as deemed sale of goods and that the said definition as to deemed sale will have to be read in every provision of the constitution. (see BSNL [2006] 3 SCC 45). In *Tata Consultancy*[17], the sale of CDs containing software was held as goods whereas in *Sunrise*[18], the sale of lottery tickets or rail tickets was not held as sale of goods.

Prior to tax reforms initiated in early 1990, sales tax was characterized by a multiplicity of rates and exemptions, lack of uniformity across States, large numbers of exemptions and concessions, and differing procedures of tax collection. Nation-wise efforts to redesign commodity taxation and the implementation of CENVAT at the level of the centre, the states have modified their sales tax regime to value-added tax[19]. The value-added tax that prevails in the European Union was favoured for two reasons. First, it is obviously superior to the prevailing cascading excise taxes which it replaced but which in many administrative aspects it resembled. Secondly, the relative ease with which jurisdiction to tax issues can be resolved.

State excise - States are empowered to levy, under entry 51 of list II of the Seventh Schedule of the Constitution, duties of excise on liquors for human consumption; on opium; Indian hemp and other narcotic drugs and narcotics (but not including medicinal and toilet preparation containing alcohol).

Taxes on motor vehicles - States are empowered to levy tax on motor vehicles under entry 57 of list II of the Seventh Schedule of the Constitution. The legislation enacted under this entry includes the Andhra Pradesh Motor Vehicles Taxation Act, 1963; the Karnataka Motor Vehicles Taxation Act, 1957; the Tamil Nadu Motor Vehicles Taxation Act, 1974; the Madhya Pradesh Motoryan Karadhan Adhiniyam, 1991.

Entertainment tax before GST - States were empowered to levy Tax under entry 62 of List II of the Seventh Schedule of the Constitution on luxuries, including taxes on entertainment, amusement betting, and gaming. Tax was levied on the price charged for admission to any place of entertainment under the legislative field exclusively reserved for the state legislature. The levy of tax by more than one statute on different taxable objects and taxable persons is not prohibited by the Constitution. In the West Bengal, there is the Bengal Amusement Tax Act, 1922; the West Bengal Entertainment and Luxuries (Hotels and Restaurants) Tax Act, 1972; and the West Bengal Entertainment Tax Act, 1982. The areas of application of each Act are different. Further, a tax on entry under entry 62 of List II of the Seventh Schedule of the Constitution may be imposed not only on the persons providing the entertainment but also on the act of the person entertaining or the subject of entertainment. It is well-settled that tax may be levied on the person offering or providing entertainment or the person enjoying

17. *Tata Consultancy Services* v. *State of AP* (2004) 271 ITR 401/192 CTR 257/141 Taxman 132/137 STC 620(SC)/(2005) 1 SCC 308 (SC)/AIR 2005 SC 371.
18. *Sunrise Associates* v. *Govt. of NCT of Delhi* (2006) 5 SCC 603/[2006] 4 STT 105 (SC).
19. Sixty Years of India Economy 1947 to 2007 by CS Prasad, Vibha Mathur and Anup Chatterjee, New century Publications, New Delhi, India.

it.[20] It was held that the operator and the person transmitting signals to him are also the giver of entertainment. The word 'luxuries' in entry 62 of List II means the activity of enjoyment of or indulgence in that which is costly or which is generally recognised as beyond the necessary requirement of an average member of society and not articles of luxury and, on that basis, the Supreme Court came to the conclusion that this entry does not permit levy of tax on goods or articles.[21] In the Ghodawat the constitutional validity of section 3B of the Maharashtra Tax on Luxury Act, 1987 was challenged as that section provided for the levy of luxury tax on tobacconist and the court held the said provision unconstitutional.

Stamp Duty and Registration Fee - Under entry 63 of List II of the Seventh Schedule of the Constitution the states levy stamp duty on the registration of property and on conveyance. The Registration Act, 1908 mainly deals with the necessity of getting a document registered in India so as to make them valid and even if they are executed outside India to provide for registration thereof after their first arrival in India. Section 17 of the Act enumerates the instruments registration of which is compulsory under the Act whereas section 49 encompasses the effect of failure to register. Registration of documents, however, is not confined only to documents relating to immovable property but also to documents dealing with other matters. Section 32 provides for the presentation of documents for registration and section 33 deals with power of attorney. (*State of Rajasthan* v. *Basant Nahata*[22]). In Basant Nahata, the constitutional validity of section 22A of the Registration Act, 1908, as amended by the State of Rajasthan and notification issued thereunder was held unconstitutional by the High Court. High Court held section 22A of the Act confers arbitrary powers on the State Government to determine as regards declaring a particular document being opposed to public policy. The impugned legislation invades the right of a citizen to deal with the property and thus is wholly arbitrary and unreasonable.

Section 22A reads as under

22A. Documents registration of which is opposed to public policy - (1) The State Government may by notification in the official gazette declare that the registration of any document or class of documents is opposed to public policy. (2) Notwithstanding anything contained in this Act, the registering Officer shall refuse to register any document to which a notification issued under sub-section (1) is applicable.

By virtue of the notification issued the registration of any power of attorney authorising the attorney to transfer any immovable property for a term in excess of six months (raised to three years) or irrevocable or where the term is not mentioned was declared opposed to public policy. The Supreme Court held:

> "Para 61. It becomes amply clear that it is not possible to define public policy with precision at any point in time. It is not for the executive to fill these grey areas as

20. *State of West Bengal* v. *Purvi Communications Ltd.* (2005) 3 SCC 711, 730.
21. *Ghodawat Pan Masala Product Ltd.* v. *State of Maharashtra* (2005) 4 SCC 415.
22. (2005) 12 SCC 77.

> the said power rests with the judiciary. An interpretation of the concept of 'public policy' is required to be considered it is for the judiciary to do so and in doing so even the power of the judiciary is very limited."

The court found the provision to be *ultra vires* articles 14 and 246 of the Constitution.

Electricity duty - Entry 53 of List II of the Seventh Schedule of the Constitution enables states to levy electricity duty. In *National Thermal Power Corporation Limited*[23] the Supreme Court held that the power of the state legislature to enact a law to levy tax by reference to list II to the Seventh Schedule has two limitations; one arising out of the entry itself and the other flowing from the restriction embodied in the Constitution. Article 288 of the Constitution exempts from state taxation in respect of water and electricity in certain cases. In *Damodar Valley Corporation* v. *State of Bihar*[24], clause (2) of article 288 was interpreted to include therein river valley authorities like the Damodar Valley Corporation.

The concept of tariff and tax is different whereas a tariff would include a list of charges a tax must be actual basis. The distinction between entry 53 of List II and entry 38 of List III was brought in these words: —

> "Entry 53 of List II provides for a taxation entry, whereas entry 38 of List III provides for a non-taxation entry dealing with general aspects of electricity excluding taxes. The 1998 Act empowers the commission only to fix the electricity tariff for the charges for the consumption of electricity. The legislation made by the State is independent of the actual tariff for electricity charges. Tariff would mean a cartel of commerce and normally is a book of rates."[25]

Entry 53 of List II of the Seventh Schedule which deals with 'Taxes on consumption or the sale of electricity' must be read as 'Taxes on consumption or sale for consumption of electricity'.[26]

In Brahmputra Metallics Ltd.[27], the Industrial Policy 2012 announced an incentive in the form of a rebate or deduction on electricity duty for a period of five years from the commencement of production. The policy document spelt out: (*i*) The nature of the incentives; (*ii*) The period during which the incentives would be available; and (*iii*) The time limit within which follow-up action would be taken by the State Government through its departments for implementing the Industrial Policy 2012. The Supreme Court held that the State having held out a solemn representation, it would be manifestly unfair and arbitrary to deprive industrial units within the State of their legitimate entitlement.

---

23. *State of AP* v. *National Thermal Power Corporation Ltd.* (2002) 5 SCC 203/[2002]2002 taxmann.com 2376 (SC).

24. (1976) 3 SCC 710.

25. *Southern Petrochemicals Co. Limited* v. *Electricity Inspector* (2007) 5 SCC 447.

26. *State of AP* v. *National Thermal Power Corporation Ltd.* (2002) 5 SCC 203/[2002] 2002 taxmann.com 2376 (SC).

27. *State of Jharkhand* v. *Brahmputra Metallics* (2020) SCC OnLine SC 968/[2020]122 taxmann.com 21 (SC).

1.10 New Tax Laws

1.10.1 The Black Money (Undisclosed Foreign Income and Assets) and Imposition of Tax Act, 2015

The Black Money (Undisclosed Foreign Income and Assets) and Imposition of Tax Act, 2015 has introduced a tax compliance provision under Chapter VI of the Act. As per section 2(11) of the Act "undisclosed asset located outside India" means an asset held by the person in his name or in respect of which he is a beneficial owner. A company can file a declaration under Chapter VI of the Act. The Directors of the company shall not be liable for any offence under the Income-tax Act, Wealth-tax Act, FEMA, Companies Act, and the Customs Act in respect of declaration made in the name of the company. Where an undisclosed foreign asset is declared under Chapter VI of the Act and tax and penalty is paid on its fair market value. Section 67 provides immunity from prosecution under the five Acts *viz.* the Income-tax Act, Wealth-tax Act, FEMA, Companies Act, and the Customs Act. It does not provide immunity from prosecution under any other Act. For example- if the undisclosed asset has been acquired out of the proceeds of the sale of protected animals the person will not be eligible for immunity under the Wildlife (Protection) Act, 1972. Section 71(*d*)(*i*) provides that declaration cannot be made where an undisclosed asset has been acquired during any previous year relevant to an assessment year for which a notice under section 142, 143(2), 148, 153A or 153C of the Income-tax Act has been issued.

The Black Money (Undisclosed Foreign Income and Assets) and Imposition of Tax Rules, 2015 provides for the determination of fair market value. It also provides for declaration in respect of any undisclosed asset located outside India. Such declaration shall be made in Form 6 and The Principal Commissioner or the Commissioner shall grant an acknowledgement in Form 7 to the declarant within fifteen days of the submission of proof of payment of tax along with penalty by the declarant under sub-section (2) of section 63 of the Act in respect of the undisclosed asset located outside India.

1.10.2 The Direct Tax Vivad se Vishwas Act, 2020

With the objective to *inter alia*, reduce pending income tax litigation, generate timely revenue for the Government, and benefit taxpayers by providing them peace of mind, certainty, and savings on account of time and resources that would otherwise be spent on the long-drawn and vexatious litigation process, the Direct Tax Vivad se Vishwas Act, 2020 was enacted on 17th March, 2020. Sections 10 and 11 of Vivad se Vishwas empower the Central Government/Central Board of Direct Taxes to issue directions or orders in the public interest or to remove difficulties. It has been clarified that a 'search case' means an assessment or reassessment made under section 143(3)/144/147/153A/153C/158BC of the Income-tax Act in the case of a person referred to in section 153A or section 153C or section 158BC or section 158BD of the Income-tax Act on the basis of search initiated under section 132, or requisition made under section 132A of the Income-tax Act. The provisions of Vivad se Vishwas had been amended by the Taxation and Other Laws (Relaxation and Amendment of Certain Provisions) Act, 2020 to provide certain relaxation in view of the COVID-19 pandemic and also to empower the Central Government to notify certain dates. Under the existing provisions of sub-section (2) of section 5 of the Vivad se Vishwas, the declarant is required to pay the amount within a period of 15 days from the date of receipt of the certificate from the designated authority. However, as per the notification, a declarant who files a declaration on or before 31st December 2020 can make payment without an additional amount on or before 31st March 2021. Sub-section (1) of section 5 provides that the designated authority shall pass a determination order within fifteen days from the date of receipt of the declaration. The DA is also required to pass another order under sub-section (2) of section 5 for full and final settlement of the tax arrears.

1.10.3 The Taxation Laws (Amendment) Act, 2021 (Act No. 34 of 2021)

The Taxation Laws (Amendment) Act, 2021, which received the assent of the President on the 13th August, 2021, has, *inter alia*, amended the Income-tax Act, 1961 so as to provide that no tax demand shall be raised in future on the basis of the amendment to section 9 of the Income-tax Act made *vide* Finance Act, 2012 for any offshore indirect transfer of Indian assets if the transaction was undertaken before 28th May, 2012 (*i.e.*, the date on which the Finance Bill, 2012 received the assent of the President).

The amendment made by the 2021 Act also provides that the demand raised for offshore indirect transfer of Indian assets made before 28 May, 2012 (including the validation of demand provided under section 119 of the Finance Act, 2012) shall be nullified on fulfilment of specified conditions such as withdrawal or furnishing of undertaking for withdrawal of pending litigation and furnishing of an undertaking to the effect that no claim for cost, damages, interest, etc. shall be filed and such other conditions are fulfilled as may be prescribed. The amount paid/collected in these cases shall be refunded, without any interest, on fulfilment of the said conditions. The aim of the amendment made by the 2021 Act is to bring tax certainty and ensure that once specified conditions are fulfilled, the pending Income-tax proceedings shall be withdrawn, demand, if any, raised shall be nullified, and amount, if any, collected shall be refunded to the taxpayer without any interest.

To implement the amendment made by the 2021 Act, rules have been notified to amend the Income-tax Rules, 1962 which specify the conditions to be fulfilled and the process to be followed to give effect to the amendment made by the 2021 Act.

The Income-tax (31st Amendment) Rules, 2021 *inter alia* inserted rule 11UE and rule 11UF. (*See* **Appendix 1**)

Taxation Laws (Amendment) Act, 2021

Taxation Laws (Amendment) Act, 2021 provides for an extension of various time limits for completion or compliance of actions under the specified Acts and reduction in interest, waiver of penalty, and prosecution for delay in payment of certain taxes or levies during the specified period. The Act makes amendments to the Income-tax Act, 1961 which, *inter alia*, include providing tax incentives for Category-III Alternative Investment Funds located in the International Financial Services Centre (IFSC) to encourage relocation of foreign funds to the IFSC, deferment of a new procedure of registration and approval of certain entities introduced through the Finance Act, 2020, providing for deduction for donation made to the Prime Minister's Citizen Assistance and Relief in Emergency Situations Fund (PM CARES FUND) and exemption to its income, incorporation of Faceless Assessment Scheme, 2019 therein, empowering the Central Government to notify schemes for faceless processes under certain provisions by eliminating physical interface to the extent technologically feasible and to provide deduction or collection at source in respect of certain transactions at three fourth's rate for the period from 14th May, 2020 to 31st March, 2021. The Act amends the Direct Tax Vivad se Viswas Act, 2020 to extend the date for payment without additional amount to 31st December, 2020 and to empower the Central Government to notify certain dates relating to filing of declaration and making of payment.

The Sabka Vishwas (Legacy Dispute Resolution) Scheme, 2019

The Finance Act (No. 2) 2019 enabled the Central Government to notify the Sabka Vishwas (Legacy Dispute Resolution) Scheme, 2019. The Scheme is a One-time measure for the liquidation of past disputes of Central Excise and Service Tax. The Scheme seeks to provide an opportunity for voluntary disclosure to non-compliant taxpayers. The period of the scheme was from 1st September, 2019 to the 31st December, 2019.

2 Constitutional provisions relating to taxation

2.1 What is tax?

The word "tax" in its widest sense includes all money raised by taxation. It therefore includes taxes levied by the central and state legislatures, and also those known as rates or other charges levied by local authorities under statutory powers. Taxation has been defined in clause (28) of article 366 of the Constitution to include the imposition of any tax or impost whether general or local or special and it has been directed that "tax "shall be construed accordingly[1].

The primary meaning of taxation is raising money for purposes of government by means of contributions from individual persons, a compulsory exaction of money by a public authority for public purpose enforceable by law, and not a payment for services rendered[2].

In an earlier case of *Commissioner Hindu Religious Endowments* v. *Sri Lakshmindra Tirtha Swamiar of Sri Shirur Mutt*[3], Mukherjee J., opined:

> "A neat definition of what tax means has been given by Latham CJ of the High Court of Australia in Matthew v. Chicory Marketing Board. A 'tax' according to the learned Chief Justice, is a compulsory exaction of money by public authority for public purposes enforceable by law and is not payment for services rendered. It is said that the essence of taxation is compulsion, that is to say, it is imposed under his statutory power without the taxpayer's consent and the payment is enforced by law. The second characteristic of tax is that it is an imposition made for public purpose without reference to any special benefit to be conferred on the payer of the tax. Another feature of taxation is that as it is a part of the common burden the quantum of imposition upon the taxpayer depends generally upon his capacity to pay."

The Matthew has been revisited by the High Court of Australia. In Roy Morgan[4], the appellant argued that the charge was not a "tax" because it

1. *D.G. Gouse & Co* v. *State of Kerala* AIR 1980 SC 271, 275. (The Kerala Building Tax Act, 1975) Five judges bench.
2. *Om Parkash* Agarwal v. *Giriraj Kishori* AIR 1986 SC 726, 730 (The Haryana Rural Development Fund Act, 1983).
3. AIR 1954 SC 282, 295. (The Madras Hindu Religious and Charitable Endowment Act, 1951 -Settlement of a Scheme in connection with Shirur Math) Seven judges bench.
4. *Roy Morgan Research Pty Ltd.* v. *Commissioner of Taxation* [2011] HCA 35.

was not imposed for "public purposes". The High Court held unanimously that the charge was a tax, and that the appellant's constitutional challenge to the Superannuation Guarantee (Administration) Act, 1992 (Cth) and the Superannuation Guarantee Charge Act, 1992 (Cth) failed. The receipt of funds into the Consolidated Revenue Fund established that the charge was imposed for "public purposes". Where other necessary constitutional criteria of a tax are met, as they were in this case, the receipt of funds into the Consolidated Revenue Fund establishes the character of the charge as a valid tax.

In *Australian Tape Manufacturers Association Ltd.* v *Commonwealth of Australia* (1993) 112 ALR 53 the issue was whether the "royalty" levied on the vendors of blank tapes is a tax. The majority held that it is not essential to the concept of a tax that the exaction should be by a public authority. A tax is valid even if it is not paid to a public authority. The majority also held that the 'public purpose' element can be satisfied by the legislature identifying a public interest.

2.2 The authority of law is essential for the levy and collection of any tax

Article 265 of the Constitution provides: No tax shall be levied or collected except by authority of law. The term 'law' means statute law. Thus, a tax cannot be imposed by an executive action. The law imposing a tax must be a valid law. It must be within the legislative competence of the legislature enacting the law. Such a law should not be violative of any provision of the constitution. Recently, the Supreme Court[5-6] held that the refund of taxes is neither a fundamental right nor a constitutional right. The Constitution only guarantees that the levy should be legal and that the collection should be in accordance with the law. There is no constitutional right to refund. Refund is always a matter of a statutory prescription and can be regulated by the statute subject to conditions and limitations.

If a tax law violates any of the fundamental rights, such law will be void. The other provisions of the constitution that place limitations on the taxing power of a state are contained in articles 276, 285, 286, 289, 301 and 304.

2.3 Constitutional remedies in tax matters

Article 32 of the Constitution provides a remedy for the enforcement of fundamental rights, the validity of a tax law can be challenged by filing a writ petition directly before the Supreme Court under Article 32 of the Constitution. In an early case[7], the state sales tax law was challenged under Article 32. The validity of the Special Bearer Bonds (Immunities and Exemption) Act, 1981 was challenged in *RK Garg* v. *Union of India*[8].

5-6. *Union of India* v. *VKC Footsteps India (P) Ltd.* (2022) 2 SCC 603/[2021] 130 taxmann.com 193/52 GSTL 513 (SC).

7. *M.P. V. Sundaramier & Co.* v. *State of Andhra Pradesh* AIR 1958 SC 468.

8. (1981) 4 SCC 675/1981 AIR 2138 (SC)/1982 SCR (1) 947/(1982) 133 ITR 329/[1981] 7 Taxman 53 (SC).

Recently, while disposing of petitions filed under Article 32 of the Constitution, the Supreme Court observed as under—

> "Para 6...Undoubtedly, the jurisdiction of this Court under Article 32 is a salutary constitutional safeguard to protect the fundamental rights of citizens. The Court must be solicitous in exercising it where a breach of fundamental human rights is in issue. But equally, whether recourse to the jurisdiction under Article 32 should be entertained in a particular case is a matter for the calibrated exercise of judicial discretion. There is regime of well-established remedies and procedures under the laws of criminal procedure. Revenue legislation also provides its own internal discipline. Short circuiting this should not become a ruse for flooding this court with petitions which can, should and must be addressed before the competent fora. Hence we are of the view that it would be appropriate to relegate the petitioner to the remedy of a petition under Article 226 so that this Court has the benefit of the considered view of the jurisdictional High Court." [9]

In *Devendra Dwivedi*[10], there was a challenge to the constitutional validity of certain provisions of the Central Goods and Services Tax Act, 2017; a direction for compliance with the procedure for investigation enunciated in Chapter XII of the Code of Criminal Procedure 1973; and declaring the investigations which have been instituted against the petitioner as illegal.

Writ jurisdiction of High Court under article 226 of the Constitution

Normally the rule of alternate remedy acts as a bar to recourse to writ jurisdiction in tax matters. However, the existence of an alternate remedy does not by itself bar the High Court from exercising its jurisdiction in certain contingencies. [11] In *Radha Krishan*[12], the law has been summarised as under—

> "28. The principles of law which emerge are that: (*i*) The power under Article 226 of the Constitution to issue writs can be exercised not only for the enforcement of fundamental rights, but for any other purpose as well; (*ii*) The High Court has the discretion not to entertain a writ petition. One of the restrictions placed on the power of the High Court is where an effective alternate remedy is available to the aggrieved person; (*iii*) Exceptions to the rule of alternate remedy arise where (*a*) the writ petition has been filed for the enforcement of a fundamental right protected by Part III of the Constitution; (*b*) there has been a violation of the principles of natural justice; (*c*) the order or proceedings are wholly without jurisdiction; or (*d*) the vires of a legislation is challenged; (*iv*) An alternate remedy by itself does not divest the High Court of its powers under Article 226 of the Constitution in an appropriate case though ordinarily, a writ petition should not be entertained when

9. *Devendra Dwivedi* v. *Union of India* [Writ Petition(s)(Criminal) No(s). 272/2020]/(2022) 11 SCC 455/[2021] 123 taxmann.com 153/84 GST 606 (SC).

10. *Ibid.*, Writ Petition(s)(Criminal) No(s). 272/2020.

11. *Whirpool Corporation* v. *Registrar of Trademarks*, Mumbai (1998) 8 SCC 1 and *Harbanslal Sahni* v. *Indian Oil Corporation Ltd.* (2003) 2 SCC 107. *Pimpri Chinchwad Municipal Corporation* v. *Gayatri Construction Company* (2008) 8 SCC 172.

12. *Radha Krishan Industries* v. *State of Himachal Pradesh* 2021 SCC OnLine SC 334/127 taxmann.com 26/86 GST 665 (SC).

> an efficacious alternate remedy is provided by law; (*v*) When a right is created by a statute, which itself prescribes the remedy or procedure for enforcing the right or liability, resort must be had to that particular statutory remedy before invoking the discretionary remedy under Article 226 of the Constitution. This rule of exhaustion of statutory remedies is a rule of policy, convenience and discretion; and (*vi*) In cases where there are disputed questions of fact, the High Court may decide to decline jurisdiction in a writ petition. However, if the High Court is objectively of the view that the nature of the controversy requires the exercise of its writ jurisdiction, such a view would not readily be interfered with."

A writ petition is maintainable before the High Court if the taxing authorities have acted beyond the scope of their jurisdiction.[13]

In *Seetaram Rice Mill*[14], the following observations were made as under—

> "82. It is argued and to some extent correctly that the High Court should not decline to exercise its jurisdiction merely for the reason that there is a statutory alternative remedy available even when the case falls in the above-stated class of cases. It is a settled principle that the courts/tribunal will not exercise jurisdiction in futility. The law will not itself attempt to do an act which would be vain, lex nil frustra facit, nor to enforce one which would be frivolous—*lex neminem cogit ad vana seu inutilia*—the law will not force anyone to do a thing vain and fruitless. In other words, if the exercise of jurisdiction by the tribunal *ex facie* appears to be an exercise of jurisdiction in futility for any of the stated reasons, then it will be permissible for the High Court to interfere in the exercise of its jurisdiction. This issue is no longer *res integra* and has been settled by a catena of judgments of this Court, which we find entirely unnecessary to refer to in detail..."

In *Magadh Sugar & Energy Ltd.*[15], the Supreme Court observed that the High Court made an error in declining to entertain the writ petition and it would be appropriate to restore the proceedings back to the High Court for a fresh disposal.

In Godrej, the issue was whether the High Court was justified in declining interference on the ground of the availability of an alternative remedy of appeal to the appellant under section 33 of the Haryana VAT Act, which it had not pursued. Supreme Court explained the difference between maintainability and entertainability. The objection as to "maintainability" goes to the root of the matter and if such objection were found to be of substance, the courts would be rendered incapable of even receiving the lis for adjudication. On the other hand, the question of "entertainability" is entirely within the realm of discretion of the high courts, writ remedy being discretionary. A writ petition despite being maintainable may not be entertained by a high court for very many reasons or relief could even be refused to the petitioner, despite setting up a sound legal point, if grant of the claimed relief would not further public interest. Hence,

13. *Assistant Commissioner of State Tax* v. *Commercial Steel Limited* [Civil Appeal No. 5121 of 2021]/[2021] 130 taxmann.com 180/88 GST 799 (SC); *State of HP* v. *Gujarat Ambuja Cement Ltd.* (2005) 6 SCC 499/[2006] 2006 taxmann.com 1823 (SC).
14. *Executive Engineer* v. *Sri Seetaram Rice Mill* (2012) 2 SCC 108.
15. *Magadh Sugar & Energy Ltd.* v. *State of Bihar* [Civil Appeal No. 5728 of 2021 decided by a Three Judges Bench on September 24, 2021].

dismissal of a writ petition by a high court on the ground that the petitioner has not availed the alternative remedy without, however, examining whether an exceptional case has been made out for such entertainment would not be proper. Supreme Court observed that the power to issue prerogative writs under Article 226 is plenary in nature. Any limitation on the exercise of such power must be traceable in the Constitution itself. One of the self-imposed restrictions on the exercise of power under Article 226 that has evolved through judicial precedents is that the high courts should normally not entertain a writ petition, where an effective and efficacious alternative remedy is available. At the same time, it must be remembered that mere availability of an alternative remedy of appeal or revision, which the party invoking the jurisdiction of the high court under Article 226 has not pursued, would not oust the jurisdiction of the high court and render a writ petition "not maintainable". The availability of an alternative remedy does not operate as an absolute bar to the "maintainability" of a writ petition and that the rule, which requires a party to pursue the alternative remedy provided by a statute, is a rule of policy, convenience, and discretion rather than a rule of law.[15a]

2.4 Tax and fee

The traditional view that there must be actual *quid pro quo* for a fee has undergone a sea change in the subsequent decisions[16]. The distinction between a tax and a fee lies primarily in the fact that a tax is levied as a part of a common burden, and while a fee is for payment of a specific benefit or privilege although the special advantage is secondary to the primary motive of regulation in the public interest. If the element of revenue for the general purpose of the state predominates, the levy becomes a tax. In regard to fees, there is, and must always be, a correlation between the fee collected and the service intended to be rendered. In determining whether a levy is a fee, the true test must be whether its primary and essential purpose is to render specific services to a specific area of class, it may be of no consequence that the state may ultimately and indirectly benefit from it.

15a. *Godrej Sara Lee Ltd.* v. *Excise and Taxation Officer-cum-Assessing Authority* [Civil Appeal No. 5393 of 2010 two judges bench decided on 1st February 2023]/[2023] 3 Centax 49 (SC).

16. *Commissioner Hindu Religious Endowments* v. *Sri Lakshmindra Thirtha Swamiar of Sri Shirur Mutt* AIR 1954 SC 282. *Jagannath Ramanuj Das* v. *State of Orissa* AIR 1954 SC 400. *Ratilal Panachand Gandhi* v. *State of Bombay* AIR 1954 SC 388. *Kewal Krishna* v. *State of Punjab* AIR 1980 SC 1008. *Southern Pharmaceutical* AIR 1981 SC 1863.

    It is also increasingly realised that the element of quid *pro quo stricto sensu* is not always a *Sine qua non* of fee. It is needless to stress that the element of *quit Pro* who is not necessarily absent in every tax. The traditional concept of *quid pro quo* is undergoing a transformation.

    A fee may be charged for the privilege or benefit conferred or services rendered or to meet the expenses connected therewith. A fee may be levied to meet the cost of supervision and maybe something more. It is in consideration for the privilege, licence or service.

    Shrinivas General Traders v. *State of Andhra Pradesh* (1983) 4 SCC 353-392, *Municipal Corporation of Delhi* v. *Mohammed Yasin* (1983) SCC 229/AIR 1983 SC 617.

The power of any legislature to levy a fee is conditioned by the fact that it must be by and large *quid pro quo* for the services rendered. However, the co-relationship between the levy and the services rendered or expected is one of general character and not of mathematical exactitude. All that is necessary is that there should be a reasonable relationship between the levy of the fees and the services rendered.

In *Srinivas General Traders* v. *State of Andhra Pradesh*[17], the increase in the rate of market fee under the A.P. Agricultural Produce and Livestock Market Act, 1966 was assailed on the ground that there was no *Quid Pro quo i.e.*, there was no correlation between the increase in the rate of market fee and the services rendered and therefore it was illegal and invalid. On this issue, the Supreme Court observed:

> "It is wrong to take only one particular year or few years into consideration to decide whether the fee is commensurate with the services rendered. An overall picture has to be taken in dealing with the question of *Quid Pro quo*."

On behalf of the petitioner, it was argued that firstly, there was surplus money with almost all the market and, therefore, there was no justification for an increase of fee and secondly, services are not rendered outside the market and, therefore, charging of any amount from those persons is impermissible. The court answered the four sets of objections which are as follows:

(*i*) The establishment of a regulated market is itself a service rendered to persons engaged in the trade. Services are rendered which extend beyond the market area. Such services include standardised weight and measures and storage facilities, etc.

(*ii*) There was no contention that there was any unauthorized expenditure by any of the market committees and the fee was justified on the grounds of inflation.

(*iii*) There is no evidence that the market committee is rendering no service.

Another important case on the distinction between tax and fee is *Municipal Corporation of Delhi* v. *Mohammed Yasin*[18]. In this case, the MCD enhanced the rate for the slaughter of animals in its slaughterhouses. The increase was assailed as an arbitrary tax. The Court made certain observations which have a direct bearing on the distinction between "tax" and "fee". The court observed:

(1) Tax and fee properly belong to the world of public finance but since the Constitution and laws are also concerned with public finance these words have often been adjudicated upon in an effort to discover their content.

(2) Compulsion is not a sole criterion to determine the difference between tax and fee.

17. (1983) 4 SCC 353-392.

18. (1983) SCC 229/AIR 1983 SC 617.

(3) Tax is a common burden and fee is payment for special benefit or privilege. But it was noticed that special benefit is secondary to the primary motive of regulation in the public interest as for instance in the case of registration fees for documents or marriage licenses.

It was further observed that there is no generic difference between a tax and a fee, though broadly tax is a compulsory exaction as part of a common burden, without a promise of any special advantages to classes of taxpayer whereas a fee is a payment for services rendered, benefit provided or privilege conferred. Further, though a fee must have relation to services rendered or advantage conferred such relation need not be direct, a mere casual relation may be enough.

Moreover, neither the incidence of fees nor the services rendered need to be uniform. That others besides those paying the fees also benefited does not detract from the character of the fee.

In fact, the special benefit or advantage to the payer of fees may even be secondary as compared to the primary motive of regulation in the public interest. Lastly, the court is not to assume the role of cost accountant. It is neither necessary nor expedient to weigh too meticulously the cost of the services rendered etc. against the amount of fee collected so as to evenly balance the two. A broad co-relationship is all that is necessary. A broad *quid pro quo* in the strict sense is not the one and only true index of a fee; nor is it necessarily absent in a tax.

Recently in *Jalkal Vibhag Nagar Nigam*[19], the Supreme Court held that the practical and even constitutional, distinction between a tax and fee has been weathered down. As in the case of a tax, a fee may also involve a compulsory exaction. A fee may involve an element of compulsion and its proceeds may form a part of the Consolidated Fund. Similarly, the element of a *quid pro quo* is not necessarily absent in the case of every tax. The levy under section 52 of the Uttar Pradesh Water Supply and Sewerage Act, 1975 is a tax simpliciter and cannot be regarded either as a charge or a fee for a service rendered.

In *Dravya Finance Pvt. Ltd.* the levy of fees by LIC for endorsing transfer of assignment of policy was struck down by the Supreme Court. In this case, the fee of rupees two hundred and fifty was levied by a circular of LIC. The Supreme Court held that fees could be levied only under an Act, rules, or regulations.[19a]

2.5 Cess

A cess may be a tax or fee. Whether a cess in a given context is a tax or fee depends upon the purpose for which it is levied. In *Hingir Rampur Coal Co. Ltd.*[20], the Supreme Court came to the conclusion that it was an amount levied essentially

19. *Jalkal Vibhag Nagar Nigam* v. *Pradeshiya Industrial and Investment Corporation* [Civil Appeal No. 6107 of 2021 decided on October 22, 2021 by a Three Judges Bench].

19a. *Life Insurance Corporation of India* v. *Dravya Finance Pvt. Ltd.* [Civil Appeal No. 4095 of 2012 Two Judges Bench decided on September 6, 2023].

20. AIR 1961 SC 459. In this case the cess was imposed under the Orissa Mining Areas Development Fund Act, 1952.

for services rendered in the areas which were declared as mining areas in the State of Orissa. The cess collected in the Act could be spent on improving the communication, constructing good roads, supply of water and electricity, and providing other amenities of sanitation and education to the labour force in order to attract workmen in the mining area. In cess, the primary object must be to benefit a specified class or area. The ultimate result or consequences are not material.

In *Om Parkash Agarwal* v. *Giriraj Kishori*[21], the Supreme Court found that the cess payable under the Haryana Rural Development Fund Act, 1983 can be spent by the State Government at its will on any purpose which it considers to be the development of almost the entire rural area of a State of Haryana.

It was held that—

> "... if in the guise of a fee, the legislation imposes a tax it is for the Court on a scrutiny of the scheme of the levy to determine its real character. If on a true analysis of the provisions levying the amount, the court comes to the conclusion that it is, in fact, in the nature of a tax and not a fee, its validity can be justified only by bringing it under any one of the entries in list II of the Seventh Schedule to the Constitution under which the state can levy a tax."

In the above case, the court held that the levy is not a fee, as claimed by the State, but it is a tax not leviable by it. It was further observed—

> "In determining a levy as a fee, the true test must be whether its primary and essential purpose is to render specific services to a specified area or class, it being of no consequence that the State may ultimately be benefited by it." [22]

In *Vijaya Laxmi Rice Mill* v. *CTO*[23], a cess was levied under the AP Rural Development Act, 1996. The court held that the cess in question is in substance a fee as it is being levied for rendering to the rural public the service of rural development.

The scope of the Building and Other Construction Workers Welfare Cess Act, 1996 has been explained by the Supreme Court in Uttar Pradesh Power Transmission Corporation Ltd. (UPPTCL) [24]. In view of the Supreme Court, the clear statutory scheme of the BOCW Act excludes a supply contract from within its ambit. A contractor who enters into a pure Supply Contract is statutorily exempted from levy under the BOCW Act. Cess under the Cess Act read with the BOCW Act is leviable in respect of building and other construction works. The condition precedent for imposition of cess under the Cess Act is the construction, repair, demolition, or maintenance of and/or in relation to a building or any other work of construction, transmission towers, in relation *inter alia* to

---

21. AIR 1986 SC 726. A law was passed *i.e.* The Haryana Rural Development Fund Act, 1983. Under the Act, there was a provision for levy of tax on every dealer on sale proceeds of agriculture produce in notified market area at the rate of one per cent of sale proceeds.
22. *Om Parkash Agarwal* v. *Giriraj Kishori* AIR 1986 SC 726.
23. [2006] 6 SCC 763/[2007] 2007 taxmann.com 1769 (SC).
24. *Uttar Pradesh Power Transmission Corporation Ltd.* v. *CG Power and Industrial Solution Limited* 2021 SCC OnLine SC 383, decided on 12.05.2021.

generation, transmission, and distribution of power, electric lines, pipelines, etc. Mere installation and/or erection of pipelines, equipments for generation or transmission or distribution of power, electric wires, transmission towers, etc. which do not involve construction work are not amenable to Cess under the Cess Act. The Cess Act and/or statutory rules framed thereunder prescribe the mode and manner of recovery of outstanding cess under the Cess Act. It is well settled that when a statute requires a thing to be done in a particular manner, it is to be done in that manner alone. UPPTCL could not have taken recourse to the methods adopted by it. Cess could only be recovered in the manner stipulated in the Cess Act and the Rules framed thereunder.

In DIAL the issue related to the payment of service tax on UDF collected by the airport operator DIAL from the passengers. DIAL was asked to pay service tax as it was collecting fees from the passengers under the Airports Authority of India (Major Airports) Development Fees Rules 2011. Following the judgment in Online Foundation in which the Supreme Court held UDF as a statutory duty, Justice Ravindra Bhat declared that in the present case, undoubtedly, neither is there any compulsion to levy development fee nor is the collection conditional upon its deposit in the government treasury. However, the absence of these features does not render UDF any less a statutory levy. As a statutory levy, UDF is a tax in the nature of cess as the UDF is collected for financing the cost of future projects. In DIAL, the Supreme Court laid down a significant legal principle on a distinction between tax and fee, and is a landmark judgment in line with developments in common law jurisdictions. Thus, UDF is not subject to the service tax. It would however be appropriate to change the title of the Airports Authority of India (Major Airports) Development Fees Rules, 2011 to the Airports Authority of India (Major Airports) Development Cess Rules, 2011, as a cess may be in nature of a tax, as held by the Supreme Court.[24a]

2.6 Salient aspects concerning the distribution of the legislative powers between the Parliament and State Legislature

Article 246 of the Constitution deals with the distribution of legislative powers between the Union and the States. Article 246 along with the three Lists namely the Union List, the State List, and the Concurrent List allocates the legislative powers. The taxing powers of the Union as well as the States are also demarcated as separate Entries in the Union List as well as the State List *i.e.*, List I and List II respectively. The Entries in the Lists are the fields of legislative powers conferred under Article 246 of the Constitution. The Entries define the areas of legislative competence of the Union and State Legislature.

Under the Seventh Schedule of the Constitution, Lists I & II are divided essentially into two groups: One, relating to the power to legislate on specified

24a. *Central GST Delhi - III* v. *Delhi International Airport Ltd.* [Civil Appeal No(s). 8996 of 2019 [06-01-2023]]/[2023] 147 taxmann.com 261/292 Taxman 4 (SC) Two judges bench comprising of [Justice Mr. S. Ravindra Bhat and Justice Mr. Dipankar Datta].

subjects, and the other, relating to the power to tax. Taxation is considered a distinct matter for purposes of legislative competence.[25]

2.7 Competence to tax

The power of taxation is generally regarded as an essential attribute of sovereignty and constitutional provisions relating to the power of taxation are regarded not as a grant of power but as limitation upon the power which would otherwise be practically without limit[26]. The only limit on this power is, where the taxing statute is plainly discriminatory, or provides no procedural machinery for assessment and levy of tax on that, it is confiscatory. In such cases, the character of the material provisions of the impugned statute is such that the court would be justified in taking the view that, in substance the taxing statute is a cloak, adopted by the legislature for achieving its confiscatory purpose.[27]

2.8 Tax on income

Income-tax Act, 1961 and annual Finance Acts are enacted by the Parliament in exercise of the power conferred by article 246(1) read with entry 82 of list 1.

Once the Parliament has the legislative competence to enact a law with respect to a certain subject matter, the limits of that competence cannot be judged further by the form or manner in which that power is exercised. Accordingly, though it would be unconventional for the Parliament to amend the taxing statue by incorporating the amending provisions in an Act of different pith and substance, such a course would not be unconstitutional.[28]

Much more so can the Parliament introduce a charging section in a Finance Act.

In *Kesoram Industries and Cotton Mill Limited* v. *CWT*[29], it was observed:

> "True it is that the Income-tax Act is a permanent Act while the Finance Acts are passed every year and their primary purpose is to prescribe rates at which the income tax will be charged under the Income-tax Act. But that does not mean that a new and distinct charge cannot be introduced under the Finance Act. Exigencies of the financial year determine the scope and nature of its provisions. If the Parliament has the legislative competence to introduce a new charge of tax it may exercise that power either by incorporating that charge in the Income tax Act or by introducing it in the Finance Act or for that matter in any other statute. The alternative in this regard is generally determined by the consideration whether the new charge is intended to be more or less of a permanent nature or whether its introduction is dictated by financial exigencies of the particular year."

25. *Hoechst Pharmaceuticals Ltd.* v. *State of Bihar* AIR 1983 SC 1019.
26. *Assistant Commissioner of Urban Land Tax* v. *Buckingham and Carnatic Company Limited* AIR 1970 SC 169, 179.
27. *Rai Ramkrishna* v. *State of Bihar* AIR 1963 SC 1967, 1973. (Bihar Taxation of Passengers and Goods Act, 1961 (17 of 1961).
28. *MD Central Cooperative Bank* v. *ITO* AIR 1975 SC 2016, 2020.
29. AIR 1966 SC 1360.

Therefore, it was observed further, what is not "income" under the Income-tax Act can be made "income" by the Finance Act, an exemption granted by the Income-tax Act can be withdrawn by the Finance Act or the efficacy of that exemption may be reduced by the imposition of new charge.

2.9 Surcharge

The power to increase federal tax by surcharges by federal legislature was recommended for the first time in the Report of the Committee on Indian Constitutional Reform[30]. The word "surcharge" was used compendiously for the special addition to taxes on income imposed in September 1931. The provisions relating to surcharges were omitted in the Finance Acts of 1946 to 1950. It was reintroduced in the Finance Act, 1951 and the same has continued in subsequent years. Special surcharges came to be levied in the Finance Acts of 1958 to 1964 and 1966 to 1971 and the additional surcharge was levied only by the Finance Act, 1963.

The imposition of a surcharge would fall within the legislative entry 82 list 1.[31] such as may be of various kinds such as a special surcharge and additional surcharge.

Health and Education Cess is levied at the rate of 4% on the amount of income tax plus surcharge.

2.10 Excise duty on liquor

The excise duty on liquor is leviable by a State, however, a State Government is not competent to levy excise duty on liquor which the contractors have failed to lift. In this regard the validity of the notification issued by the State Government in the exercise of its power under clauses (*d*) and (*h*) of section 62 of the Madhya Pradesh Excise Act, 1915 was challenged. The legislature has levied excise duty only on those articles which come within the scope of section 25.[32] It was found that the rule-making authority has not been conferred with any power to levy duty on any article which does not fall within the scope of section 25. It was held:

> "No tax can be imposed by any by-law or rule or regulation unless the statute under which the subordinate legislation is made especially authorises the imposition even if it is assumed that the power to tax can be delegated to the executive. The basis of the statutory power conferred by the statute cannot be transgressed by

30. Vol. I. Part I.
31. *CIT* v. *K. Srinivasan* AIR 1972 SC 491, 494.
32. Section 25 reads as follows—

    Duty on excisable articles (1) An excise duty or a countervailing duty, as the case maybe, shall, if the state government so direct, be levied on excisable articles- (*a*) imported; or (*b*) exported; or (*c*) transported or; (*d*) manufactured, cultivated or collected under any licence granted under section 13; or (*e*) manufactured in any distillery established, or any distillery or brewery licenced under this Act.

> the rule-making authority. A rule-making authority has no plenary power. It has to act within the limits of the power granted to it."[33]

2.11 Sales tax

Entry 54 list II of the Seventh Schedule of the Constitution authorises the state legislature to legislate in respect of taxes on the sale or purchase of goods. A legislative entry like entry 54 list II does not merely enunciate powers. It specifies a field of legislation and the widest import and significance should be attached to it. Power to legislate on a topic includes power to legislate in respect of matters which may fairly and reasonably be said to be comprehended therein.[34] A taxing entry, therefore, confers power upon the legislature to legislate for matters ancillary or incidental including provision for preventing evasion of tax.[35] Section 42 of the Madras General Sales Tax Act, 1959 which set up the machinery of check post for prevention of sales tax and consequent confiscation of goods carried in a vehicle without document was held to be not falling within the ambit of ancillary and incidental power to tax sale of goods.[36]

In *Kasturilal Harlal* v. *State of UP*[37], the validity of section 29A of the UP-Sales Tax Act, 1948 was challenged. This section laid down the procedure for the disbursement of amounts wrongly realised by dealers as tax. This provision was held constitutionally valid, Justice Bhagwati observed:

> "It is now well settled that an entry in a legislative list must be read in its widest amplitude and the legislature must be held to have power not only to legislate with respect to the subject matter of the entry but also to make ancillary or incidental provision in the aid of main topic of legislation."

And consequently, section 29A was held to be an exercise of incidental power. The court observed further that the taking over of sums collected by dealers from the public under the guise of tax solely with a view to return them to the buyers so deprived is necessarily incidental to tax on the sale or purchase of goods. Such a provision is manifestly a consumer protection measure.

By the Constitution (One Hundred and First Amendment) Act, 2016[38], entry 54 List II has been substituted as under:

> "54. Taxes on the sale of petroleum crude, high speed diesel, motor spirit (commonly known as petrol), natural gas, aviation turbine fuel and alcoholic liquor for human consumption, but not including sale in the course of inter-State trade or commerce or sale in the course of international trade or commerce of such goods."

---

33. *B.C. Banerjee* v. *State of M.P.* AIR 1971 SC 517, 520.
34. *C.P. Officer* v. *K. P. Abdullah* AIR 1971 SC 792.
35. Shah J, in *Navinchand Mafatlal* v. *CIT* AIR 1955 SC58; *Balaji* v. *ITO* AIR 1962 SC 123.
36. *C.P. Officer* v. *K. P. Abdullah* AIR 1971 SC 792, 793.
37. AIR 1987 SC 27.
38. The Act came into force: 08-09-2016 (Date of Assent).

2.12 Interpretation of Legislative entry

There is no dispute that the heads of legislation in the various lists in the Seventh Schedule of the Constitution should be interpreted widely so as to take in all matters which are of character incidental to the topics mentioned therein. Even so, there is a limit to such incidental or ancillary power. These incidental and ancillary powers have to be exercised in aid of the main topic of legislation. Thus, the provisions of Hyderabad General Sales Tax Act, 1940 which provided under section 11(2) that the amount collected by way of tax though not exigible to tax under the Act and if not paid over shall be recovered as arrears of land revenue was held to be beyond the legislative competence under entry 54 list II.[39] All powers necessary for the levy or collection of tax concerned and for seeing that the tax is not evaded are comprised within the ambit of the legislative entry as ancillary or incidental. But where the legislation under the relevant entry proceeds on the basis that amount concerned is not a tax exigible under the law made under that entry, but even so lays down that it is not exigible under the law, it shall be paid over to the government, merely because some dealers by mistake or otherwise have collected it as a tax, it is difficult to see- how such a provision can be ancillary or incidental to the collection of tax legitimately due under a law made under the relevant taxing entry. The impact of ancillary or incidental power does not permit the legislature to provide that though the amount collected may be wrongly, by way of tax is not exigible under the law as made under the relevant taxing entry, it shall still be paid over to the government as if were a tax.

In *Assistant Commissioner of Urban Land Tax, Madras* v. *Buckingham & Carnatic Company Limited*[40], the question of the interpretation of the legislative entries and the list I of entries 86 and 87 and entry 49 list II came for consideration. The court observed that the legislative entries must be given a large and liberal interpretation, the reason being that the allocation of subjects to the lists is not by way of scientific or logical definition but by way of a mere simplex numeration of broad categories. Entries 86 and 87 of List 1 do not preclude the state legislature from taxing the capital value of land and buildings under entry 49 of List II. In fact, there is no conflict between entry 86 of List 1 and entry 49 of List II. The basis of operation under the two entries is quite distinct. As regards entry 86 of list I the basis of taxation is the capital value of the asset. It is not a tax directly on the capital value of assets of individuals and companies on the valuation date. The tax is not imposed on the components of the assets of the assessee. The tax under entry 86 proceeds on the principle of aggregation and is imposed on the totality of the value of all assets. On the other hand, Entry 49 of List II contemplates a levy of tax on lands and buildings or both as a unit. It is not concerned with the division of interest or ownership in the

39. *Abdul Quadar* v. *STO* AIR 1964 SC 922 Wanchoo J. (Gajendragadkar, Dasgupta, Shah, Ayyngar).
40. AIR 1970 SC 169. List I entry 86 reads as Taxes on the capital value of the assets exclusive of a agriculture land, or individuals and companies, taxes on the capital of the companies.
List II entry 87 reads as estate duty in respect of property.

units of land or building which are brought to tax. Tax on lands and buildings is directly imposed on land and buildings and bears a definite relation to it. For the purpose of levying tax under entry 49 list II, the state legislature may adopt for determining the incidence of tax the annual value or the capital value of the land and buildings. However, the adoption of the annual or capital value of lands and buildings for determining tax liability will not make the field of legislation under the two entries overlapping.[41]

The Supreme Court laid down the principles of interpretation of taxation Entries in List II even when regulation of an activity is provided under an Entry in List I. Legislation in the field of tax and economic activities need special consideration and are to be viewed with larger flexibility rather than measuring the propositions by an abstract symmetry. Thus, there is a distinction between power to regulate and control and power to tax, the two being distinct.[42]

Thus, the power to legislate which is dealt with under Article 246 has to be read in conjunction with the Entries in the three Lists which define the respective areas of legislative competence of the Union and State Legislatures. While interpreting these entries, they should not be viewed in a narrow or myopic manner but by giving the widest scope to their meaning, particularly, when the vires of a provision of a statute is assailed. In such circumstances, a liberal construction must be given to the Entry by looking at the substance of the legislation and not its mere form.

However, while interpreting the Entries in the case of an apparent conflict, every attempt must be made by the Court to harmonise or reconcile them. Where there is an apparent overlapping between two Entries, the doctrine of pith and substance is applied to find out the true character of the enactment and the entry within which it would fall. The doctrine of pith and substance, in short, means, that if an enactment substantially falls within the powers expressly conferred by the Constitution upon the legislature which enacted it, it cannot be held to be invalid merely because it incidentally encroaches on matters assigned to another legislature.[43]

The entries in List I and List II must be construed if possible, so as to avoid conflict. If there appears to be a conflict between Entries of List I and List II, what has to be decided is whether there is any real conflict. If there is none, the question of application of the non-obstante clause 'subject to' does not arise. If there is a conflict, the correct approach to the question is to see, whether, it is possible to effect a reconciliation between the two entries so as to avoid a conflict and overlapping. In the event of a dispute arising it should be determined by applying the doctrine of pith and substance in order to find out whether, between two Entries or legislative fields assigned to two different legislatures,

41. *Assistant Commissioner of Urban Land Tax* v. *Buckingham & Carnatic Co. Ltd.* AIR 1970 SC 169.

42. *State of Karnataka* v. *State of Meghalaya* [Civil Appeal Nos. 10466-10476 of 2011 decided on 23rd March, 2022]/[2022] 139 taxmann.com 454/60 GSTL 161 (SC).

43. *State of Karnataka* v. *State of Meghalaya* [Civil appeal Nos.10466-10476 of 2011 decided on 23rd March, 2022]/[2022] 139 taxmann.com 454/60 GSTL 161 (SC).

the particular subject of the legislation falls within the ambit of the one or the other. Where there is a clear and irreconcilable conflict of jurisdiction between the Union and a State Legislature, it is the law of the Union that must prevail.[44]

2.13 Pith and substance

When the validity of legislation is challenged on the ground of want of legislative competence and it becomes necessary to ascertain to which entry in three lists the legislation is referable, the court has evolved a theory of pith and substance[45]. If the pith and substance of legislation fall within one entry or the other but some portion of the subject matter of the legislation incidentally trenches upon and might enter a field under another list, the Act as a whole would be valid notwithstanding such incidental trenching. The pith and substance of the Act has to be looked into and an incidental trespass will not invalidate the law. For ascertaining the pith and substance the entire scheme of the Act is to be looked into. A comprehensive examination of all the provisions of the Act is to be undertaken to justify the inclusion in one entry or the other[46].

The entries in the three lists do not follow any logical classification or dichotomy. Since they are likely to overlap occasionally, it is usual to examine the pith and substance of legislation with a view to determining to which entry they can be substantially related, a slight connection with another entry in another list notwithstanding.

The Constitution divides the topics of legislation into three broad categories: (*a*) entries enabling laws to be made; (*b*) entries relating tax to be imposed, and (*c*) entries enabling fees and stamp duty to be collected, it is not intended that every entry gives a right to levy a tax. The taxes are separately mentioned and in fact, contain the whole power of taxation. Unless a tax is specifically mentioned it cannot be imposed except by parliament in the exercise of its residuary power. In regard to the validity of the Gift Tax Act, the issue arose was that whether it falls under Entry 18 List II or Entry 97 list 1[47].

Entry 18 of List II reads as follows:

> '18. land, that is to say, rights in or over land, land tenures including the relationship of landlord and tenant, and the collection of rents; transfer and alienation of agriculture land; land improvement and agriculture loans'.

The court held this entry does not confer additional power of taxation. At the most fees can be levied in respect of the items mentioned in that entry, *vide* entry 66 of the State list. But, however, wide that entry, it cannot still authorise a tax

44. *State of Karnataka* v. *State of Meghalaya* [Civil Appeal Nos. 10466-10476 of 2011 decided on 23rd March, 2022]/[2022] 139 taxmann.com 454/60 GSTL 161 (SC).

45. *Ishwari Khaitan Sugar Mills* v. *State of UP* AIR 1980 SC 1955, 1964.

46. See also, *Union of India* v. *HS Dhillon* AIR 1972 SC 1061, *KSE Board* v. *Indian Aluminium* AIR 1976 SC 1031 and *State of Karnataka* v. *R Reddy* AIR 1978 SC 215 (Karnataka contract carries acquisition Ordinance 1976).

47. *Second GTO* v. *DS Nazarath* AIR 1970 SC 999.

not expressly mentioned. Therefore, either the pith and substance of the Gift Tax Act fall within entry 49 of the state list i.e. taxes on lands and buildings or not. If it does, then the Parliament will have no power to levy the tax even under residuary powers. If it does not, then Parliament must undoubtedly possess that power under Article 248 and Entry 97 of the union list.

The court observed that the pith and substance of the Gift Tax Act is to place the tax on the gift of the property which mainly includes land and building. It is not a tax imposed directly upon lands and buildings but is a tax upon the value of the total gifts made in a year which is above the exempted limit. There is no tax on lands or buildings as units of taxation. Indeed, the lands and buildings are valued to find out the total amount of gifts and what is taxed is gift. The value of the land and building is only measure of the value of the gift. A gift tax is thus not a tax on lands and buildings, as such which is tax resting upon general ownership of land and buildings but is a levy upon a particular use, which is transmission of title by gift.

Thus, in determining whether an enactment is legislation with respect to a given power what is relevant is not the consequences of the enactment on the subject matter or whether it affects it, but whether in pith and substance it is a law upon the subject matter in question.

In *Assistant Commissioner of Urban Land Tax, Madras* v. *Buckingham and Carnatic Company Limited*[48], the limits of pith and substance principle were stated as follows:

> "It is well established that you are to look at the true nature and character of the legislation. The pith substance of the legislation. If on the view of the Statute as a whole, you find that the substance of the legislation is within the express powers then it is not invalidated if incidentally, it affects matters which are outside the authorised field. The legislation must not under the guise of dealing with one matter in fact encroach upon the forbidden field. Nor are you to look only at the object of the legislature... you may certainly consider the clauses of an Act to see whether they are passed in respect of the forbidden subject.[49]"

On the "pith and substance" test in *Gallagher* v. *Lynn*,[50] it is stated that a degree of trespass into reserved areas is inevitable because reserved and other areas are not divided into neat watertight compartments.

2.14 Retrospective operation of law

A retrospective legislation is one which gives to pre-enactment conduct a different legal effect from that which it would have had without the passage of the statute. The most obvious kind of retrospective statute is one which relates back to attaching new legal rights and duties to already completed transactions. However, the most fundamental reason why retrospective legislation is suspect

48. AIR 1970 SC 169.
49. *Ibid* at p. 179.
50. (1937) AC 863 at page 870.

stems from the principle that a person should be able to plan his conduct with reasonable certainty of legal consequences. He expects stability with respect to past transactions.

In the United States, the Supreme Court *United States* v. *Carlton* 512 US 26 (1994) analysed the due process clause on the basis of their retrospective operation. The relevant article of the Constitution is Article I, Section 10, which provides that no state shall pass any law impairing the obligations of the contract. However, the court has taken the view that only those retrospective legislation is unconstitutional which on a balancing of consideration on both sides felt to be unreasonable.

2.14.1 In the case of *Jawahar Mal* v. *The State of Rajasthan*[51], the Supreme Court held that the power to make laws involves the power to make them effective prospectively as well as retrospectively and tax laws are no exception to this rule. So, it would be idle to contend that merely because the taxing statute purports to operate retrospectively, the retrospective operation *per se* involves contravention of the fundamental rights of the citizen taxed under article 19 (f) or (g). The Supreme Court stated that it is true that cases may conceivably occur where the court may have to consider the question as to whether excessive retrospective operation prescribed by the taxing statute amounts to the contravention of the citizen's fundamental right; and in dealing with such a question, the court may have to take into account all the relevant and surrounding facts and circumstances in relation to the taxation.

2.14.2 In the case of *Assistant Commissioner of Urban Land Tax* v. *Buckingham and Carnatic Company Limited*[52], the Supreme Court held that it is not right to say as a general proposition that the imposition of tax with retrospective effect *per se* renders the law unconstitutional. In applying the test of reasonableness to a taxing statute it is of course a relevant consideration that the tax is being enforced with retrospective effect but that is not conclusive in itself.

2.14.3 In the case of *Krishna Murti and Company* v. *State of Madras*[53] Supreme Court held that the aim of the Amending and Validating Act is to effectuate and carry out the object for which the earlier principal Act has been enacted. The making of small repairs is a permissible mode of amending and validating Act and is frequently resorted to in fiscal enactments. The object of such an enactment is to remove and rectify the effect in phraseology or lacunae of other nature and also to validate the proceedings, including the realisation of tax, which has taken place in pursuance of the earlier enactment which has been found by the court to be vitiated by an infirmity.

---

51. AIR 1976 SC 764 at p. 772.
52. AIR 1970 SC 169. The petitioner contended that the retrospective operation of the law from 1st July, 1963 would make it unreasonable. The Supreme Court did not accept the contention of the petitioner.
53. (1973) 31 STC 190 at p. 197.

2.14.4 In the case of *Hiralal Ratanlal* v. *STO*[54], the Supreme Court held that a feeble attempt was made to show that the retrospective levy made under the Act is violative of article 19(1)(*f*) and (*g*). But the court found no substance in that contention. In fact, the amendment of the Act was necessitated because of the legislature's failure to bring out clearly in the principal Act its intention to separate the processed or split pulses from the unsplit or unprocessed pulses process. Further, the retrospective amendment became necessary as otherwise, the state would have to refund large sums of money.

2.14.5 In the case of *State of Gujarat* v. *Raman Lal Keshav Lal Soni*[55], the Supreme Court stated that the legislature is undoubtedly competent to legislate with prospective effect to take away or impair any vested right acquired under existing laws but since the laws are made under a written Constitution, and have to confirm to dos and don't of the Constitution neither prospective nor retrospective laws can be made so as to contravene fundamental rights. The law must satisfy the requirements of the Constitution today taking into account the accrued or acquired rights of the parties today. The law cannot say that 20 years ago the parties had no rights; therefore, the requirements of the Constitution will be satisfied if the law is dated back 20 years. We are concerned with today's rights and not yesterday's. A legislature cannot legislate today with reference to a situation that occurred 20 years ago and ignored the march of events and the constitutional rights accrued in the course of the 20 years. That would be most arbitrary, unreasonable, and a negation of history.

2.14.6 In the *Lohia Machines Limited* v. *Union of India*[55a] the Supreme Court held that the power and competence of Parliament to amend any statutory provision with retrospective effect cannot be doubted. A Validating Act validating any fiscal provision with retrospective operation is usually held not to be unreasonable or arbitrary. In the case of any Validating Act, the intention of the legislature is generally made sufficiently clear in the section or in the Act which is declared invalid on account of some flaw or defect which is within the competence of parliament to rectify. Such Validating Acts do not in fact have the effect of imposing a fresh tax with retrospective effect and they only legalise the levy already imposed. Appropriate legislation including various fiscal laws is enacted for this purpose. The imposition of any tax by parliament is, therefore, considered to be made in the public interest. It may so happen that any provision of any enactment imposing a particular levy may be held to be constitutionally invalid. If any particular provision of any statute imposing any tax which has been or is being collected, is struck down as unconstitutional, the financial arrangement of the state may become upset and the government which might have already collected and even utilised the tax may be called upon to refund tax so collected. If such a situation arises, the economy of the state may get unbalanced and difficulties may arise in meeting the various commitments and obligations. Under such circumstances, a validating Act may be passed and

54. (1973) 31 STC 178 at p. 186.

55. (1983) 2 SCC 33 at p. 62.

55a. (1985) 152 ITR 308, 381/20 Taxman 9 (SC).

is often enacted to remove the infirmity that might have led to the invalidation of the provision imposing the levy.

Any retrospective amendment to be valid must, however, be reasonable and not arbitrary and must not be violative of any of the fundamental rights guaranteed under the Constitution. The mere fact that any statutory provision has been amended with retrospective effect does not by itself make the amendment unreasonable. Unreasonableness and arbitrariness of any such amendment with retrospective effect has necessarily to be judged on the merits of the amendment in the light of the facts and circumstances under which such amendment is made. In considering the question as to whether the legislative power to amend the provision with retrospective operation has been reasonably exercised or not it becomes relevant to enquire as to how the retrospective effect of the amendment operates. In fiscal matters, in the larger interest of administration and for the promotion of public interest and welfare of the country, power has been conferred by the Constitution on Parliament to mobilise resources and to levy taxes. Because of the complexity of fiscal adjustment of diverse elements, parliament necessarily enjoys a very wide discretion in the matter of fiscal legislation. To meet various expenses for proper administration, maintenance of defense and security, for promoting peace and prosperity, and for development of social, economic, and all-round growth of the country, the government must have resources and sufficient funds at its disposal. Suitable provisions have necessarily to be made for raising revenue and for proper realisation of funds to be collected to meet such expenses.

However, Justice A. N. Sen in *Lohia Machines Limited* v. *Union of India* held the retrospective amendment violative of Article 19(1)(g) of the Constitution. Justice Sen held that it is true that in considering the question as to whether legislative power to pass an Act retrospectively has been reasonably exercised or not, it is relevant to enquire how the retrospective operation operates. The withdrawal or modification with retrospective effect of the relief properly granted by the statute to an assessee which the assessee has lawfully enjoyed or entitled to enjoy as his vested statutory right, depriving the assessee of the vested statutory right has the effect of imposing the levy with retrospective effect for the year for which there was no such levy and cannot, unless there be strong and exceptional circumstances justifying such withdrawal or modification, be held to be reasonable or in public interest. This kind of retrospective amendment, seeking to defeat an accrued statutory right is likely to affect the sanctity of any statutory provision and may create a state of confusion. To establish arbitrariness or unreasonableness it does not become necessary to prove that the undertaking of the assessee will be completely crippled that will have to be closed down in consequence of the withdrawal of the relief with retrospective effect. The operation of the retrospective amendment is bound to have with serious effect on the assessee and there is a reasonable possibility of the business of the assessee being adversely affected and seriously prejudiced.

Withdrawal with retrospective effect by amendment of any financial benefit or relief granted by a fiscal statute must ordinarily be held to the unreasonable and arbitrary. Such withdrawal makes a mockery of a beneficial statutory provision and leads to chaos and confusion. Such withdrawal in effect results in the imposition of a levy at a future date for past years for which there was no such levy in the relevant years. The imposition of any fresh tax with retrospective effect for years for which there was no levy is bound to operate unduly harshly on every assessee who is entitled to arrange and normally arranges his financial affairs on the basis of the law as it exists. Such retrospective taxation imposes an unjust and unwarranted accumulated burden on the assessee for no fault on his part and the assessee has to face unnecessary without any just reason very serious financial and other problems. Imposition of any tax with retrospective effect for years for which there was no such tax was there cannot also be considered to be just and reasonable from the point of view of the revenue. Such retrospective taxation is likely to disturb and unsettle the settled problems; and because of such imposition of retrospective levy for the years for which there was no such levy, assessment completed and concluded will get upset. If the State is in need of more funds the state instead of seeking to levy any tax with retrospective effect, can always take appropriate steps to collect any larger amount so required by the imposition of higher taxes or by other appropriate methods.

2.14.7 In *Empire Industries*[56] the Supreme Court upheld retrospective operation under the Excise Duty Act. The Court held that it is necessary that the legislature should be able to cure inadvertent defects in statute or their administration by making what has been called small repairs. Moreover, the individual who claims that a vested right has risen from the defect is seeking a windfall since the legislature's or administrator's action had the effect it intended to and could have had, no such right would have arisen.

Thus, the interest in the retrospective curing of such defect in the administration of Government outweighs the individual interest in benefiting from the defect. The court has been extremely reluctant to override the legislative judgment as to the necessity for retrospective taxation, not because of the paramount government interest in obtaining adequate revenues but also because taxes are not in the nature of the penalty or a contractual obligation but rather a means of apportioning the costs of government among those who benefit by it.[57]

2.14.8 In *D. Cawa J & Co.*[58], the constitutional validity of the Mysore Sales Tax Amendment Act, 1969 was challenged. By this amendment, section 2 was amended as follows:

Section 2. In the Second Schedule to the Mysore Sales Tax Act, 1957 in column 3 of serial number 39 for the words "six and a half per cent." the words " forty-five per cent" shall be and shall be deemed to have been substituted with effect from the 1st day of April, 1966.

---

56. *Empire Industries Ltd.* v. *Union of India* (1986) 162 ITR 846,873.

57. *Ibid*. Definition of manufacture in section 2(*f*) of the Central Excise Duty Act by an amendment included processing, dying etc. This definition was given retrospective effect.

58. *D.Cawa J & Co.* v. *State of Mysore* (1985) 58 STC 461 (SC).

It was argued that the Amending Act is arbitrary and unreasonable since it seeks to levy sales tax on the value of goods which includes excise duty and cess. Delivering the judgment, Justice A.N. Sen observed:

> "The amendment does not proceed to cure the defect or the lacuna by bringing in an amendment providing for eligibility of sales tax on excise duty, health cess, and education cess. The impugned amending Act may not, therefore, be considered to be a validating Act. A Validating Act seeks to validate the earlier Acts declared illegal and unconstitutional by courts by removing the defects or lacuna which led to invalidation of the law."

A Validating Act is usually passed with retrospective effect. The retrospective operation relieves the state of the consequences of acts done prior to the passing of the Validating Act. The retrospective operation of a Validating Act properly passed curing the defects and lacuna which might have led to the invalidity of any act done may be upheld if considered reasonable and legitimate. The Supreme Court held the enhancement of the rate of duty from 6 and a half per cent to 45% with retrospective effect is in the facts and circumstances of the case clearly arbitrary and unreasonable. It may be open to the legislature to impose the duty at a higher rate with prospective operation but levy of taxation at a higher rate which really amounts to imposition of tax with retrospective operation has to be justified on the proper and cogent reasons.

2.14.9 In *Ambae Picture Palace*[59], a limit was shown to have been put on the retrospective operation of taxation law. The Andhra Pradesh High Court observed:

> "In the principles entrenched as to reasonableness, the State is obliged to offer an explanation when retrospective effect is given to a taxing statute. In those cases where no explanation is offered, no proper or cogent reasons are suggested the retrospectivity of an Act cannot be sustained. In such cases, retrospectivity is penal in character. It is no argument that there is no equity about the tax or that the government has the power to impose a tax with a retrospective effect. The constitutional requirement as to reasonableness must be satisfied."

2.14.10 Retrospective operation and rule of law

The rule of law will insist on changes enacted openly through procedures that are transparent and clear, changes that are formulated prospectively in general terms, and changes that take the form of established schemes that people can expect to see upheld and enforced in the medium and long term, changes set out publicly in intelligible legal texts and then given to independent judicial tribunals for interpretation, administration, and enforcement. In recent years more and more changes in tax laws—direct and indirect—namely income tax, central excises, and customs, have been carried out through the Finance Act. The basic objective of a Finance Bill/Act is to prescribe rates of tax/duties. However, amendments in the statutory tax laws through the Finance Acts have

---

59. *Ambae Picture Palace* v. *ETO* (1986) 162 ITR 772 (AP) The Andhra Pradesh Entertainment Tax Act, 1985 passed on October 24th, 1984 that it will take effect from September 7, 1984. No cogent reasons were given for retrospective operation of the statute.

so far found favour with the courts. The number of retrospective amendments made in the Income Tax Act, 1961 through the Finance Act has been quite large. Some of these amendments are under challenge before the courts. At present in India, transparency and accountability are ensured in all legislations as they are referred to the Committees of Parliament (Select Committee, Joint Committee, Department Related Parliamentary Standing Committees) for scrutiny and report. Like other legislation, a Finance Bill amending tax laws and more particularly giving retrospectively to a number of provisions for a period which goes from a year to a period going back to the date of commencement of the Income-tax Act, 1961 is also required to undergo scrutiny by a Committee of Parliament. Such a measure will ensure transparency in the law-making process. The recent practice in the United Kingdom is that provisions of a Finance Bill other than rates of tax are scrutinized by a Committee of Parliament. In India, a time has come to confine the provisions of a Finance Bill to rates only and this will silence critics of retrospective amendments including foreign investors— who like an average Indian require our laws to be stable and predictable.

Supreme Court recently in R. Gandhi[59a] has observed that legislature is presumed not to legislate contrary to the Rule of Law and observed further that though the validity of the provisions of a legislative Act cannot be challenged on the ground that it violates the basic structure of the Constitution, it can be challenged as violative of constitutional provisions which enshrine the principles of Rule of Law, separation of power and independence of the judiciary. The rule of Law demands that changes in laws ought to be enacted openly through procedures that are transparent and clear. Changes in law ought to be formulated prospectively in general terms and changes set out publicly in intelligible legal texts and then given to independent judicial tribunals for interpretation, administration, and enforcement. That seems to be the spirit of the Rule of Law. The spirit of legislative due process that changes in law ought to be formulated prospectively in general terms was not followed by Parliament in overturning the Supreme Court verdict in Vodafone[59b]. By the Taxation Laws (Amendment) Act, 2021, retrospectivity to section 9 of the Income-tax Act, 1961 was rationalised. The Taxation Laws (Amendment) Act, 2021 amends the Income-tax Act, 1961 so as to provide that no tax demand shall be raised in the future on the basis of the said retrospective amendment for any indirect transfer of Indian assets if the transaction was undertaken before 28th May 2012 (*i.e.*, the date on which the Finance Bill, 2012 received the assent of the President). It is further proposed to provide that the demand raised for indirect transfer of Indian assets made before 28th May, 2012 shall be nullified on fulfilment of specified conditions such as withdrawal or furnishing of undertaking for withdrawal of pending litigation and furnishing of an undertaking to the effect that no claim for cost, damages, interest, etc., shall be filed.

59a. *Union of India* v. *R. Gandhi, President, Madras Bar Association* [2011] 11 SCC 1

59b. Chaturvedi, Kameshwar Nath, Legislative Retrospectivity and Rule of Law, Statute Law Review, Vol. 34, Issue 3, pp. 207-220 .

2.15 Delegation of Taxing Power

The legislature is required to perform its essential legislative functions. Once the skeletal structure of the policy is framed by the legislature, the details can emerge through delegated legislation.[60] It is a settled position that the legislature cannot delegate its 'essential legislative functions.'[61] The essential legislative functions with respect to the tax law are the levy of tax, subject matter of tax, taxable person, rate of taxation, and value for the purpose of taxation. However, the power to frame rules, regulations, and notifications which are essentially legislative in character is entrusted to the executive. Under delegated legislation or subordinate legislation, the legislature must lay down the policy.

Essential legislative functions are the determination of legislative policy and its formation as a rule of conduct. There is excessive delegation when there is (*a*) no legislative policy; (*b*) vague legislative policy; (*c*) absence of any standard for guidance; (*d*) absence of control; (*e*) wide powers of modification. However, legislative policy is laid down if there is specific mention of the purpose, object, and limits of taxation.

Rules - They may be defined as minor laws. The legislature may give out the list of topics on which rules are to be made. They are made by the government. They are general in character.

Regulation - They are inferior to rules. They are made by a board or statutory bodies and have limited application.

By-laws - Municipal bodies are authorized to frame on a specific matters by-law. For instance, building bye-laws.

Order - They must have the force of law. They are specific and limited in duration. For instance, price control orders under the Essential Commodities Act.

2.15.1 Necessity of delegated legislation

On the necessity of delegated legislation in *Pandit Banarasi Das*[62] it was observed:—

> "... it is not unconstitutional for the legislature to leave it to the executive to determine details relating to the working of taxation laws, such as the selection of persons on whom the tax is to be laid, the rate at which it is to be charged in respect of different classes of goods and the like."

2.15.2 Requirements of law

Taxation can be made in India by subordinate legislation also provided they are authorized by the statute. In such cases, the legislature must lay down the policy. A statute may authorise the executive to vary the list of taxable commodities by

60. *Municipal Corporation of Delhi* v. *Birla Cotton Spinning and Weaving Mills* AIR 1968 SC 1232; *Avinder Singh* v. *State of Punjab* [1979] 1 SCC 137/[1979] 1979 taxmann.com 93 (SC).

61. *In re* Delhi Laws Act 1912, AIR 1951 SC 332; *Edward Mills Co. Ltd.* v. *State of Ajmer* AIR 1955 SC 25; *A.N. Parasaran* v. *State of Tamil Nadu* (1989) 4 SCC 683.

62. *Pandit Banarasi Das Bhanot* v. *State of M.P.* AIR 1958 SC 909 at 913.

addition or deletion and even to fix the rate of taxation. If the discretion of the executive in fixing the rate of tax is allowed to play over a wide range and there is a wide gap between minimum and maximum, it will amount to excessive delegation. Fixation of rates of tax not being an essential legislative function could be validly delegated to a non-legislative body but when it is left to such a body, the legislature must provide guidance for such fixation.

2.15.3 Liberty Cinema

In *Corporation of Calcutta* v. *Liberty Cinema*[63], section 548(2) of Calcutta Municipal Act, 1951 empowered the corporation to levy fees at such rates as may from time to time be fixed by the Corporation. In this case, the Court found the guidance in the monetary needs of the corporation for carrying out the function entrusted to it under the Act.

2.15.4 Municipal Board Hapur[64]

UP Municipality Act, 1913 conferred power on the municipality to fix the rate of tax. It was found by the court that the checks on municipality- (*a*) the fact that the board was a representative body; and (*b*) there were other safeguards by way of checks and control by the state government which could veto the action of the Board in case it did not carry out the mandate of the legislature.

2.15.5 Devidas Gopal Krishna[65]

Section 5 of the East Punjab Sales Tax Act, 1948 empowered the State government to fix sales tax at such rate as thought fit. On the issue of whether the legislature has sufficient control over the executive or not, Justice Subbarao observed:

> "The needs of the state and the purpose of the Act would not provide sufficient guidance for the fixation of the rate of tax."

2.15.6 Birla Cotton Spinning and Weaving Mill[65a]

In this case the court observed that the nature of the body to which delegation is made is also a factor to be taken into consideration in determining whether there is sufficient guidance in the matter of delegation. The fact that the delegation was made to an elected body responsible to the people including those who paid taxes provided a great check on the elected Councillor imposing an unreasonable rate of tax. The guidance may take the form of providing maximum rates of tax up to which local body may be given the discretion to make its choice or it may take the form of providing consultation with the people of local area. It may also take the form of subjecting the rate to be fixed by the local body to the approval of the government which acts as a watchdog on the actions of the local body. There may be other ways in which guidance may be provided.

63. AIR 1965 SC 1107.

64. *Municipal Board Hapur* v. *Raghuvendra Kripal* AIR 1966 SC 693.

65. *Devidas Gopal Krishna* v. *State of Punjab* AIR 1967 SC 1895.

65a. *Municipal Corporation of Delhi* v. *Birla Cotton Spinning and Weaning Mills Ltd.* AIR 1968 SC 1232.

2.15.7 Avinder Singh[66]

In this case the validity of a tax on foreign liquor was an issue. An order for tax on India-made Foreign Liquor was issued by the state government under section 90 of the Punjab Municipal Act, 1976. It was challenged, *inter alia*, on grounds of excessive delegation of legislative power. It was held that it is now well-settled that the essentials of legislative functions shall not be delegated but the inessentials, however numerous and significant they may be handed over to appropriate agencies subject to parliamentary control.

In the above case, the Supreme Court held that "for the purpose of this Act "provides a sufficient answer as to legislative policy.

2.15.8 Gwalior Rayon case[67]

In this case, the court upheld the validity of Section 8(2)(*b*) of the Central Sales Tax Act and ruled that Parliament can make a provision that Central sales tax shall be levied at the same rate at which the sale tax is being levied in the State Act, when there is a special reason for purpose exist.

2.15.9 International Cotton Corporation[68]

In this case, the validity of section 8(2)(*a*) of the Central Sales Tax Act, 1956 was upheld. It was held that section 8(2)(*a*) applies the rate of tax under the appropriate State Act to sales of declared goods in the course of interstate trade or commerce.

2.16 Limitations on the taxing power

The Constitution is the law of the land. All laws are to be in conformity with the provisions of the Constitution. The Constitution places certain limitations on the law-making power of the legislature. Various entries of the seventh schedule to the Constitution demarcate taxing power between the union and states. Further, constitutional limitations are provided in the chapter on fundamental rights, in article 265, in articles 301 to 307, and in articles 285 and 289 of the Constitution.

As far as fiscal legislation is concerned, the limitation is implicit in Article 265 of the Constitution which provides that no tax shall levied on collected except by the authority of law. The Supreme Court in *Chhotabhai Jethabhai Patel*[69] held that if by reason of article 265, every tax has to be imposed by the law it would appear to follow that it could only be imposed by law which is valid and is in conformity to criteria laid down in relevant articles of the Constitution. These are that the law should be (1) within the legislative competence of the legislature being covered by the legislative entries in Schedule VII of the Constitution;

---

66. *Avinder Singh* v. *State of Punjab* AIR 1979 SC 321.
67. *Gwalior Rayon Silk Mfg.* Co. v. *Asstt. Commissioner of Sales Tax* AIR 1974 SC 1660.
68. *International Cotton Corpn. (P.) Ltd.* v. *Commercial Tax Officer, Hubli* AIR 1975 SC 1604.
69. *Chhotabhai Jethabhai Patel and Company* v. *Union of India* AIR 1962 SC 1006.

(2) The Law should not be prohibited by any particular provision of the Constitution such as for example articles 276(2), 286 etc. and (3) the law or relevant provisions thereof should not be invalid under article 13 for repugnancy to those freedoms which are relevant to the subject matter of the law.

A provision of tax law may be challenged as violative of Article 14 or any other provision of the Constitution by way of a writ under Article 32, before the Supreme Court, and under Article 226 before the High Court. A writ petitioner may make a prayer for an appropriate writ, direction, or order. Article 14 forbids class legislation but permits reasonable classification for the purpose of legislation, which classification must satisfy the twin tests of classification being founded on an intelligible differentia that distinguishes persons or things that are grouped together from those that are left out of the group and that differentia must have a rational nexus to the object sought to be achieved by the statute in question. Further, a law that is manifestly arbitrary also violates Article 14.[70]

In *Madras Bar Association*[71], the National Tax Tribunal Act, 2005 was held unconstitutional. The precise question formulated on behalf of the petitioners is whether a tribunal can substitute the High Court in its appellate jurisdiction when it comes to deciding substantial questions of law. Justice Nariman in his concurring opinion observed that one of the objects for enacting the National Tax Tribunals Act, as stated by the Minister on the floor of the House, is that the National Tax Tribunal can lay down the law for the whole of India which then would bind all other authorities and tribunals. In view of the Court, this is a direct encroachment on the High Court's power under Art. 227 to decide substantial questions of law which would bind all tribunals. The decisions of the Supreme Court[72] have allowed tribunalization at the original stage subject to certain safeguards. The boundary has finally been crossed in this case.

Justice Nariman held that the National Tax Tribunals Act is unconstitutional, being the ultimate encroachment on the exclusive domain of the superior Courts of Record in India. Justice Khehar on his behalf and on behalf (of Lodha C.J., Chelameswar J, and AK Sikri J) held Sections 5, 6, 7, 8, and 13 of the National Tax Tribunal Act, 2005 to be unconstitutional, and held that the "basic structure" of the Constitution will stand violated, if while enacting legislation pertaining to transfer of judicial power, Parliament does not ensure, that the newly created court/tribunal, conforms with the salient characteristics and standards, of the court sought to be substituted. Constitutional conventions, pertaining to constitutions styled on the Westminster model, will also stand breached, if while enacting legislation, pertaining to the transfer of judicial power, conventions and

---

70. *Shayara Bano* v. *Union of India* (2017) 9 SCC 1.

71. *Madras Bar Association* v. *Union of India* [Transferred Case (C) No. 150 of 2006 date of decision 25-9-2014]/(2014) 10 SCC 1/[2014] 49 taxmann.com 515/227 Taxman 151 (Mag.) (SC).

72. *L. Chandra Kumar* v. *Union of India* (1997) 3 SCC 261/[1997] 1997 taxmann.com 1023 (SC).

salient characteristics of the court sought to be replaced, are not incorporated in the court/tribunal sought to be created.

2.16.1 Fundamental rights are those rights which are supreme and the State shall not make any law which takes away or abridges the rights conferred under part 3 of the constitution and any law made in the contravention of articles 14, 19 and 27 shall to the extent of the contravention be void.

Fundamental rights are given to citizens and non-citizens by the Constitution. Before the Constitution, there was a system of government *i.e.* Parliamentary form, under the Government of India Act, 1935 but there were no such provisions similar to the chapter on fundamental rights. Though all fundamental rights are important but greater emphasis is placed upon rights guaranteed under Article 14 and Article 19. Article 14 confers a right of equality on all persons-citizen and non-citizen and Article 19 confers six freedoms on all citizens only. Yet another important article is article 27.

Article 27 reads as follows:

> "No person shall be compelled to pay any taxes, the proceeds of which are specifically appropriated in payment of expenses for the promotion or maintenance of any particular religion or religious denomination."

The prohibition is in respect of tax and not in relation to fees.

2.16.2 Under Article 19 tax laws are frequently challenged as violative of Article 19(1)(*f*) and (*g*). However, in some cases, tax laws may violate other freedoms, *i.e.*, speech and expression. For example, a statute which imposes a tax on the business of advertisements in the newspaper would be void if it was found to be a deliberate and calculated device in the guise of a tax to limit the circulation of information to which the public is entitled by virtue of the constitutional guarantee.[73] Retrospective validation of tax laws does not amount to imposing unreasonable restrictions on fundamental rights. Provisions of taxing laws designed to prevent evasion of tax do not amount to unreasonable restrictions.

2.16.3 Taxation Laws and Article 14

Power of taxation cannot be used arbitrarily and, in a manner, inconsistent with fundamental rights guaranteed under the Constitution. No tax may be levied and collected under our constitutional setup except by the authority of law and the law must not only be within the legislative competence but it must also not be inconsistent with any other provisions of the Constitution. The State can make a reasonable classification for the purpose of legislation. The classification in order to be reasonable must satisfy two tests: (*i*) the classification must be founded on intelligible differentia and (*ii*) the differentia must have a rational relation with the object sought to be achieved by the legislation in question. The object itself should be lawful. The object itself cannot be discriminatory, for otherwise, for instance, if the object is to discriminate against one section of

73. *Express Newspaper* v. *Union of India* AIR 1958 SC 578.

the community the discrimination cannot be justified on the ground that there is a reasonable classification because it has a rational relation to the object sought to be achieved.[74]

2.17 Statute held constitutional

It is now a settled law that the legislature enjoys a wide latitude in framing taxation laws suitable for the economic policies of the state. The Special Bearer Bonds scheme was held constitutional in *R.K. Garg* case[75]. In RK Garg the provisions of Special Bearer Bonds (Immunities and Exemption Act, 1981) were challenged on the grounds of discrimination and violation of Article 14. It was laid down by the Constitution bench of five judges that laws relating to economic activities should be viewed with greater latitude than laws touching civil rights such as freedom of speech, religion, etc. RK Garg has been cited in a large number of cases. Some of the landmark judgments in this field are Bhavesh D. Parish, Indian Oil Corporation Limited, Goel Bus Service, and in Cosmo Films Limited.

In *Bhavesh D. Parish*[76], the challenge was to the validity of section 9 of Reserve Bank of India Act as amended by the Amendment Act, 1997 on the ground that it was violative of Article 14 and Article 19(1)(*g*) of the Constitution.

Indian Oil Corporation Limited[77], the Bihar Tax on Entry of Goods into Local Areas for Consumption, Use or Sale Act, 1993, was under challenge. Justice Nariman speaking for the Bench observed that when it comes to taxing statute, the law laid down by this Court is clear that it can be said to be breached only when there is perversity or gross disparity resulting in clear and hostile discrimination without any rational justification for the same.

In *Goel Bus Service*[78] Justice Vikram Nath speaking for the Court observed that it is by now well settled that any tax legislation may not be easily interfered with. The Courts must show judicial restraint to interfere with tax legislation unless it is shown and proved that such taxing statute is manifestly unjust or glaringly unconstitutional. Taxing statutes cannot be placed or tested or viewed on the same principles as laws affecting civil rights such as freedom of speech, religion, etc. The test of taxing statutes would be viewed on more stringent tests and the lawmakers should be given greater latitude.

---

74. *Nagpur Improvement Trust* v. *Vithal Rao* (1973) 3 SCR 39/(1973) 1 SCC 500.
75. *R.K. Garg* v. *Union of India* (1981) 4 SCC 675/[1982] 1982 taxmann.com 240 (SC).
76. Para 27 In matters of economic policy should be best left to the wisdom of the legislature. Further, it went on to state that in the context of a changed economic scenario the expertise of the people dealing with the subject should not be lightly interfered with.
77. *Indian Oil Corporation Limited* v. *State of Bihar* (2018) 1 SCC 242/[2017] 88 taxmann.com 76/ [2018] 65 GST 83 (SC).
78. *State of Himachal Pradesh* v. *Goel Bus Service* [Civil appeal No.(s) 5534-5594 of 2011 date of decision January 13, 2023. (Three Judge's Bench)].

More recently, in *Cosmo Films*[79] Justice S. Ravindra Bhat speaking for the Court observed that there is no constitutional compulsion that whilst framing a new law, or policies under a new legislation – particularly when an entirely different set of fiscal norms are created, overhauling the taxation structure, concessions hitherto granted or given should necessarily be continued in the same fashion as they were in the past. When a new set of laws are enacted, the legislature's effort is to, on the one hand, assimilate as far as practicable, the past regime. On the other hand, the object of the new law is creation of new rights and obligations, with new attendant conditions. Inevitably, this process is bound to lead to some disruption. In this case, the disruption is in the form of exporters needing to import inputs, pay the two duties, and claim refunds. Yet, this inconvenience is insufficient to trump the legislative choice of creating an altogether new fiscal legislation, and insisting that a section of assessees order their affairs, to be in accord with the new law. Therefore, the exclusion of benefit of imports in anticipation of AAs, and requiring payment of duties, under Section 3(7) and (9) of the Customs Tariff Act, 1975, with the 'pre-import condition', cannot be characterized as arbitrary or unreasonable.

2.18 Statute held unconstitutional

In *Suraj Mall Mohta*[80], the Supreme Court struck down Section 5(4) of the Taxation on Income (Investigation Commission) Act, 1947 on the ground that the procedure prescribed was substantially more prejudicial and more drastic to the assessee than the procedure contained in the Indian Income-tax Act, 1922.

Judging the validity of Kerala Building Tax Act, 1961 which provided for the levy of tax on the basis of the floor area of the building irrespective of its being situated either in a village or City or irrespective of its use either as residential or commercial irrespective of the nature of the construction, it was held that:

In enacting the Kerala Building Tax Act no attempt at any rational classification has been made by the legislature. The legislature has not taken into consideration the class to which a building belongs, the nature of construction, the purpose for which it is used, it's situation, its capacity for profitable user and other relevant consideration which have a bearing on matters of taxation. They have adopted merely the floor area of the building as the basis of taxes irrespective of all other consideration. Where objects, persons or transactions essentially dissimilar are treated by the imposition of a uniform tax, discrimination may result. In our view, refusal to make a rational classification in some cases operates as denial of equality.[81]

79. *Union of India* v. *Cosmo Films Limited* [Civil appeal No(s). 290 of 2023 date of decision April 28, 2023.(Two Judges Bench)].

80. *Suraj Mall Mohta and Co.* v. *A.V. Visvanatha Sastri* (1955) 1 SCR 448.

81. *State of Kerala* v. *Haji K. Kutty* AIR 1969 Supreme Court 378, 380. Tax on factory building in Municipal Area on the basis of floor area was had illegal. *Manik Chowk Spinning and Weaving Mill* v. *Municipal Corporation* Ahmedabad AIR 1967 SC 801.

Moopil Nair's case[82]

A tax law cannot be challenged merely on the ground that the rate of tax is very high unless the tax is a colourable device to confiscate property. For example, a law imposing an income tax of 100 Paisa in the Rupee would be *void* because it does not tax income but confiscates it. In Moopil Nair's case, a tax on land was declared *void* as violative of Article 14 and Article 19(1)(*f*). In this case, a tax of ₹ 2 per acre of land under the Travancore-Cochin Land Tax Act, 1955 was imposed which resulted in inequality since all lands were taxed equally without any reference to their yield. Further, the tax was imposed on forest land whereas the forest land had no yield. Thus, it resulted in the tax being confiscatory. The forest land was unproductive because there was an Act in operation *viz.*, the Madras Preservation of Private Forest Act, 1949.

The Supreme Court struck down the Travancore-Cochin Land Tax Act, 1955 as violative of Article 14 on the grounds that unequal's were treated equally. By the impugned Act, all lands in the State held under whatever tenure were to be charged and levied a uniform rate of tax to be called the basic tax.

Manik Chowk case[83]

In *Manik Chowk* case, Supreme Court struck down the assessment of property tax by the Municipal Corporation, *inter alia*, on the ground that the method of levy of tax on the basis of floor area was against the provisions of the Act and rules made thereunder.

Raja Jagannath Baksh Singh[84]

Another important decision is *Raja Jagannath Baksh* v. *State of U.P.* In this case, the court observed:

> "A taxing statue can be held to contravene Article 14 if its purports to impose on the same class of property similarly situated an incidence of taxation which leads to obvious inequality. There is no doubt that it is for the legislature to decide on what objects to levy what rate of tax and it is not for the court to consider whether some other objects should have been taxed or whether a different rate should have been prescribed for the tax. It is also true that the legislature is competent to classify persons or properties into different categories and tax them differently, and if the classification thus made is rational, the taxing statute cannot be challenged merely because different rates of taxation are prescribed for different categories of persons or objects. But, if in its operation, any taxing statute is found to contravene Article 14, it would be open to the courts to strike it down as denying to the citizens the equality before the law guaranteed by Article 14."

Similarly, if it taxing statute makes no specific provision about the machinery to recover tax and the procedure to make the assessment of the tax and leaves it entirely to the executive to device such machinery as it thinks fit and to prescribe such procedure as appears it to be fair, an occasion may arise for the courts

82. *Moopil Nair* v. *State of Kerala* AIR 1961 SC 552.
83. *New Manek Chowk Spg. and Wvg. Mills Co. Ltd.* v. *Municipal Corpn. of the City of Ahmedabad* AIR 1967 SC 1801.
84. *Raja Jagannath Baksh* v. *State of U.P* AIR 1962 SC 1563.

to consider whether the failure to provide for a machinery and to prescribe a procedure that does not tend to make the imposition of the tax an unreasonable restriction within the meaning of article 19(5). Imposition of a tax which, in the absence of a prescribed machinery and prescribed procedure would partake the character of purely administrative affairs can, in a proper case be challenged as contravening article 19(1)(*f*).

Lawrence Singh Ingty[85]

Section 10(26) of the Income-tax Act, 1961 which exempts income of members of scheduled tribe excluding government servant was struck down as violative of article 14 of the Constitution.

The court observed:

> "... It may be that for the purpose of taxation, a classification can be made on the basis of administrative convenience.... administrative convenience which can offer a just basis for classification must be real and substantial one... classification can also be justified on the basis of past legislative practice and history..."

Finally, the court observed:

> "For the purpose of classification what is required is not some imaginary difference but a reasonable and substantial distinction having regard to the purpose of the law."

Raja Reddy[86]

In Raja Reddy the court held the classification based upon Ayacut under the Andhra Pradesh Land Revenue (Additional Cess Assessment and Cess Revision) Act, 1962 has no reasonable relation to the duration of water supply. Further, the whole imposition of assessment was left to arbitrary discretion of officers, not named in the Act without giving any remedy to the assessee for questioning the correctness of any of the important stages in the matter of assessment. Arbitrary power under the Act enables the appropriate officers to make unreasonable discrimination between persons and land. The Act, therefore, clearly violates Article 14.

Anant Mill[87]

In this case, the issue related to the constitutional validity of the Bombay Municipal Corporation Act, 1949 as amended by the Gujarat Acts, 1968 and 1970, so far as they relate to the assessment of the property tax of large premises like textile mills, factories, etc. Section 127(1) requires the Corporation to impose property tax *i.e.*, water tax, conservancy tax, and general tax. Delivering the judgment, Justice Khanna observed:

> "... In permissible classification mathematical nicety and perfect equalities are not required. Similarly, not identity of treatment is enough. If there is equality and uniformity within each group, the law will not be condemned as discrimination,

85. *SK Dutta* v. *Lawrence Singh Ingty* (1968) 68 ITR 272 (SC).

86. *State of Andhra Pradesh* v. *Raja Reddy* AIR 1967 SC 1458, 1469.

87. *Anant Mill Co.* v. *State of Gujarat* AIR 1975 SC 1234.

> though due to some fortuitous circumstances arising out of peculiar situation some included in a class get an advantage over others, so long as they are not singled out for a special treatment. Taxation law is not exception to this doctrine. But, in the application of the principles, the courts in view of the inherent complexities of fiscal adjustment of diverse elements permit a larger discretion to the legislature in the matter of classification, so long as it adheres to the fundamental principles underlying the said doctrine. The power of the legislature to classify is of wide range and flexibility so that it can adjust its system of tax in all proper and reasonable ways..."

The court further observed:

> "... In case any party assails the validity of any provision on the ground that it is violative of Article 14 of the Constitution, it is for that party to make the necessary averments and adduce material to show discrimination violative of Article 14... It was, therefore, in our opinion, essential to ascertain and find out a correct factual position before recording a finding that the impugned provision is violative of Article 14."

In *A. Sanyasi Rao*[88], the Supreme Court struck down Section 44AC of the Income Tax Act as being discriminatory when only particular trades were singled out for discriminatory treatment, reliefs under Sections 28 to 43C of the Income Tax Act being denied only to such trades.

In *Pepsi Foods Ltd*[89], the third proviso[90] to section 254(2A) of the Income-tax Act, introduced by the Finance Act, 2008, was held both arbitrary and discriminatory and, was struck down as offending Article 14 of the Constitution of India. Since the object of the third proviso to Section 254(2A) of the Income-tax Act is the automatic vacation of a stay that has been granted on the completion of 365 days, whether or not the assessee is responsible for the delay caused in hearing the appeal, such object being itself discriminatory was struck down as violating Article 14 of the Constitution of India.

Old Settlers of Sikkim[91]

Proviso to Section 10(*26AAA*) of the Income-tax Act, 1961, insofar as it excludes from the exempted category, "a Sikkimese woman, who marries a non-Sikkimese after 1-4-2008" was struck down being *ultra vires* to Articles 14, 15 and 21 of the Constitution of India. At present benefit of exemption

88. *Union of India* v. *A. Sanyasi Rao* (1996) 3 SCC 465/[1996] 85 Taxman 321 (SC).

89. *Deputy Commissioner of Income tax* v. *Pepsi Foods Ltd.* [Civil Appeal No. 1106 of 2021]/ (2021) 7 SCC 413/[2021] 126 taxmann.com 69/282 Taxman 10 (SC).

90. **Provided also** that if such appeal is not so disposed of within the period allowed under the first proviso or the period or periods extended or allowed under the second proviso, which shall not, in any case, exceed three hundred and sixty-five days, the order of stay shall stand vacated after the expiry of such period or periods, even if the delay in disposing of the appeal is not attributable to the assessee.

91. *Association of Old Settlers of Sikkim* v. *Union of India* [Writ Petition (C) No. 59 of 2013 date of decision 13-1-2023]/[2023] 146 taxmann.com 271/292 Taxman 73 (SC).

is restricted only to those Sikkimese who fall within the three clauses of the *Explanation* to Section 10(*26AAA*) of the Income-tax Act, 1961, or those persons domiciled in Sikkim, or are Sikkimese as covered under the 1961 Regulation.

By the Finance Act, 2023, the existing clause (*26AAA*) was substituted[92] retrospectively with effect from 1st day of April, 1990.

92. '(*26AAA*) in case of an individual, being a Sikkimese, any income which accrues or arises to him—

(*a*) from any source in the State of Sikkim; or

(*b*) by way of dividend or interest on securities.

Explanation.—For the purposes of this clause "Sikkimese" shall mean—

(*i*) an individual, whose name is recorded in the register maintained under the Sikkim Subjects Regulation, 1961 read with the Sikkim Subject Rules, 1961 (hereinafter referred to as the "Register of Sikkim Subjects"), immediately before the 26th day of April, 1975; or

(*ii*) an individual, whose name is included in the Register of Sikkim Subjects by virtue of the Government of India Order No. 26030/36/90- I.C.I., dated the 7th August, 1990 and Order of even number dated the 8th April, 1991; or

(*iii*) any other individual, whose name does not appear in the Register of Sikkim Subjects, but it is established beyond doubt that the name of such individual's father or husband or paternal grand-father or brother from the same father has been recorded in that register; or

(*iv*) any other individual, whose name does not appear in the Register of Sikkim Subjects but it is established that such individual was domiciled in Sikkim on or before the 26th day of April, 1975; or

(*v*) any other individual, who was not domiciled in Sikkim on or before the 26th day of April, 1975, but it is established beyond doubt that such individual's father or husband or paternal grand-father or brother from the same father was domiciled in Sikkim on or before the 26th day of April, 1975;'

Various stages of law-making and their relevance as an aid to interpretation

3.1 Scheme of the chapter

In this chapter, stages of law-making, both prior to the introduction of a bill and the consideration of the bill in the houses of parliament including its committee, have been discussed. This chapter also covers the relevance of documents in the interpretation of an Act, mainly, the law commission reports, the statement of objects and reasons appended to the bill, the speech of the minister, and reports of the parliamentary committees.

3.2 Law-making process

The preparation of legislation involves three stages namely:

(*a*) the formulation or determination of legislative policy;

(*b*) the creation of the legislative scheme; and

(*c*) the composition of sentences.

The formulation or determination of legislative policy takes place in the respective administrative departments of the government in case of public bills.

3.3 Relation between policy and drafting

Initial responsibility for finalising the policy lies in the matter of direct taxes with the Central Board of Direct Taxes and in the matter of indirect taxes with the Central Board of indirect taxes and Customs. Policy decisions can be changed up to the last point till the bill is finalized. The next two stages *i.e.*, the creation of the legislative scheme and the composition of sentences are reached in the legislative department of the Ministry of Law and Justice. During the drafting process, the constitutional validity of each proposal is to be examined and it is also to be seen that the statute is complete. The form, arrangement, and wording of the bill are the primary concerns of the draughtsman; however, it is to be ensured that the legislative scheme is sound and workable. The manner in which courts are likely to interpret a provision is another safeguard which is to be taken into account.

At this stage it is appropriate to refer to the following observations:

> "Just as any piece of writing is modified to cater to its audience, the manner in which laws are drafted should take into account how courts are expected to interpret them. For example, the Renton committee distinguished in general terms between the Civil law system and the common law system. It found that under the Civil law system legislature tends to be drafted in the form of a broad statement of principle, with the application of these principles to particular cases being left to the judgment of the court. Classic civil law drafting practices a deliberate restraint in the proliferation of the detail rules. In contrast, common law drafting tends to be much more detailed, trying to cover each possible case, with the Court taking the corresponding narrower reading of a particular provision of a statute."[1]

3.4 Introduction of a bill

Once a legislative proposal is formulated in the form of a bill, the detailed procedure laid down in the Constitution of India regarding the introduction and passing of the bill as an Act is followed.

Before an Act is passed, it is introduced in the form of a bill in either House and both the houses are to be agreed upon such bill, with or without any amendment. When it receives the assent of the President or the Governor as the case may be, it become into law. For coming into force of the law either there is a specific mention of the date in the Act itself or it comes into force on the date it receives the assent of the President. Since the imposition, remission, alteration, or regulation of any tax falls within the definition of "Money Bills", a special procedure is laid down.

3.5 Money bill

A Money Bill shall not be introduced in the Council of State. Whether the Council of State have any power in regard to the Money Bill, except that it is received for its recommendation from the House of People? The House of the People is free to either accept or reject the recommendations of the Council of State. As defined in article 110 of the Constitution a bill shall be deemed to be a Money Bill if it contains only provisions dealing with all or any of the matters specified in sub-clauses (*a*) to (*f*) of clause (*1*) of article 110 or dealing with any other matter incidental to any of the above-mentioned matter.

Incidental matters must be indispensable for giving effect to the main provisions, such as, for the imposition or regulation of any tax. Thus, under the taxing law, the matters pertaining to assessment and machinery thereof are incidental matters. likewise, penalties imposed also fall within the category of incidental matters.

1. Victor Thuronyi, ed, Tax law design and drafting, Volume 1, International Monetary Fund 1996, Chapter 3 at pages 13-14.

3.6 Financial bill

Article 117 of the Constitution makes special provisions as to Financial Bills. Financial Bills other than Money Bills are those bills which make provision for any of the matters contained in sub-clauses (*a*) to (*f*) of article 110 of the Constitution but which do not consist exclusively of such matters but consist of other matters also in addition to for example a Bill which contains taxing clause but deal with other matters also.

Such bills have features common with Money Bills namely they should not be introduced in Rajya Sabha and they should not be introduced except on the Recommendation of the President.

Financial bills other than Money Bills are not subject to clauses (2) to (5) of Article 109 of the Constitution. Such bills have to be passed in the Rajya Sabha like ordinary Bills and provisions of joint sitting apply in the case of disagreement.

An ordinary bill may contain a provision which if passed would involve expenditure from the Consolidated Fund of India but in such cases, the bill must be passed in each house provided the President has recommended the consideration of the bill.

Other requirements provided under article 117 of the Constitution is that a bill or amendment in respect of Money Bills shall not be introduced or moved except on the recommendation of the President. However, no recommendations shall be required for moving an amendment for the reduction or abolition of any tax. The provisions of Article 117 shall not apply where a bill or amendment provides for:

(*i*) the imposition of fines or other pecuniary penalties; or

(*ii*) the demand or payment of fees for licence or fees for services rendered; or

(*iii*) for the imposition, abolition, remission, alteration, or regulation of any tax by any local authority or body for local purposes.

3.7 Finance bill

Taxation proposals feature annually in the Finance Bill. The proposals of the government for the levy of new taxes or the modification of the existing tax structure are submitted through the Finance Bill. The Finance Bill is an important component of the Union budget. Union budget means a statement of estimated receipts and expenditure which has to be laid before Parliament for the financial year beginning 1st April to 31st March of the succeeding Year.

The budget statement shows receipt and expenditure in three parts. (*i*) Consolidated fund of India; (*ii*) Contingency Fund of India; and (*iii*) Public accounts of India.

Consolidated fund of India - It consists of all revenue's government, loans raised by it, and also its receipts from the recovery of loans granted by it. All expenditure of the government is incurred from the consolidated fund of India and no amount can be withdrawn from the funds without the authorisation of the Parliament.

Contingency fund - It is an imprest placed at the disposal of the President of India to meet urgent unforeseen expenditure pending authorisation from the Parliament.

Public accounts - It means a fund where in certain amount received as bankers by the government is kept, such amounts include provident funds, small savings collections, and other deposits.

The Finance Bill means the bill ordinarily introduced every year to give effect to the financial proposals of the Government of India for the following financial year and includes a Bill to give effect to supplementary financial proposals for any period.

In view of the declaration under the Provisional Collection of Taxes Act, 1931[1a] the finance bill has to be passed by Parliament and assented to by the President before the expiry of the 75th day after the day on which it was introduced.

3.8 Recommendation of President

The recommendation of the President is necessary for the consideration and passing of a bill involving expenditure from the Consolidated Fund of India. [Article 117(3)] Recommendations for consideration would also be necessary in the following cases—

(*i*) if the bill would, if enacted involve expenditure indirectly;

(*ii*) In the case of continuous bills involving expenditure from the consolidated fund of India although the recommendation was not obtained when the original bill was passed;

(*iii*) in the case of a bill consolidating an existing Act or Acts which involve expenditure from the consolidated fund;

(*iv*) for an amending bill seeking to convert an existing Act into a permanent one, if the recommendation was necessary for the consideration of the principal Act.[2]

3.9 Documents to accompany the Finance Bill or any other Taxation Bill

A Finance bill or any other taxation bill requires the recommendation of the President for the introduction and passing of the bill. Other documents are:

Financial memorandum;

The statement of objects and reasons;

1a. Now the Provisional Collection of Taxes Act, 2023, *see* **Appendix 2**.

2. MN Kaul and SL Shakdhar, Practice and Procedure of Parliament (1968) pp. 613-614.

Notes on clauses; and

The memorandum on delegated legislation.

3.10 Financial memorandum

A Bill involving expenditure from the consolidated fund of India is required to be accompanied by a financial memorandum, which outlines the object on which the expenditure is likely to be involved. The memorandum has to invite particular attention to the clauses involving the expenditure and also to give an estimate of the recurring and non-recurring expenditures involved in case the bill is passed into law.

3.11 Statement of objects and reasons

When a bill is finalized and is approved by the Union Cabinet, the Ministry sponsoring it prepares a statement of objects and reasons which is signed by the Minister who is to be in charge of the bill in the Parliament. The statement of objects and reasons is vetted by the concerned draftsman so that it truly reflects the objects of the bill. The statement of object and reasons is attached to the bill when it is introduced in the Lok Sabha or in the Rajya Sabha.

3.12 Memorandum on delegated legislation

A Memorandum of delegated legislation explains whether the delegation is of normal character or of exceptional nature.

3.13 Notes on Clause

Notes on clauses are appended when the bill is of a complicated nature. Every bill containing more than 25 clauses is accompanied by notes on clauses. Finance bills are invariably accompanied by notes on clauses.

3.14 Explanatory Memorandum to the Finance Bill

The explanatory memorandum to the Finance Bill is prepared in the Finance Ministry to explain in detail the proposals contained in the Finance Bill. These are more elaborate than notes on clauses.

3.15 The Finance Bill and the Provisional Collection of Taxes Act, 1931[2a]

Section 3 provides that where a Bill to be introduced in Parliament on behalf of the Government provides for the imposition or increase of a duty of customs or excise, the Central Government may cause to be inserted in the Bill a declaration that it is expedient in the public interest that any provision of the Bill relating to such imposition or increase shall have immediate effect under this Act.

2a. Now the Provisional Collection of Taxes Act, 2023, *see* **Appendix 2**.

A declared provision shall have the force of law immediately on the expiry of the day on which the Bill containing it is introduced. (2) A declared provision shall cease to have the force of law under the provisions of this Act—(*a*) when it comes into operation as an enactment, with or without amendment, or when the Central Government, in pursuance of motion passed by Parliament directs, by notification in the Official Gazette, that it shall cease to have the force of law or (*c*) if it has not already ceased to have the force of law under clause (*a*) or clause (*b*), then on the expiry of the seventy-fifth day after the day on which the Bill containing it was introduced.

3.16 Statutory interpretation and reports of the law commission

On taxation, The Law Commission of India has so far forwarded following recommendations:

Parliamentary legislation relating to sales tax (second report)

Income-tax Act (12th report)

Proposal for inclusion of Agricultural income in total income for purposes of determining the rate of Income Tax under the Income-tax Act, 1961 (49th report)

Certain problems connected with the power of the state to levy tax on the sale of goods and with the Central Sales Tax Act, 1956 (61st report)

The second report has been implemented by enacting the Central Sales Tax Act. The twelfth report was implemented by enacting the Income-tax Act, 1961. The 49th report has been implemented by including agricultural income in the non-agricultural income of the taxpayer since 1972. The 61st report has been implemented into the Constitution 46 Amendment Act.

In the interpretation of an enactment, the reports of the law commission may be valuable as a matter of history, but it cannot be a legitimate guide for the construction of a section of the statute. In Santa Singh[3], Fazal Ali J. considered the extent and import of the word ' hear' used in section 235(2) of the Code of Criminal Procedure, 1973. Does it indicate, that the accused should enter into a fresh trial by producing oral and documentary evidence on the question of the sentence which naturally will result in the delay of the trial? The learned judge observed:

> " ... The Parliament does not appear to have intended that the accused should adopt dilatory tactics under the cover of these new provisions but contemplated short and simple opportunity has to be given to the accused to place materials, if necessary, by leading evidence before the court hearing on the question of sentence and the consequent opportunity to the prosecution to rebut those materials."

---

3. *Santa Singh* v. *State of Punjab* AIR 1976 SC 2386. Section 235(2) read as:

   '(2) if the accused is convicted, the judge shall, unless he proceeds in accordance with the provisions of section 360, hear the accused on the question of the sentence, and then past sentence on him, according to law.'

The Law Commission was fully aware of this anomaly and accordingly suggested:

> "we are aware that a provision for an opportunity to give evidence in this respect may necessitate an adjournment; and to avoid delay, adjournment for the purpose should ordinarily be for not more than 14 days, it may be so provided in the relevant clause."

The court observed that it may not be practicable to keep up to the time limit suggested by the law commission with mathematical accuracy but the court must be vigilant to exercise proper control over the proceedings so that the trial is not unavoidably or unnecessarily delayed.

In Balchand[4], while interpreting section 438 of the Code of Criminal Procedure, 1973 on anticipatory bail, the court observed that while the law commission recommended that a provision for an order of anticipatory bail to be effective when a person is arrested should be made, at the same time it stressed that this being an extraordinary power should be exercised sparingly and only in special cases. It also recommended that this power should not be exercised without giving notice to the other side. I think this is why the legislature has entrusted this power to the high authorities like the sessions judge and the high court and we also feel that in the interest of justice, it would be desirable if a final order is made only after hearing the prosecution. Although this condition is not mentioned in section 438 of the Code but having regard to the setting in which the section is placed and the statement of the objects and reasons which is actually based on the recommendation of the law commission, we think that rule of prudence requires that notice should be given to the other side before passing a final order for anticipatory bail so that anticipatory bail is not obtained by a party by placing incorrect or misleading facts or suppressing material facts.

3.17 Statutory interpretation and reports of the taxation committees

Referring to the report of the administration enquiry committee as an aid in the interpretation of a provision of the statute, in *Delhi Flour Mills*[5], it was observed that the views expressed in such reports need not necessarily be taken as reflecting the intention of the legislature. In fact, it may well be that, if the views expressed by the committee were not clearly reflected in the statute, it may be understood that the legislature did not accept such views.

However, the Report of the Taxation Enquiry Committee was relied upon in interpreting the words ' warehouses and godown' in Section 80P of the Income-tax Act, 1961. Negativing the contention that the 'shops' are also included within the words 'warehouse and godown' the court in Ahmedabad Cloth Dealers Co-operative Society Limited[6] observed:

---

4. *Balchand* v. *State of M.P.* AIR 1977 SC 366.
5. *Delhi Flour Mills Company Limited* v. *CIT* (1974) 95 ITR 151 (Delhi).
6. *CIT* v. *Ahmedabad Maskati Cloth Dealers Co-operative Warehouses Society Limited* (1986) 50 CTR 283 (Gujarat).

It will appear from the recommendation made by the Taxation Enquiry Committee that it considered the extension of a system of warehouses in rural areas of importance and with a view to construct warehouses which are likely to prove useful in the development of the rural economy, it was thought that such cooperative society should enjoy exemption from tax on such part of their income as is derived from the letting of godown and warehouses. In other words, the committee was of the view that unless total exemption is granted so far as income derived from the letting of godowns and warehouses are concerned, co-operative societies will not be encouraged to construct godowns and warehouses and that in the long run prove detrimental to rural economy. There cannot be doubt that legislature desired to extend the benefit of exemption of the whole income to cooperative society if derived from the letting of godowns and warehouses needed for the development of rural economy. It is for this reason that the legislature limited the benefit to income from Godown and warehouses for if it was the intention of the legislature to extend the benefit to income derived by the letting of shops, etc. nothing would have been easier than to substitute the words 'any premises' for the words 'godowns or warehouses'.

3.18 Statutory interpretation and the statement of objects and reasons

The reports of the Law Commission of India and of the taxation committee are useful while formulating tax policies. The statement of objects and reasons is appended to the bill. It is well settled that when the language of the statute is clear and admits of no ambiguity, recourse to the statement of objects and reasons for the purpose of construing the statutory provision is not permissible[7].

In Khandelwal Metal[8], counsel for the appellant relied strongly on the objects and reasons of section 3 of the Customs Tariff Act, 1975 in support of their contention that the said section is a charging section and imposes a countervailing duty. The Supreme Court observed that the statement of objects and reasons leads *prima facie* support to the contention of the appellant but, in the absence of any ambiguity in the wordings of section 3, we cannot treat the additional duty referred to therein as countervailing duty. Nor, indeed, can we regard that provision charging section merely because the statement says that section 3 provides for the levy. The statement of objects and reasons errs in being common to sub-sections (1) and (3) of section 3. It is more apposite to sub-section (3) though even there, it may not be correct to say that it is a charging provision.

In S.C. Prashar[9], judges expressed their opinion on the admissibility of the statement of object and reasons in interpreting a provision. Justice SK Das observed that it is indeed true that the statement of objects and reasons for introducing a particular piece of legislation cannot be used for interpreting the legislation if the words used therein are clear enough. But the statement of objects and

7. *Govind Sharan* v. *ST Commissioner* AIR 1985 SC 1041, 1045.
8. *Khandelwal Metal and Engineering Works* v. *Union of India* AIR 1985 SC 1211.
9. *S.C. Prashar* v. *Vasantsen Dwarkadas Hungerford Investment Trust Ltd.* (1963) 49 ITR 1 (SC).

reasons can be referred to for the purpose of ascertaining the circumstances which led to the legislation in order to find out what was the mischief which the legislation aimed at.

In the same case, Justice Kapur observed that in construing an enactment and determining its true scope it is permissible to have regard to all such factors as can legitimately be taken into account to ascertain the intention of the legislature such as the history of the Act, the reason which led to its being passed, the mischief which had to be cured as well as the other provisions of the statute... taking this principle into account it appears that the object of the amendment was to validate certain notices after the amendment after the lapse of 8 years from the end of the assessment year.

In the same case, Justice Sarkar (on behalf of the majority) observed that, however, strange, if at all, the result may be, I do not think the Courts can alter the plain meaning language of the statute only on the ground of incongruity if there is nothing in the words justify the alteration.

3.19 Statutory interpretation and reports of parliamentary committees

On a motion moved in and adopted by the house, bills are from time to time, referred to the select committee, joint committee, or department-related standing committee[10]. A bill is referred to a joint committee with the concurrence of the Rajya Sabha, composed of members of both the houses. A select committee is composed of members of either Lok Sabha or Rajya Sabha. Such select committees or joint committees are *ad hoc* committees which are appointed for consideration of a particular bill referred to them. The function of a select or joint committee on a bill is to go through the text of the bill, clause by clause, in order to see that the provisions of the Bill bring out clearly the intention behind the measure, that there will be no procedural defect in its working, that the Bill does not offend the provisions of the existing law, and that the object proposed to be achieved is adequately brought out. A committee may, before or at the time of taking a decision on any provision of the bill, invite written memorandum or take oral evidence of, experts or interested persons and organisations, and require government officials to explain the policy behind the cause of the bill and give such information as the committee may desire. Parliamentary committees are constituted with certain purposes. The formation of the committee has a history. "Committees have been described as a primary organizational device whereby legislatures can accommodate an increase in the number of bills being introduced, while continuing to scrutinize legislation; handle the greater

10. *Kalpana Mehta* v. *Union of India* (2018) 7 SCC 1.

[Founded on English traditions, the Indian Parliament's committee system has a vital role in the parliamentary democracy. Generally speaking, the Parliamentary committees are of two kinds; standing committees and *ad hoc* committees. Standing Committees are permanent and regular committees which are constituted from time to time in pursuance of the provisions of an Act of Parliament or Rules of Procedure and Conduct of Business in Lok Sabha]

complexity and technical nature of bills under review without an exponential growth in size; develop "division of labours" among members for considering legislation..."[11] Today parliamentary committee systems have emerged as a creative way for parliaments to perform their basic functions. They serve as the focal point for legislation and oversight.[12]

In India, earlier the courts were of the view that the draft of the bill and the report of a Commission or of a select committee are not admissible as constructing the provisions of the Act. In Srinivasan[13], reference was made in the judgment of an Appellate Tribunal to the views of the select committee, but it was held by the High Court that it was not a permissible consideration in the interpretation of the statute. In the *State Bank of India*[14], the court held that what is relevant is the intention of the Legislature and not the intention of any committee (meaning thereby select committee).

In *Sodra Devi*[15], while interpreting section 16(3) of the Income-tax Act, 1922, the majority decision referred to the recommendation of the Enquiry Committee 1936 and held that the term individual included only male persons. The court observed that the mischief which the enquiry report sought to remedy by its recommendations was one which was the result of husbands entering into nominal partnership between themselves and their wives and minor children. Admitting their minor children to the benefit of such partnership. The mischief, if any, resulting from the mother's admitting their minor children to the benefits of partnership in which they were member was farthest from the thoughts of the enquiry committee and was nowhere sought to the remedied. Having regard to the circumstances which prevailed at the time when the enquiry committee made its report, the only mischief which they sought to remedy by their recommendation was the one resulting from the male assessees indulging in such tactics for the evasion of income tax by creating nominal partnership between themselves and their wives on the one hand and their minor children on the other.

Placing a limit on the use of the report of the committee in Sodra Devi, Mr. Justice SK Das in his dissenting opinion observed:

> "It is clear, however, that the report is of very little help in the construction of section 16(3) because the legislature did not accept in full the recommendation made in the report."

However, in *Vadilal Lallubhai*,[16] the Supreme Court stated that it will not be inappropriate to find out the reasons which persuaded the select committee to recommend the inclusion of a provision if such provision is considered ambiguous.

---

11. Entering the Committee System: State Committee Assignments, Ronald D. Hedlund, Political; Research Quarterly, Vol. 42, Issue 4, pp. 597-625.
12. *Kalpana Mehta* v. *Union of India* (2018) 7 SCC 1.
13. *CIT* v. *K. Srinivasan and K. Gopalan* (1953) 23 ITR 87 (SC).
14. *CIT* v. *State Bank of India* (1957) 31 ITR 545 (Calcutta).
15. *CIT* v. *Sodra Devi* (1957) 32 ITR 615 (SC).
16. *CIT* v. *Vadilal Lallubhai* (1972) 86 ITR 2 (SC).

In constitutional interpretation the reports **of the Parliamentary Committee and the statement made by the Minister while moving the Bill are relevant aids for a construction of constitutional provision**[17]. In *Surat Art Silk*[18], Supreme Court held:

> "It is legitimate to look at the state of law prevailing leading to the legislation so as to see what was the mischief at which the Act was directed. This Court has on many occasions taken judicial notice of such matters as the reports of parliamentary committees, and of such other facts as must be assumed to have been within the contemplation of the legislature when the Acts in question were passed."

In *Dharam Dutt*[19], the Supreme Court took note of the three Parliamentary Standing Committees appointed at different points of time which had recommended the taking over of Sapru House on the ground of declining standard of the Institution.

In *Kalpana Mehta*[20], the issue was to whether a Parliamentary Standing Committee (PSC) report can be placed reliance upon for adjudication of a fact in issue and also for what other purposes it can be taken aid of. The Supreme Court held:

> "... the reports or speeches have been referred to or not referred to for the purposes indicated therein and when the meaning of a statute is not clear or ambiguous, the circumstances that led to the passing of the legislation can be looked into in order to ascertain the intention of the legislature. It is because the reports assume significance and become relevant because they precede the formative process of a legislation... the Court can take aid of the report of the parliamentary committee for the purpose of appreciating the historical background of the statutory provisions and it can also refer to committee report or the speech of the Minister on the floor of the House of the Parliament if there is any kind of ambiguity or incongruity in a provision of an enactment."

In *Jignesh Shah*[21] Supreme Court referred to the Report of the Insolvency Law Committee of March, 2018. In another case[22], it was stated as under:

> "11. Having heard the learned counsel for both sides, it is important to first set out the reason for the introduction of Section 238A into the Code. This is to be found in the Report of the Insolvency Law Committee of March 2018,..."

---

17. *Dr. Jaishri Laxman Rao Patil* v. *The Chief Minister* [Civil Appeal No. 3123 of 2020 decided on 5 May 2021].

18. *Additional Commissioner of Income Tax, Gujarat* v. *Surat Art Silk Cloth Manufacturers' Association, Surat*, (1980) 2 SCC 31.

19. *Dharam Dutt* v. *Union of India* (2004) 1 SCC 712.

20. *Kalpana Mehta* v. *Union of India*, (2018) 7 SCC 1, [Chief Justice Dipak Misra held that reports of the Parliamentary Committees and the speeches made in the Parliament can be referred to identify the circumstances that led to the enactment of the legislation along with the intention of the legislature: "129. We have referred to these authorities to highlight that the reports or speeches have been referred to or not referred to for the purposes indicated therein and when the meaning of a statue is not clear or ambiguous, the circumstances that led to the passing of the legislation can be looked into in order to ascertain the intention of the legislature. It is because the reports assume significance and become relevant because they precede the formative process of a legislation."]

21. *Jignesh Shah* v. *Union of India* (2019) 10 SCC 750/109 taxmann.com 486/156 SCL 542 (SC).

22. *B.K. Educational Services (P.) Ltd.* v. *Parag Gupta and Associates* (2019) 11 SCC 633/[2018] 98 taxmann.com 213/150 SCL 293 (SC).

There are a number of judgments[23] wherein reference to the parliamentary committee was made. In the construction of statutes parliamentary debates have also been referred to appreciate the context relating to the construction of a statute.[24]

In Abhiram Singh[25], the report of the select committee was referred to and Mohit Mineral[25a] is a landmark judgment. It was observed:

> "Though the traditional view of interpretation of statutes is that legislative history is not readily used in interpreting a law, the modern trend of thinking on the subject has enabled courts to look into the history of a legislation to understand the full purport of the words used and the mischief sought to be remedied by the law."

The Court held: -

> **'The Statement of Objects and Reasons and the debates and speeches in the legislature indicate the intent behind the introduction of the Bill. The legislative history, the statement of objects and reasons of the Bill and the speech made when the bill was introduced indicate the mischief that Articles 246A and 279A to the Constitution sought to remedy, which is to simplify the indirect tax regime to prevent the complexities inherent in and the cascading effect of a multiplicity of taxes.'**

3.20 Statutory interpretation and speech of the members of the legislature

A speech made in the course of the debate on a bill could at best be indicative of the subjective intent of the speaker, but it could not reflect the inarticulate mental process lying behind the majority vote which carried the bill[26]. In *State of West Bengal*[27] it was observed that a statute is the expression of the collective intention of the legislature as a whole, and any statement made by an individual, albeit a Minister, of the intention and objects of the Act cannot be used to cut down the generality of the words used in the statute. Later on, Debates in the Constituent Assembly were used as an aid to the interpretation of a constitutional provision.[28]

---

23. *Gujarat Electricity Board* v. *Hind Mazdoor Sabha* (1995) 5 SCC 27, *Modern Dental College and Research Centre* v. *State of Madhya Pradesh* (2016) 7 SCC 353; and *Krishan Lal Gera* v. *State of Haryana* (2011) 10 SCC 529.

24. *Novartis AG* v. *Union of India* (2013) 6 SCC 1/[2013] 32 taxmann.com 1/119 SCL 217 (SC), *State of Madhya Pradesh* v. *Dadabhoy's New Chirimiri Ponri Hill Colliery Co. Pvt. Ltd.* (1972) 1 SCC 298, *Union of India* v. *Steel Stock Holders Syndicate, Poona* (1976) 3 SCC 108, *K and Surana Steels Pvt. Ltd.* v. *Dy. Commissioner of Income Tax* (2008) 6 SCC 1.

25. *Abhiram Singh* v. *C.D. Commachen (Dead)* [Civil Appeal No. 37 of 1992 decided on 2nd January 2017 (Five judges)]/(2017) 2 SCC 629. The Select Committee held four meetings and adopted a Report on the scheduled date. It was observed in the Report that the proposed amendment to Section 123(3) of the Representation of People Act "does not clearly bring out its intention."

25a. *Union of India* v. *Mohit Minerals (P.) Ltd.* [Civil Appeal No. 1390 of 2022, decided on May 19, 2022]/[2022] 138 taxmann.com 331/61 GSTL 257/92 GST 101 (SC).

26. *State of Travancore Co.* v. *Bombay Co.* AIR 1952 SC 366.

27. *State of West Bengal* v. *Union of India* (1964) 1 SCR 371.

28. *Indra Sawhney* v. *Union of India* AIR 1993 SC 477.

In *K.P. Varghese*[29], the Supreme Court, while referring to the budget speech of the Minister, ruled that speeches made by members of legislatures on the floor of the House where a Bill for enacting a statutory provision is being debated are inadmissible for the purpose of interpreting the statutory provision. But the Court made it clear that the speech made by the mover of the Bill explaining the reasons for introducing the Bill can certainly be referred to for ascertaining the mischief sought to be remedied and the object and the purpose of the legislation in question.

This view was held by the Court in Kalpna Mehta[30] in consonance with the juristic thought not only in the Western countries but also in India as in the exercise of interpretation of a statute, everything that is logically relevant should be admitted.

---

29. *K.P. Varghese* v. *Income Tax Officer, Ernakulam* (1981) 4 SCC 173/[1981] 7 Taxman 13 (SC) [Court held that the "speech made by the mover of the Bill explaining the reason for the introduction of the Bill can certainly be referred to for the purpose of ascertaining the mischief sought to be remedied by the legislation and the object and purpose for which the legislation is enacted.]
30. *Kalpana Mehta* v. *Union of India* (2018) 7 SCC 1.

4 Structure of a Taxing Statute

4.1 Drafting of a taxing statute

An Act or a Statute expresses the will of the legislature in carefully chosen words. Drafting tax laws is a subspecialty of legislative drafting in general. The approach to drafting a tax law will vary widely from country to country because languages and local drafting styles differ.

Victor Thuronyi in Drafting Tax Legislation[1] states the techniques of drafting a taxing statute. In view of Victor Thuronyl, in the most general terms, the tax laws should be drafted so as to best fulfil their role in the tax system, which is to specify such matters as how much each taxpayer is liable to pay and what the taxpayer's rights and obligations are. A well-drafted tax law spells out with precision the matters that are within its scope. But precision is not enough. A law should not be precise at the expense of being complicated and impossible to understand. The easier a tax law is to understand, the lower will be the compliance costs, both for taxpayers and for tax administrators. It is particularly important that a tax law be easy to apply (compared with other public law, for example, a law governing the generation of toxic waste or one governing building codes) because the tax law applies to nearly every physical and legal person in the country with respect to countless transactions every day. The fact that tax law must be applicable to so many transactions in an efficient manner has an important influence on how the law must be drafted. In particular, there is little room for sloppiness. Finally, a tax law must be effective in achieving the policy goals of the legislator, both in terms of the amount of revenue to be raised—with an eye to equity, efficiency, and simplicity—and the items and persons to be taxed. Good drafting goes hand in hand with the specification of policy. These criteria sometimes conflict. For example, a simple statute may be rejected as inequitable, because it does not recognize the differences in situation of different taxpayers. A statute that provides too much certainty may conflict with the goals of equity and revenue raising (because the certainty can be exploited by tax planners). In many cases, however, there is no conflict; complexity that

1. https://www.imf.org/external/pubs/nft/1998/tlaw/eng/ch3.pdf accessed on 26th August, 2023. at pp. 2-3 Chapter 3. **Tax Law Design and Drafting** Editor: Victor Thuronyi ©1996 International Monetary Fund Volume 1: 1996.

is merely the result of bad drafting can be eliminated while at the same time providing greater certainty and a clearer articulation of the policy.

4.2 Title

Every bill has a title that describes the nature of the proposed measure. The long title is different from the short title, which is embodied in the first section of the Act itself. The long title of an Act indicates the main purpose of the enactment. It cannot control the express operative portion of the Act[2] or it cannot limit the plain meaning of the text[3]. Every Act of Parliament should have a short title ending with the date of the Year in which it is passed. Modern statutes generally contain a section enacting that the Act may be cited by some short title. The short title is, however, given to the Act only for the purpose of facility of reference.

The title is not conclusive of the intent of the Legislature but constitutes only one of the numerous sources from which assistance must be obtained in the ascertainment of that intent in the case of doubt. It will not rectify the defects or omission in the enacting part but may be resorted to merely as an aid in the ascertainment of the legislative intent where the meaning is uncertain by reason of the use of general language of indefinite signification or of words of doubtful import.[4]

4.3 Preamble

The Preamble is a clause at the beginning of a statute, following the title and preceding the enacting clause. The proper function of the preamble is to explain certain facts which are necessary to be explained before the enactment contained in the Act can be understood. The inclusion of a Preamble in a bill has now become out of fashion[5] but in many statutes, Preamble is given. The preamble of an Act refers to finding out whether there is delegation of the legislative power or it is discretionary power conferred upon the executive authorities.

In *Thangal Kunju*[6] the question arose whether there was any guidance for selective application of Section 5 of the Travancore Taxation on Income Investigation Commission Act. Section 5 enacted that the government might at any time before the last day of Makaram refer to the Commission for investigation and report any case or points in a case in which the government had, *prima facie*, reasons for belief that a person had to a substantial extent evaded payment of tax on income together with such materials as might be available in support of such belief.

2. *Manohar Lal* v. *State of Punjab* AIR 1961 SC 418.
3. *Aswini Kumar Ghosh* v. *Arabinda Bose* AIR 1952 SC 269.
4. Craford, Statutory construction at p. 359.
5. Kaul, MN and Shakdhar S.L., Practice and Procedure in Parliament (1969) at p. 415.
6. *A. Thangal Kunju Musaliar* v. *M. Venkatachalam Potti* (1956) 29 ITR 349 (SC).

The Supreme Court observed that in order to ascertain the scope and purpose of the impugned section reference was made to the Act itself. The Preamble of a statute was held as a good means of finding out its meaning as if it was key to the understanding of it. The Supreme Court, however, concluded that the Preamble of the Act gave no assistance to the solution of the problem.

In *Kathi Raning*[7] the Supreme Court held that the preamble to the Saurashtra Ordinance gave definite guidance to the state government to choose for reference to a special judge only such offences or cases as affected public safety, maintenance of public order and preservation of peace and tranquility.

In *RK Garg* v. *Union of India*[8], it was stated that the preamble of the Act affords useful light as to what the statute intends to reach or in other words afford a clue to the scope of the statute. The Preamble to the Special Bearer Bonds Immunities and Exemptions Act, 1981 made it clear that the Act is intended to canalise for productive purposes black money which has become a serious threat to the national economy.

In the course of the judgment, Justice Bhagwati observed that it is an undisputed fact that there is a considerable amount of black money in circulation that is unaccounted or concealed. The menace of Black Money has reached such staggering proportions that it is causing havoc to the economy of the country and poses a serious challenge to the fulfilment of our objective of distributive Justice and setting up or an egalitarian society. The generation of black money through tax evasion throws a greater burden on the honest taxpayer and leads to economic inequality and concentration of wealth in the hands of unscrupulous, few in the country. Thus, in view of the Supreme Court, there is no exaggeration to say that black money is causing cancerous growth in the country's economy which if not checked in time is certain to lead to chaos and confusion.

In an English case *i.e.*, *Lord Chetwode* v. *IRC*[9] the Court of Appeal took recourse to the preamble in construing the word 'income' in the expression 'income of' and 'income becomes payable' occurring in 412(1) of the Income-tax Act, 1952. The principal question, in this case, was whether in computing the income of a foreign company for the purposes of section 412 of the Income-tax Act, 1952 it is proper to take expenses of management into account.

Justice Sir John Pennycuick observed that on the natural construction of section 412(1) read in conjunction with the Preamble, the word 'income' should be treated as denoting profit *i.e.*, the excess of receipts over outgoing. That means, of course, receipts and outgoings properly attributable to the revenue account.

7. *Kathi Raning Rawat* v. *State of Saurastra* AIR 1952 SC 123.
8. AIR 1981 SC 2138.
9. (1976)1 All E R 641 (Court of Appeal).

4.4 Interpretation of definition clause

The interpretation clause usually comes immediately after the short title, extent, and commencement. Where the definition is necessary only for a particular part of the chapter, it is given in that part of the chapter. Otherwise, at the beginning of the Act definition section is given.

Definitions are required:

(*a*) to avoid tedious paraphrases;

(*b*) to explain terms which are ambiguous or of uncertain meaning;

(*c*) to give to a term which has been judicially interpreted a sense other than that given by such interpretation; or

(*d*) to include or exclude, for the purposes of the Act, something in regard to the inclusion or exclusion of which there might otherwise be doubt.

When a word or phrase is defined as having a particular meaning, it is that meaning and that meaning alone which must be given to it, in interpreting a section of the Act, unless the context otherwise requires.

The definition clause uses expressions such as 'includes' or 'means' or 'include and means'.

On the exact connotation of the word 'includes' the judicial practice is now firmly established. Includes is generally used in interpretation clauses in order to enlarge the meaning of the words or phrases occurring in the body of the statute. When it is so used these words or phrases must be construed as comprehending not only such things as they signify according to their nature and import but also those things which the interpretation clause declares that they should include.

In *Dilworth* v. *Commissioner of Stamps*,[10] the interpretation to be given to such an inclusive definition had been clearly laid down by the House of Lords. The House of Lords held that in the interpretation of statutes, it is well known that when the legislature wants to enlarge the natural meaning of the words or phrases, it uses the word includes and in such a context an inclusive definition means that over and above the natural meaning of the words. The House of Lords further held that the specially provided meaning of the words will also have to be attributed for the purpose of interpretation of that particular chapter of the Act as the case may be.

Thus, the word 'includes' in the definition or interpretation clause that extends the meaning of the word does not take away its ordinary meaning. The word 'includes' is often used in interpretation clauses in order to enlarge the meaning of the words and phrases occurring in the body of the Statute. When it is so used, these words and phrases must be construed as comprehending not only

10. Law Reports (1899) Appeal Cases 99 quoted in *CIT* v. *Premanand Industrial Cooperative Limited* [1980] 124 ITR 772/3 Taxman 498 (Guj.).

such things as they signify according to their nature and import, but also those things which the interpretation clause declares that they include[11].

The Karnataka High Court in *Patil Vijay Kumar*[12] held that the encashment of leave although it is not specifically included within the expression 'salary' as defined in section 17(1) or in the expression 'profit in lieu of salary' as defined in section 17(3)(*ii*) of the Income-tax Act, 1961 nevertheless it falls within the meaning of the term 'profit in lieu of salary' under clause (*ii*) of sub-section (3) of section 17 of the Income-tax Act. The court observed that the leave salary and allowances and salary and allowances an employee receives for the same period are one and the same. The payment of leave salary and allowances to an employee who surrendered his leave is related to or flows from the relationship between employer and employee and from the terms and conditions of employment.[13]

In N.S. Chettiar[14], the Supreme Court stated that an interpretation clause which extends the meaning of a word does not take away its ordinary meaning. An interpretation clause is not meant to prevent the word from receiving its ordinary, popular, and natural sense, whenever that would be applicable, but to enable the word as used in the Act, when there is nothing context in the subject matter to the contrary, to be applied to something to which it would not be applicable ordinarily.

The judicial decisions mentioned above get support from the views of *Maxwell*.[15] He observed:

> "Sometimes, however, the word 'include' is so used in order to enlarge the meaning of words and phrases occurring in the body of the Statute; and when it is so used these words or phrases must be construed as comprehending, not only such things as they signify according to their natural import but also those things which the interpretation clause declares that they shall include. In other words, the word in respect of which 'includes' is used bears both its extended statutory meaning and its ordinary, popular, and natural sense, whenever that would be properly applicable."

Craies on statute law[16] observed:

An interpretation clause which extends the meaning of a word does not take away its ordinary meaning. An interpretation clause is not meant to prevent

---

11. *CIT* v. *Taj Mahal Hotel* (1971) 82 ITR 44 (SC). In this case sanitary fittings and pipelines in the hotel was held covered in the definition of plant referred to in section 10(5) of the Indian Income-tax Act 1922. Plant includes vehicles, books, scientific apparatus, surgical equipment for the purpose of business or profession. It was observed that the very fact that even books have been included shows that the meaning intended to be given to plant is wide. The court held that we are unable to see how the sanitary fittings in the bathrooms in a hotel will not be plant within section 10(2)(*vib*). Legislature intended to give it a wide meaning and that is why articles like books and surgical instruments were expressly included in the definition of plant.
12. *Patil Vijaykuraar* v. *Union of India* (1985) 151 ITR 48/20 Taxman 363 (Kar.).
13. *Ibid* at p. 64.
14. *CGT* v. *N.S. Getty Chettiar* [1971] 182 ITR 599, 605; AIR 1971 SC 2410.
15. Maxwell, interpretation of statute at 270 quoted in *CIT* v. *Straw Board Manufacturing Company Limited* (1975) 98 ITR 78 (P&H).
16. Craies, Statute law (6th edition) at p. 213.

a word from receiving its ordinary, popular, and natural sense whenever that would be properly applicable, but to enable the word as used in the Act, when there is nothing in the context or subject matter to the contrary, to be applied to some things to which it would not ordinarily be applicable.

In *Mahalakshmi Oil Mills*[17], the controversy was whether the term "tobacco" and the inclusive clause were wide enough to cover tobacco seeds. In the first place, tobacco seeds hardly answer to the description of either the expression "manufactured tobacco" or the expression "unmanufactured tobacco" in their ordinary connotation; and the expression "cured or uncured" cannot also be associated with tobacco seeds. The expression used in the first part of the definition, though very wide, is, therefore, singularly inappropriate to take within its purview tobacco seeds as well. Secondly, the definition occurs in a statute levying excise duty which is concerned not with the parts of a plant grown on the field but with the use to which those parts are put or can be put after severance.

The other cases in which the word 'include' has been construed are *P. Kasilingam*[18], *Hospital Mazdoor Sabha*,[19] and *Taj Mahal Hotel*[20]. Recently, in Orator Marketing[21], the Supreme Court held that of course, depending on the context in which the word 'includes' may have been used, and the objects and the scheme of the enactment as a whole, the expression 'includes' may have to be construed as restrictive and exhaustive. Thus, in *Orator* Supreme Court preferred the contextual interpretation.

4.5 Legal fiction or the use of the expression 'deemed'

The word "deemed" is used a great deal in modern legislation. Where the legislature says that something should be deemed to have been done which in truth has not been done it creates a legal fiction and in that case, the court is entitled and bound to ascertain for what purposes and between what persons the statutory fiction is to be resorted to and full effect must be given to the statutory fiction and it should be carried to its logical conclusion.[22]

In the Income-tax Act, 1961 legal fiction is used in the definition of many terms and phrases at more than one occasion. Sometimes it is used to impose for the purpose of the statute an artificial construction of a word or phrase. sometimes it is used to put beyond doubt a particular construction. the effect of a legal fiction is that a position that would otherwise not be obtained is being deemed to be obtained under these circumstances.[23]

17. *Mahalakshmi Oil Mills* v. *State of Andhra Pradesh* AIR 1989 SC 335.
18. *P. Kasilingam* v. *P.S.G. College of Technology* 1995 Supp (2) SCC 348/[1995] 2 SCR 1061.
19. *State of Bombay* v. *Hospital Mazdoor Sabha* AIR 1960 SC 610.
20. *CIT Andhra Pradesh* v. *Taj Mahal Hotel Secunderabad* (1971) 3 SCC 550.
21. *Orator Marketing (P.) Ltd.* v. *Samtex Desinz (P.) Ltd.* [Civil Appeal No. 2231 of 2021 decided on July 26, 2021]/[2021] 128 taxmann.com 424/167 SCL 610 (SC).
22. *CIT* v. *Bombay Corporation* AIR 1930 PC 54; *ITO* v. *Alfred* AIR 1952 SC 663.
23. *K. Kamaraj Nadar* v. *Kunju Thevar* AIR 1958 SC 687.

A well-established rule of interpretation is that the legal fiction should be carried to its conclusion but the fiction cannot be extended beyond the language of the section. In Mother India Industries[24], the issue that came up for consideration was that what is the true scope and purpose of the legal fiction created under proviso (*b*) to section 10(2) of the Income-tax Act, 1922. The counsel for the assessee urged that full effect must be given to the legal fiction created and that the above-mentioned statutory provisions and therefore between the aggregate amount of depreciation and unabsorbed carried forward losses the priority has to be given to the latter matter of set off. Justice Tulzapurkar speaking for the court observed:

> " It is not possible to accept the contention of the counsel for the assessee that because of the legal fiction, the unabsorbed carried forward losses should be given preference not merely over the unabsorbed carried forward depreciation but also over current year depreciation. In other words, it clearly emerges that in the matter of set-off, the unabsorbed business losses of the earlier years will have preference over unabsorbed depreciation that is required to be carried forward under proviso (*b*) to Section 10(2)(*vi*) of the Indian Income-tax Act, 1922 and no preference over the current depreciation is intended".

In *Narayanrao Deshmukh*[25] Supreme Court observed that a legal fiction should no doubt be carried out to its logical end to carry out the purposes for which it is enacted but it cannot be carried beyond that. It is no doubt true that the right of a female heir to the interest inherited by her in the family property gets fixed on the death of a male member under section 6 of the Hindu Succession Act, 1956, but she cannot be treated as having ceased to be a member of the family without her volition as otherwise it will lead to strange results which could not have been in the contemplation of Parliament when it enacted that provision(*i.e.* section 6, *Explanation 1* of the Hindu Succession Act, 1956) which might also be in the interest of such female heirs.

In a decision of the Bombay High Court,[26] the exact scope of the legal fiction created under section 41 of the Income-tax Act, 1961 came up for consideration. The legal fiction created under section 41 of the Income-tax Act, 1961 treats something which is a capital receipt as income of the business. The question arose in this case was that whether expenditure admissible as a deduction under section 37 of the Income-tax Act, 1961 is also allowed in computing income under section 41 or not. The Bombay High Court held that as a matter of fact, the brokerage and the traveling expenses are directory referable to and related to the sale and we see no reason why the fiction cannot be extended to cover expenses directly referable to the realisation of the sale price.

---

24. *CIT* v. *Mother India Refrigeration Industries (P.) Ltd.* (1985) 155 ITR 711/23 Taxman 8 (SC).
25. *State of Maharashtra* v. *Narayan Rao Shyam Rao Deshmukh* AIR 1985 SC 716/(1985) 2 SCC 321/[1985] 22 Taxman 38 (SC).
26. *CIT* v. *Bharat lines Ltd.* (1986) 159 ITR 541/29 Taxman 76 (Bom.).

4.6 Heading

The heading is prefixed to sections or a set of sections is preamble to those sections. It (heading) is a shorthand reference to the general subject matter involved. However, though the heading refers to a particular subject, it neglects to reveal allied or cognate matters. Thus, the law is established that the heading of a section cannot limit the plain meaning of the text. In *Chandroji Rao*[27] the question arose was that whether interest payable in respect of compensation under the Madhya Pradesh Abolition of Jagir Act, 1951 is taxable or not. The Supreme Court upholding the decision of the high court observed that the marginal heading cannot control the interpretation of the words of the section particularly when the language of the section is clear and unambiguous. The legislature being well aware of the distinction between compensation and interest thereon employed clear language which leaves no room for doubt that under sub-section (2) interest was payable in its well-known and well under sense and it could never form a part of the compensation money.[28]

4.7 Marginal notes

Marginal notes are inserted as a matter of convenience. They intend to condense the section to a short and accurate phrase. As pointed out by the Privy Council in *Balraj Kumar*[29], marginal notes in an Indian statute, as in an English Act of Parliament, cannot be relied upon for interpreting a section unless there is some ambiguity in the section. The marginal note is not decisive of the true intention.[30] It cannot assist the court in arriving at the true meaning of the section.[31] although marginal note cannot be relied upon for the purpose of interpreting a section it certainly helps the court to resolve that doubt.[32]

The marginal note may give an indication as to exactly what was the mischief that was intended to be remedied[33]. In Navanagar Transport[34] the court observed

---

27. *Chandroji Rao* v. *CIT* AIR 1970 SC 1582 "In our opinion, the High Court rightly rejected the contentions. Section 8 clearly provided that compensation shall be due from the date of resumption. Thus, the amount of compensation became ascertained and payable from the date of resumption. The provision for interest was made simply because the compensation was to be paid in ten annual instalments. A clear distinction has been made between the compensation payable under sub-section (1) and the interest which is payable under sub-section (2). The compensation has to be determined in accordance with the principles laid down in Schedule 1. That schedule indicates that the determination of compensation had nothing to do with the payment of interest."
28. *Chandroji Rao* v. *CIT* AIR 1970 SC 1582 at pp. 1583-1584.
29. *Balraj Kumar* v. *Jagat Pal Singh* ILR 26 All 393 at p. 406 quoted in *CIT* v. *Ahmedbhai Umarbhai & Co.* (1950) 18 ITR 472 (SC).
30. *CIT* v. *Lokenath & Co.* (1984) 40 CTR 297/17 Taxman 209 (Delhi).
31. *Sutlej Cotton Mills Ltd.* v. *CIT* (1950)18 ITR 112 (Cal.).
32. *Sanjiv V Kudva* v. *CIT* (1981) 20 CTR (Kar.) 1.
33. *CIT* v. *Vadilal Lallubhai* (1972) 86 ITR 2 (SC)
34. *Navanagar Transport and Industries Limited* v. *ITO* (1964) 54 ITR 271 (Guj.).

that the marginal note cannot be regarded as an aid to the construction of the section and it cannot affect the plain and natural meaning of the language used in the section but it can certainly be referred to as furnishing a clue the meaning and purpose of the section. In Navanagar Transport case, the marginal note to the amended Section 23A of the Income-tax Act, 1922 was titled "Power to assess companies to super tax on distributed income in certain cases". It was held that the marginal notes clearly indicate the drift of the section, namely, that the section is intended for the assessment of companies to super-tax all undistributed profits in certain cases and in the body of the section one finds that such meaning and effect of the section and the section does not authorize the assessment of companies to super- tax on undistributed income in the cases specified in the section.

In *Sajjan Mills Limited*[35] the proper interpretation 40A(7) came up before the Court. This provision was inserted in 1975 and provided for disallowance in respect of payment of gratuity. On a literal/strict construction put on this clause, it was contended by the assessee that the above-mentioned provision *i.e.* section 40A(7) could only apply if the assessee had made provision for Payment of Gratuity and not in other cases *i.e.* where Payment of Gratuity is made without making any provision for the same in books of account. This argument was negatived by their lordship of the Supreme Court on the following grounds namely:

"(*i*) Section 40A contains a marginal note under the heading 'expenses or payment not deductible in certain circumstances'. Read with the marginal notes of section 40A, the *non-obstante clause* of sub-section (1) of section 40A has an overriding effect over the provisions of any other section that will have effect notwithstanding anything contained in sections 28 to 37 of the Income-tax Act, 1961.

(*ii*) On a plain construction of clause (*a*) of sub-section (7) of section 40A, what it means is that whatever is provided for future use by the assessee out of gross profits of the year of account for payment of gratuity to employees would not be allowed as deduction in the year of account. The embargo is on deductions of amounts provided for future use in the year of account for meeting the ultimate liability to the payment of gratuity. This is subject to exemptions provided in clause (*b*) of section 40A(7). Clause (*b*)(*i*) excludes from the operation of clause (*a*) contributions to approved gratuity fund and the amount provided for or set apart for payment of gratuity which would be payable during the year of account. Clause (*b*)(*ii*) deals with a situation where the assessee might provide by spread-over method and provides that such provisions would be excluded from the operation of clause (*a*) provided the three conditions laid down by the sub-clause are satisfied.

(*iii*) The interpretation as suggested by the assessee would entitle the assessee who made no provision to claim a deduction unless the requirement down in the sub-section is fulfilled. This interpretation, if accepted, will lead to a curious result, and if one may venture to say an absurd result, even the assessee who has made no provision from the gross profits of the year will get relief out of payment made towards gratuity to employees.

35. *Shree Sajjan Mills Ltd.* v. *CIT* (1985) 156 ITR 585/23 Taxman 37 (SC).

(*iv*) Where the intention of the Legislature in enacting the provision in question was to put an embargo on the deduction, the interpretation suggested by the assessee defeats that purpose.

(*v*) Interpretation suggested by the assessee would lead to a conclusion which would be extraordinary and repugnant to common sense. It will also cause gross injustice to the assessee who has been prudent enough to set apart a sum for payment of gratuity. The principle that fiscal statute should be strictly construed does not rule out the application of the principle of reasonable construction to give effect to the purpose or intention of any particular provision as apparent from the scheme of the Act with the assistance of such external aids as are permissible under the law."

4.8 Explanation

The purpose of explanation is often to explain some concept or expression or phrase occurring in the main provision and it is not uncommon for the legislature to accord extended meaning or restricted meaning to such concept or expression or phrase by inserting an appropriate explanation. In Warangal Industries[36], the issue arose was whether, under section 41(2) of the Income-tax Act, 1961, the assessee could claim a deduction in respect of unabsorbed depreciation out of the deemed income under section 41 of the Income-tax Act. The income tax officer took the plea that since no business was in existence when the deemed profit under section 41 arose therefore no allowance for depreciation could be granted because depreciation is related to the business which is carried on. Negativing the aforesaid contention, the Bombay High Court observed that by virtue of *Explanation* to Section 41(2), deeming fiction is created and by virtue of that deeming fiction, the business is no longer in existence for the purposes of Section 41(2) and is deemed to be in existence in the previous year in the course of which the machinery, plant, or furniture in respect of which depreciation has been allowed in an earlier year is sold, discarded, demolished, or destroyed.

The object of explanation was summarised in a *Sundaram*[37] as follows: -

(1) It is to explain the meaning and intendment of the Act itself.

(2) When there is any obscurity or vagueness in the main enactment, to clarify the same so as to make it consistent with the dominant object which it seems to subserve.

(3) To provide additional support to the dominant object of the Act in order to make it meaningful and purposeful.

(4) An explanation cannot in any way interfere with or change the enactment or any part thereof but, where some gap is left which is relevant for the purpose of preventing the mischief and advancing the object of the Act it can help or assist the true purpose and intendment of the enactment, and

36. *CIT* v. *Warangal Industries (P.) Ltd.* [1977] 110 ITR 756 (AP).

37. *S. Sundaram* v. *Pattibhiraman* AIR 1985 SC 582, 593.

(5) It cannot curtail statutory right which any person under a statute has been clothed with or by becoming an hindrance in the interpretation of the same.

In *Khandelwal Metal*[38], an issue arose as to the interpretation of an *Explanation* to the Customs Tariff Act,1975. Section 3(1) of the Tariff Act, 1975 was sought to be interpreted as levying countervailing duty independently of the provisions of the Customs Act,1962. It was contended on behalf of the petitioner that brass scrap which is not capable of being produced or manufactured cannot be subject to duty under section 3(1) of the Tariff Act. Rejecting the argument, the Supreme Court observed:

> "Any doubt on this point is resolved by... explanation furnishes a dictionary for the interpretation of section 3(1) and provides a clue to its understanding. The explanation provides in so many words that the excise duty for the time being leviable on a like article if produced or manufactured in India means the excise duty for the time being in force which would be leviable on a like article if produced or manufactured in India ... The explanation even goes further and provides that if a like article is not so produced or manufactured, then, the duty leviable means the duty which would be leviable on the class or description of articles to which imported article belongs."

In *Vrajlal*[39], the levy of sales tax on Tendu leaves disposed of by the state government was challenged on the ground, *inter alia*, that neither the state government nor any of its departments including the forest department or its officers was a dealer within the meaning of the term defined under section 2(*a*) of the Madhya Pradesh General Sales Tax Act, 1958 as none of them carried on the business of buying, selling, supplying or distributing goods and that *Explanation* II which was inserted in the said clause (*a*) did not have the effect of enlarging the concept of dealer as defined in that clause. In this context, it is pertinent to note that for a person to be a dealer within the meaning of clause (*a*), he must be one who carries on the business of buying, selling, supplying, or distributing goods, and the definition as originally enacted included within its scope the Central Government, State government or any of their departments which carried on such business. This definition was amended by the 1971 Act retrospectively and reference to the central government or State government or any of their departments in sub-clause (*i*) of clause (*a*) was omitted from that sub-clause and an explanation was added.

Commenting upon the exact nature and scope of the explanation their lordship of the Supreme Court Justice Madon observed that merely because a particular provision in a statute is labeled as an explanation it does not mean that it is inserted merely with a view to explain the meaning of the words contained in the section of which it forms a part. The true scope and effect of an explanation can only be judged by its expressed language and not merely by the label given

---

38. *Khandelwal Metal and Engineering Works* v. *Union of India* (1985) 3 SCC 620/[1985] 1985 taxmann.com 418 (SC)/AIR 1985 SC 1211.

39. *Vrajlal Manilal and Company* v. *State of Madhya Pradesh* (1986) 63 STC 1 (SC).

to it. The language of the explanation shows that its purpose is to create a legal fiction and that while under the main clause, for a person to be a dealer, he must carry on the business of buying, selling, supplying, or distributing goods, even if the central government or State government or any of their departments or offices does not carry on such business if it buys, sales, supplies or distributes good, it is to be deemed to be a dealer the purpose of the Madhya Pradesh Sales Tax Act, that is, for the purpose of the levy and collection of Tax under the Madhya Pradesh Sales Tax Act[40].

Sometimes the explanation is to be given a retrospective effect if the language permits such construction. Explanation giving the meaning to the phrase 'when an assessee is in default' under section 221 of the Income-tax Act, 1961, by section 53 the Taxation (Amendment) Act, 1975 was given retrospective effect. The effect of the explanation was held that of declaratory in nature and therefore it was given retrospective effect[41]. The declaratory Act may be defined as an Act to remove doubts existing as to common law or the meaning or effect of any statute. Such Acts are usually held to be retrospective. The usual reason for passing a declaratory Act is to set aside what Parliament seems to have been a judicial error, whether in the statement of common law or in the interpretation of statute. Usually, if not invariably, such an Act contains a preamble, and also the words 'declared as well as enacted.

4.9 Proviso

The word provided is an enacting word and it means it is provided. Usually, it is confined to taking a special case out of general enactments and providing specially for them.

In *Indo-Mercantile Bank*[42], Justice Kapoor observed that the proper function of a proviso is that it qualifies the generality of the main enactment by providing an exception and taking out as it were, from the main enactment, a portion which, but for the proviso would fall within the main enactment. Ordinarily, it is foreign to the proper function of a proviso to read it as providing something by way of an addendum, for dealing with the subject which is foreign to the main enactment...

The scope of the proviso has been dealt with by the Supreme Court in many cases[43]. in *Bezwada Municipality*[44], Lord Macmillan observed that the proper function of the proviso is to except and deal with a case which would

40. *Vrajlal Manilal and Company* v. *State of Madhya Pradesh* (1986) 63 STC 1 (SC) pp. 10-11.

41. *CIT* v. *Sriram Agrawal* (1986) 54 CTR (Patna) 367/28 Taxman 81 (Patna).

42. *CIT* v. *Indo Mercantile Bank Limited* (1959) 36 ITR 1, 7 (SC).

43. *CIT* v. *Bipinchandra Maganlal & Co. Ltd.*, Bombay AIR 1961 SC 1040/(1961) 2 SCR 493/(1961) 41 ITR 290 (SC); *Sundaram Pillai* v. *V R Pattabiraman* [1985] 1 SCC 591; *Hiralal Rattanlal* v. *State of UP* (1973) 1 SCC 216;

44. *SM Railway* v. *Bezwada Municipality* AIR 1944 Privy Council 71.

otherwise fall within the general language of the main enactment, and its effect is confined to that case... where the language of the main enactment is clear and unambiguous, proviso can have no repercussion on the interpretation of the main enactment, so as to exclude from it by implication what clearly falls within its express terms.

In *Madurai Mills*[45], the Supreme Court observed that a proviso cannot be construed as enlarging the scope of an enactment when it can be fairly and properly construed without attributing to it that effect. Further, if the language of the main part of the statute is plain and unambiguous and does not contain the provisions which are said to occur in it, one cannot derive those provisions by implication from a proviso.

In *Madurai Mills*, Mr. Manchanda on behalf of the appellant has invited the attention of the court to the third proviso to sub-section (1) of section 12B as originally enacted in 1946 wherein it was enacted, *inter alia*, that any distribution of a capital asset on the dissolution of the firm or other association of persons on the liquidation of the company shall not for the purposes of section 12B be treated as sale, exchange, or transfer of capital assets. It was argued that the omission of such distribution of capital assets in the first proviso to Section 12B(1) under the Finance (No. 2) Act of 1956 would show that the legislature wanted the distribution of capital assets on the dissolution of a firm or other association of persons on the liquidation of the company to be treated as sale, exchange or transfer. The Supreme Court refused to accept the aforesaid contention and laid down the law as stated above.

The Bombay High Court in *Jhumar Mal*[46] held that normally the proviso should be looked upon as a proviso to the section in which it appears and, before the proviso can have application, the section itself must apply and cannot be regarded as an independent enacting clause.

It was stated further that it is equally clear that the legislature may enact a substantive provision in the garb of the proviso and if it appears from the language of the proviso that its application could not be restricted to the main section, the court must look upon it as a substantive provision if it has a clear meaning[47].

The proviso may become a substantive provision of the Act itself. In *Leela Jain*[48], the question arose whether the proviso in the Act was a limiting provision to the main provision or was a substantive provision in itself.

The court observed that so far as a general principle of construction of a proviso is concerned, it has been broadly stated that the function of a proviso is to limit the main part of the section and carve out something which but for the proviso would have been within the operative part.

---

45. *CIT* v. *Madurai Mills Company Limited* (1973) 89 ITR 45 (SC).
46. *Jummarlal Suraj Karan* v. *CIT* (1963) 47 ITR 809 (AP).
47. *Ibid* at p 812.
48. *State of Rajasthan* v. *Leela Jain* AIR 1965 SC 1296.

In *Ramkrishna Javer*[49], it was contended that on a proper construction of section 41 of the Madras General Sales Tax Act, 1959 the officer of the department had no authority to search the premises and seize either account books or the goods found there. The Supreme Court while rejecting the contention held that the proviso to Section 41 of the Act gave such power. Speaking for the Court Wanchoo, CJ observed:

> "As we have already held, there is no provision in the main part of the sub-section for searching purely residential premises. Therefore, when the proviso provides for such a search, it is providing for something independent of the main part of the sub-section. Thus, in exceptional circumstances, a proviso may not be really a proviso in the accepted sense but may be a substantive provision itself. Further, the second part of the proviso which talks of searches made under this sub-section shows that the power of inspection provided in the main part of the sub-section is tantamount to a power of search."

As traditionally understood proviso acts as an exception to the main enactment. However as discussed in the case of *R.S. Javer*[50], a proviso may act as a substantive provision of the main enactment also.

A proviso may have four separate functions[51], namely:—

(*a*) Qualifying or excepting certain provisions from the main enactment;

(*b*) It may entirely change the very concept of the intendment of the enactment by insisting on certain mandatory conditions to be fulfilled in order to make the enactment workable;

(*c*) It may be so embedded in the Act itself as to become an integral part of the enactment and thus acquire the tenor and colour of the substantive enactment itself; and

(*d*) It may be used merely to act as an optional addendum to the enactment with the sole object of explaining the real intendment of the statutory provision.

Very recently in *VKS Footsteps*[52], the Supreme Court stated that provisos in a statute have multi-faceted personalities. Multi-faceted aspects of provisos have been explained in the above-quoted judgments and in the report of the Direct Tax Laws Committee (1978).

4.10 Schedule

Some Acts contain schedules appended to them. Income-tax Act, 1961, the Wealth-tax Act, 1957, the Gift-tax Act, 1958, and legislation on tax on goods and services contain schedules appended to them. As a rule, a matter of details

---

49. *Board of Revenue* v. *Ram Kishan Shri Kishan Javer* AIR 1968 SC 59.

50. *Ibid.*

51. Report of the Direct Tax Laws Committee (1978) at p. 43.

52. *Union of India* v. *VKC Footsteps India Pvt. Ltd.* (2022) 2 SCC 603/[2021] 130 taxmann.com 193/52 GSTL 513 (SC).

is relegated to the schedule. the schedule contains sometimes substantive provisions of law. The Direct Tax Laws Committee (1978)[53] recommended:

> "We, accordingly recommend that provisions of a substantive nature presently contained in the rules of the fourth schedule be included in the sections of the law dealing with the computation of income from salaries."

The rule of interpretation, which ought to be applied to the combination of Act and schedule was stated by Lord Sterndale as follows:

> "If the Act says that the schedule is to be used for certain purposes and the heading of the part in the schedule in question shows that it is *prima facie* at any rate devoted to that purpose, then you must read the Act as though the schedule is operating for the purpose, and if you can satisfy the language of the section without extending it beyond that purpose you ought to do it. But if in spite of that, you find with the language of the schedule, words and terms that go clearly outside the purpose, then you must give effect to them and you must not consider them as limited by the heading of that part of the schedule mentioned in the Act for which the schedule has provided and you cannot refuse to give effect to clear words simply because *prima facie* they seem to be limited by the heading of the schedule and definition of the purpose of the schedule contained in the Act."[54]

In *Indira Bai*[55], Madras High Court observed that it is axiomatic that the statute was to be read as a whole and that the schedule to the Act is as much part of the Act as any other provision thereof. Rules of interpretation even require that if an enactment in a schedule other than one merely of form contradicts an earlier clause it is the schedule that would prevail.

In this case, the petitioner contended that under the charging provisions of the Act, the tax is payable only on each gift subject to the exceptions and exemptions provided in the Act and there is no provision in the Act for aggregating the value of all gifts made by a person during the previous year. The court held reading section 3 and schedule to the Act the logical result would appear to be that the total value of all gifts is to be computed and the appropriate rate of tax applied to any particular assessment. The court further stated, "Not only is the schedule to the Gift Tax Act clear and specific in its requirement that the tax is in respect of the total value of the taxable gifts made during the previous year but the other relevant provisions of the Act including in particular the charging section itself give no room for entertaining the contrary view.

An important decision on the interpretation of an entry in a schedule is that of *Premiere Mills Limited*[56]. Justice Bala Subramaniam observed:

> "... I believe that ordinary rules of statutory construction should not be applied to an understanding of the entries in the schedule of this kind. It is true that a schedule to an Act is enacted by the hand of the Legislature and it is very much

53. Report of the Direct Tax Laws Committee (1978) at p. 43.

54. *IRC* v. *Gittus* (1920) 1 KB 563.

55. *Indira Bai* v. *GTO* (1962) 44 ITR 66 (Madras).

56. *Premiere Mills Limited* v. *CIT* (1985) 152 ITR 457 (Madras).

part of the Act. Even so, its construction calls for a difference in approach. Rules of interpretation, such as the *ejusdem generis* rule, the rule of expression *unius alterius exclusio alterius*, and the like are all very good, in their own way, for construing sections.... But their wholesale adoption, without qualification, to the construction of entries on a schedule is open to question. There is, in our opinion, a functional difference between the body of the Statute, on the one hand, and the schedule, which is attached thereto on the other. The sections in an Act are enacting provisions. They contain the legislature's do's and don'ts. They confer rights. They impose obligations. They prescribe conditions, limitations, and restrictions. They lay down sanctions, they concern in short, with acts that may be either positive or negative and their consequences. In contrast, a schedule for an Act merely sets down things and objects and contains their names and descriptions. The schedule does not enact anything. The entries therein derive their sustenance only from the relevant sections in the body of the Act. The fifth schedule to the Income-Tax Act is no exception. It is nothing but a list of entries."

How entries should be interpreted? Another important point is how the entries in a schedule are to be interpreted.

Whether they are to be understood in their technical sense or in their ordinary sense.

In *Pai and Company*[57] the issue was whether if the ornaments and other articles of gold purchased by the assessee fall within the entry 56 First Schedule to the Kerala General Sales Tax Act, 1963, the turnover of purchase of these goods would be liable to be taxed at the rate of 1%, while it would have to suffer tax at the rate of 3% if these goods do not fall within this entry and are taxable under section 5A read with section 5(1)(*ii*) of the Act.

Justice Bhagwati observed that there is one cardinal rule of interpretation which has always to be borne in mind while interpreting entries in sales tax legislation and it is that the words used in the entries must be construed not in any technical sense nor from the scientific point of view but as understood in common parlance. We must give the words used by the legislature their popular sense meaning that sense which people conversant with the subject matter with which the statute is dealing would attribute to it. The word 'bullion' in entry 56 of the First Schedule to the Kerala General Sales Tax Act, 1963, must, therefore, be interpreted according to ordinary parlance and must be given a meaning which the people conversant with this commodity would ascribe to it. Now, it is obvious that bullion in its popular sense cannot include ornaments and other articles for gold even if old and antiquated. They are not raw or unwrought gold or gold in mass but they represent manufactured and finished products of gold.

Classification

The Customs Tariff Act, 1975, in section 2 provides that the rates at which duties of customs shall be levied under the Customs Act, 1962, are specified in the First and Second Schedules. Similarly, the Central Excise Tariff Act, 1985 specifies

57. *Deputy Commissioner of Sales Tax* v. *Pai and Company* (1980) 45 STC 58, 61 (SC).

rates in the schedules. Classification under the Harmonised System is done by placing the good under the most apt and fitting sub-heading. This is done by choosing the appropriate Chapter, Heading, and sub-heading respectively. To facilitate interpretation and classification, each of the 97 Chapters in the HSN contains corresponding Chapter Notes, General Notes, and Explanatory Notes applicable to the Headings and sub-headings within that Chapter. In addition, there are six General Rules of Interpretation applicable to the Harmonised System as a whole[58].

GRI 1 states that the titles of Sections, Chapters, and sub-chapters are provided for ease of reference only. Therefore, they have no legal bearing on classification. Classification is to be effected: (*a*) according to the terms of the Headings and any relative Section or Chapter Notes; and, (*b*) provided the Headings or Chapter Notes do not otherwise require according to the provisions hereinafter contained, *viz*., GRIs 2 to 6. Thus, it is clear from the above that: (*i*) the Headings, and, (*ii*) the relative Section or Chapter Notes must be considered before classification is done. Only after this exercise is done, if a conflict in classification still persists, the subsequent GRIs are to be resorted to.

GRI 3 provides for classification in the event when the goods are classifiable under two or more Headings. As per GRI 3, when by application of GRI 2(*b*) or for any other reason, the goods are, *prima facie*, classifiable under more than one Heading, then; (*a*) the 'most specific description' is preferred, (*b*) a mixture of different goods will be classified as that good which gives the mixture its 'essential characteristic', and (*c*) when goods cannot be classified with reference to (*a*) or (*b*), they should be classified under the Heading which occurs last in the numerical order.

The order of priority therefore is; (*a*) specific description, (*b*) essential character, and (*c*) the Heading which occurs last in numerical order. However, GRI 3 can only take effect provided the terms of the Heading or Section or Chapter Notes do not otherwise require.

GRI 4 states that when the goods cannot be classified in accordance with the aforementioned rules, they shall be classified under the heading appropriate for the goods "to which they are most akin".

GRI 5 applies exclusively to cases and packing material.

GRI 6 states that the classification of goods in the sub-headings of a Heading shall be determined according to the terms of those sub-headings and any related Notes, and *mutatis mutandis* to the above GRIs, on the understanding that only sub-headings at the same level are comparable.

The General Rules of Interpretation and the role of interpretative rules, which guide the appropriate classification of products, were explained in *Simplex*

58. *Commissioner of Customs and Central Excise* v. *D.L. Steels* [Civil Appeal Nos. 2360-2376 of 2009 decided on 11th July, 2022]/2022 (381) ELT 289/[2022] 140 taxmann.com 253 (SC).

Mills[59]. In Simplex Mills the Supreme Court observed that for legal purposes, classification "shall be determined according to the terms of the headings and any relevant section or chapter notes". If neither the heading nor the notes suffice to clarify the scope of a heading, then it must be construed according to the other following provisions contained in the Rules. Rule 1 gives primacy to the section and chapter notes along with terms of the headings. They should be first applied. If no clear picture emerges then only can one resort to the subsequent rules. The appellants have relied upon Rule 3. Rule 3 must be understood only in the context of sub-rule (*b*) of Rule 2 which says *inter alia* that the classification of goods consisting of more than one material or substance shall be according to the principles contained in Rule 3. Therefore, when goods are *prima facie*, classifiable under two or more headings, classification shall be effected according to sub-rules (*a*), (*b*) and (*c*) of Rule 3 and in that order.

Pan masala or gutka/gutkha

In *M/s Trimurthi Fragrances*[60] It was held that on a **plain application of the interpretive rules**, especially Rule 3(*a*) it is clear that the heading which provides the most accurate description has to be followed. In the present case, there is no doubt, that before 2001, pan masala and gutkha fell within Chapter 21, as pan masala, regardless of whether they contained tobacco. Goods classifiable under Chapter 24, *i.e.* tobacco items were more general; also they did not include pan masala.

Talcum Powder

In *Heinz India*[61] it was held that there can be no two opinions that talcum powder *ipso facto* is classifiable as a cosmetic. Yet, the expression "including" used in Entry 127 has the effect of bringing in [or "pulling in"] an entirely different product, which ordinarily may not have been in the same class, *i.e.* medicated powder. To rule out any ambiguity, the legislature specifically referred to a sub-class of medicated powders, *i.e.* medicated talcum powder. Such specific entries have not come up for consideration, before this court; as noticed, predominantly, the courts have ruled that in the context of broad descriptions such as cosmetics or medications, if there are medical ingredients, in a product, which is meant as a curative or prophylactic product, it would be classifiable as drugs or medicines.

Anardana

In *D.L. Steels*[62], a question arose that should dried pomegranate seeds, domestically known as 'anardana', be classified under Heading 0813 of the Tariff entries

59. *Commissioner of Central Excise, Nagpur* v. *Simplex Mills Co. Ltd.* [2005] 2 SCR 441/(2005) 3 SCC 51/[2005] 2005 taxmann.com 777 (SC).

60. *Trimurthi Fragrances (P) Ltd.* v. *Govt. of N.C.T. of Delhi* [Civil Appeal No(s). 8486 OF 2011 decided on 4th May, 2023]/[2023] 6 Centax 65 (SC).

61. *Heinz India Limited* v. *State of Kerala* [Civil Appeal No(s). 2338-2339 of 2010 decided on 4th May, 2023]/[2023] 6 Centax 64 (SC).

62. *Commissioner of Customs and Central Excise* v. *D.L. Steels* [Civil Appeal Nos. 2360-2376 OF 2009 decided on 11th July, 2022]/2022 (381) E.L.T. 289/[2022] 140 taxmann.com 253 (SC).

issued under the Customs Tariff Act, 1975, as claimed by the Commissioner of Customs, Amritsar, or under Heading 1209 as claimed by the importers? Thus, for taxation the issue involved the classification of the goods under the tariff sub-heading 1209.99.90, attracting basic custom duty at the rate of 5% plus education cess at the rate of 2%. However, the customs authorities contend that the goods must fall under sub-heading 0813.40.90, and accordingly, are liable for basic custom duty at the rate of 30% plus education cess at the rate of 2%. The Court explained that pomegranates are rather unusual fruits and their structure is unlike other fruits. The outermost layer is a hard and inedible shell. The edible part consists of the seeds and arils. Arils are the sweet, juicy, and crunchy covering that encases the seeds. However, the finding of the CESTAT is that wild pomegranates from which 'anardana' is made are different from the pomegranate fruit… 'Anardana', therefore, can be defined as Sun-dried seeds of a ripe sour pomegranate, and is predominantly used as an acidulant in Indian and Persian cuisines, and for its health benefits in the Ayurvedic system of medicine. After a scholarly analysis by Justice Sanjiv Khanna, the Court held that the revenue, it may be advisable, should take a considered policy decision after examining the data and ascertaining the views of the trade associations on the classification of 'anardana' or by fixing a specific customs duty. Till the said exercise is undertaken, the classification as determined by the CESTAT may be continued to avoid confusion and litigation.

Recently, In M/S Videocon Industries[63], the interpretation of entry in the Schedule to the Customs Tariff Act was an issue. The issue was in which entry of the schedule LCD falls. The Supreme Court held that the LCD sets were under Chapter 90, Entry 9013. 8010. The relevant norms of interpretation under the First Schedule of the Customs Tariff Act, *i.e.* "The General Rules of Interpretation of this Schedule" are given in Rules 1[64], 2,[65]

---

63. *CCE Aurangabad* v. *Videocon Industries Ltd.* [Civil Appeal No. 5622 of 2009 decided on 29th March, 2023]/[2023] 5 Centax 108 (SC).

64. Classification of goods in this Schedule shall be governed by the following principles: 1. The titles of Sections, Chapters, and Sub-Chapters are provided for ease of reference only; for legal purposes, classification shall be determined according to the terms of the headings and any relative Section or Chapter Notes and, provided such headings or Notes do not otherwise require, according to the following provisions.

65. 2. (a) Any reference in a heading to an article shall be taken to include a reference to that article incomplete or unfinished, provided that, as presented, the incomplete or unfinished article has the essential character of the complete or finished article. It shall also be taken to include a reference to that article complete or finished (or falling to be classified as complete or, finished by virtue of this rule), presented unassembled or disassembled. (b) Any reference in a heading to a material or substance shall be taken to include a reference to mixtures or combinations of that material or substance with other materials or substances. Any reference to goods of a given material or substance shall be taken to include a reference to goods consisting wholly or partly of such material or substance. The classification of goods consisting of more than one material or substance shall be according to the principles of rule 3.

and 3[66]. Supreme Court found that on a reading of the General Interpretive rules and the notes to the concerned chapters (85 and 90, in the present case), it is evident that: (a) classification has to be in accord with "the terms of the headings and any relative Section or Chapter Notes" (Note 1) (*b*) Reference in a heading to "an article" includes "that article incomplete or unfinished" provided, such incomplete or unfinished article has "the essential character of the complete or finished article." [Note 2(*a*)] 15 (*c*) If on an application of Rule 2(*a*), an article is classifiable in more than one heading "the heading which provides the most specific description shall be preferred to headings providing a more general description." [Note 3(*a*)].

The correct manner of interpreting the notes, chapters, and the General rules of interpretation was explained in Simplex[67] by stating that the Rules for the Interpretation of the Schedule to the Central Excise Tariff Act are framed pursuant to the powers under Section 2 of that Act.

Whether "Car matting" fell within Chapter 57 of the First Schedule to the Central Excise Tariff Act under the heading "Carpets and Other Textile Floor Coverings" or were to be classified under Chapter 87, as "vehicles other than railway or tramway rolling-stock and parts and accessories thereof". In *UNI Products India Ltd.*[68], it was held on detailed analysis of various entries, Rules, and Notes that they fit the description of goods under chapter heading 570390.90. Once the

66. 3. When by application of rule 2(*b*) or for any other reason, goods are, *prima facie*, classifiable under two or more headings, classification shall be effected as follows: (*a*) the heading which provides the most specific description shall be preferred to headings providing a more general description. However, when two or more headings each refer to part only of the materials or substances contained in mixed or composite goods or to part only of the items in a set put up for retail sale, those headings are to be regarded as equally specific in relation to those goods, even if one of them gives a more complete or precise description of the goods. (*b*) mixtures, composite goods consisting of different materials or made up of different components, and goods put up in sets for retail sale, which cannot be classified by reference to (*a*), shall be classified, as if they consisted of the material or component which gives them their essential character, insofar as this criterion is applicable. (*c*) when goods cannot be classified by reference to (*a*) or (*b*), they shall be classified under the heading which occurs last in numerical order among those which equally merit consideration.".

67. *Commissioner of Central Excise, Nagpur* v. *Simplex Mills Co. Ltd.* [2005] 2 S.C.R. 441/(2005) 3 SCC 51/[2005] 2005 taxmann.com 777 (SC). "The Rules for the Interpretation of the Schedule to the Central Excise Tariff Act, 1985 have been framed pursuant to the powers under Section 2 of that Act. According to Rule 1 titles of sections and chapters in the Schedule are provided for ease of reference only. But for legal purposes, classification 'shall be determined according to the terms of the headings and any relevant section or chapter notes. If neither the heading nor the notes suffice to clarify the scope of a heading, then it must be construed according to the other following provisions contained in the Rules. Rule 1 gives primacy to the section and chapter notes along with terms of the headings. They should be first applied. If no clear picture emerges then only can one resort to the subsequent rules. The appellants have relied upon Rule 3. Rule 3 must be understood only in the context of sub-rule (b) of Rule 2 which says *inter alia* that the classification of goods consisting of more than one material or substance shall be according to the principles contained in Rule 3. Therefore, when goods are *prima facie*, classifiable under two or more headings, classification shall be effected according to sub-rules (*a*), (*b*) and (*c*) of Rule 3 and in that order."

68. *Commissioner of Central Excise, Delhi-III* v. *UNI Products India Ltd.* [2020] 13 S.C.R. 295/2020 (19) SCC 742/[2020] 116 taxmann.com 401 (SC).

subject goods are found to come within the ambit of the sub-heading, for the sole reason that they are exclusively made for cars and not for "home use" (in broad terms), those goods cannot be transplanted to the residual entry against the heading 8708.

Automatic Data Processing Machines (ADP)

In Hewlett Packard India[69], the issue related to the correct classification of Automatic Data Processing Machines popularly known as All-in-One Integrated Desktop Computers. While interpreting the word 'portable' the Supreme Court observed that the word 'portable' is to be defined in reference to Automated data processing instead of relying on dictionary meaning and the concerned goods were held not portable. The significant observations of the Supreme Court are on two aspects. One is the caution on the use of online material for legal dispute resolution[70] and observed that the courts and adjudicating authorities should rather make an endeavour to persuade the counsels to place reliance on more reliable and authentic sources. Secondly, the meaning of the word 'portable' has changed with technological advancement. For example, faster microchips have made it possible for mobile phones to have performance specifications which a decade ago was possible on high-end laptops.

4.11 Power to remove difficulties

The power to remove difficulty is legislative power and is conferred upon the executive for a limited duration *i.e.*, for 2 years, 3 years, or 5 years. Since the power is legislative in nature, therefore, mostly in the Acts it is limited to 2 years. This extraordinary power of the Executive is also known as the Henry VIII Clause.

In Gautam Khaitan,[71] a removal of difficulty order under the Black Money Act[72] was held legal. The Black Money Act was passed on 11-05-2015. Sub-section (1) of section 3 provides that save otherwise provided, it shall come into force on 1st April, 2016. By the removal of the difficulty order[73] it has been provided that the Black Money Act shall come into force on 01-07-2015. The Court observed-

> "The date has been changed only for the purpose of enabling the assessee(s) to take benefit of section 59 of the Black Money Act. The power has been exercised only in order to remove difficulty."

69. *Hewlett Packard India Sales Pvt. Ltd. (Now HP India Sales Pvt. Ltd.)* v. *Commissioner of Customs (Import), Nhava Sheva* [Civil Appeal No. 5373 of 2019 decided on 17-1-2023]/[2023] 2 Centax 236 (SC).
70. Para 14.
71. *Union of India* v. *Gautam Khaitan* 2019 INSC 1143.
72. The Black Money (Undisclosed Foreign Income and Assets) and Imposition of Tax Act, 2015.
73. 86. *Power to remove difficulties*.—(1) If any difficulty arises in giving effect to the provisions of this Act, the Central Government may, by order, not inconsistent with the provisions of this Act, remove the difficulty:

    Provided that no such order shall be made after the expiry of a period of two years from the date on which the provisions of this Act come into force. (2) Every order made under this section shall be laid before each House of Parliament.

5 Tax Interpretation of Exemption Provisions

5.1 Preliminary

Literally, exemption from tax is freedom from tax liability. For instance, total exemption from tax or conditional tax exemption or tax holiday to new units, or concessional rate of tax to goods or persons for a limited period. An exemption from tax liability is granted with specific objectives. Exemption provisions are often contained in the Constitution, and statutes, and sometimes exemption from tax is provided by a rule, order, or notification.

5.2 Constitutional provisions on tax exemption

There are a number of articles of the Constitution of India on exemption from tax. These are Article 285(Exemption of property of the Union from State taxation) Article 287 (Exemption from taxes on electricity) Article 288 (Exemption from taxation by States in respect of water or electricity in certain cases), and Article 289(Exemption of property and income of a State from Union taxation).

In the *NDMC* case,[1] the issue before a bench of nine judges was whether, by virtue of Article 289(1) of the Constitution, the property of the State is exempt from Union Taxation; and the undefined phrase "Union Taxation" in Article 289(1) would mean all taxes which the Union is empowered to impose; under the Constitutional scheme and, specifically under Part VIII of the Constitution. For the NDMC, it was contended: that the phrase "Union Taxation" would not extend to legislations in Union Territories and interpretation should be restricted to laws made by Parliament in respect of the entries in List I. The Supreme Court held that property taxes levied by municipalities within Union Territories are properly within the ambit of the exemption provided in Article 289(1) and the States can avail of the exemption. The term "Union Taxation" used in Article 289(1) will ordinarily mean "all taxes leviable by the Union" and it includes within its ambit taxes on property levied within Union Territories; therefore, the States can avail of the exemption provided in Article 289(1) in respect of their properties situated within Union Territories.

1. *New Delhi Municipal Committee* v. *State of Punjab* (1997) 7 SCC 339; AIR 1997 SC 2847.

5.3 The complexity of exemption provisions

It is often argued that tax laws are complex as they contain a multitude of provisos, explanations, and exemptions. Complexities of tax laws have been studied in common law jurisdictions including the United Kingdom, Canada, Australia, and in India. There is no one-size formula as the social, economic, and political systems of each country differ from one country to another. For example, the Income-tax Bill, 1961 as introduced, contained twenty-six clauses under section 10 of the Income-tax Act, 1961. Now, there are fifty clauses in section 10, and in between many clauses have been added. For example, between clause (23) and clause (24) there are **thirty additional or new clauses**, numbered clause (23A) to clause (23FD). Clause (23C) of section 10 contains **twenty-two provisos**. Chapter III of the Income-tax Act, 1961 is titled "Income not to be included in the total income of the assessee." An income is granted exemption subject to the fulfilment of conditions stated in the provision of the law or under the notification granting an exemption.

In the Customs Act, 1962, exemption is granted by a notification issued under section 25 of the Customs Act,1962. In the indirect taxes, a mega exemption notification[2] was issued. Mega exemption contains a list of services that are exempted from service tax leviable under Section 66B. The Central Goods and Services Tax Act, 2017[3] empowers the Central Government on being satisfied that it is necessary in the public interest to do, on the recommendations of the Council, grants exemption on the *intra State* supply of services. Under the GST regime, an exemption notification was issued in 2017[4] and amended in 2019[5]. A clarificatory circular has also been issued[6].

5.4 Procedural safeguards

The power to grant exemption is an unusual, extraordinary, and exceptional power given to the executive and it is imperative that adequate safeguards should be there to ensure that the powers are used sparingly and there are no chances of their being misused. Under Sections 25 and 66 of the Customs Act, 1962 power has been conferred on the Central Government to exempt items from duty of customs. These Notifications are required to be laid on the Table of the House within seven days of the commencement of the session if such Notifications are issued when Parliament is not in session, and if issued when Parliament is in session, on the same day, or on the next day. These Notifications

2. On 20th June 2012, Mega Exemption Notification No. 25 of 2012-ST (for short, 'the Mega Exemption Notification') was issued containing several exemptions.
3. Section 11 of the Central Goods and Services Tax Act, 2017.
4. Notification No. 12/2017-CT(R) dated 28-06-2017.
5. Notification No. 20/2019-CT(R) dated 30-09-2019.
6. Circular No. 164/20/2021-GST.

are laid on the Table under Section 159 of the Customs Act under which power has been given to Parliament to annul these Notifications or modify them in any respect as the Parliament may deem necessary. These notifications are also examined by the Committee on Subordinate Legislation, Lok Sabha, and Rajya Sabha respectively.

5.5 Judicial review of exemption provisions

In a recent case[7], a question arose whether the exclusion of a woman who married after 1st April, 2008 to a non-Sikkimese man from the definition of "Sikkimese" in Section 10(*26AAA*) of the Income-tax Act, 1961 is violative of Article 14 of the Constitution? The Court held that the proviso to Section 10(*26AAA*) inasmuch as it excludes from the provision of exemption a Sikkimese woman merely because she marries a non-Sikkimese after 1-4-2008 is totally discriminatory and violative of Articles 14, 15, and 21 of the Constitution of India, which requires to be struck down.

Justice M.R. Shah held that section 10(*26AAA*) to the extent that it excludes old Indian settlers from the benefit of exemption from payment of income tax *i.e.*, those who have settled in Sikkim prior to the merger of Sikkim with India on 26th April, 1975 but whose names are not recorded as "Sikkim Subjects" from the definition of Sikkimese is *ultra vires* as, being arbitrary, discriminatory, and violative of Article 14 of the Constitution of India. Hence, persons who are old Indian settlers who have settled in Sikkim prior to the merger of Sikkim with India on 26th April, 1975 shall also be entitled to the exemption under Section 10(*26AAA*) of the I.T. Act, 1961.

Justice Nagarathna in her separate opinion observed that clause (*26AAA*) of section 10 states that in case of an individual, being a Sikkimese, any income, which accrues or arises to him (*a*) from any source in the State of Sikkim; or (*b*) by way of dividend or interest on securities, shall not be income falling within total income of any person. The proviso, however, states that nothing contained in this clause shall apply to a Sikkimese woman who, on or after 1st April, 2008, marries an individual who is not a Sikkimese... The proviso runs counter to the *Explanation* and is thus manifestly arbitrary. This is because the *Explanation* intends to give the benefit of section 10(*26AAA*) of the I.T. Act, 1961 to all Sikkimese who are defined under the said *Explanation* as those individuals whose names have been recorded and registered in the Register of Sikkim Subjects immediately before 26th April, 1975 or included pursuant to the Government of India Order No. 26030/36/90/I.C.I. dated 7th August, 1990 and Order of even number dated 8th April, 1991, or those persons whose names do not appear in the Register of Sikkim Subjects but it has been established that the name

7. *Association of Old Settlers of Sikkim* v. *Union of India* [Writ Petition (C) No. 59 of 2013 date of decision 13th January, 2023]/[2023] 146 taxmann.com 271/292 Taxman 73 (SC).

of such individual's father or husband or paternal grandfather or brother from the same father had been recorded in that Register. Hence, the benefit of the *Explanation* must be extended to all Sikkimese women, irrespective of whether they have married a Sikkimese or a non-Sikkimese after the 1st April, 2008.

The Finance Act, 2023 substituted clause (26AAA)[8] with effect from the 1st day of April 1990, and the offending part was removed from the new clause (26AAA).

5.6 Flexibility in Designing Exemption Provisions

There are a few cases where a provision has been struck down as violative of Article 14. These cases have been discussed in Chapter 2. Article 14 permits the classification of persons or objects for the purposes of tax exemptions. A classification is bad if it is under-inclusive or over-inclusive. When a State benefits or burdens persons in a manner that furthers a legitimate purpose but does not confer the same benefit or place the same burden on others who are similarly situated such classification is bad in law. Similarly, a classification is over-inclusive when it includes not only those who are similarly situated with respect to the purpose but others who are not so situated as well. In other words, this type of classification imposes a burden upon a wider range of individuals and is bad in law.[9]

A wider latitude is given in policy formulation to the State. Ideally, a uniform policy may be devised by the Centre or by a State. However, there is no constitutional requirement that any such policy must be implemented at one go. Policies are capable of being implemented in a phased manner. More so, when the policies have far-reaching implications and are dynamic in nature, their implementation in a phased manner is welcome for it receives gradual willing acceptance and invites lesser resistance.[10]

The law need not apply to all the persons in the sense of having a universal application to all persons. A law can be sustained if it deals equally with the people of well-defined class-employees of insurance companies as such and such a law is not open to the charge of denial of equal protection on the ground that it had no application to other persons. Article 14 does not prevent legislature from introducing a reform *i.e.*, by applying the legislation to some institutions or objects or areas only according to the exigency of the situation and further classification of selection can be sustained on historical reasons or reasons of administrative exigency or piecemeal method of introducing reforms.[11]

---

8. Clause (*26AAA*), for full details, *see* page 49.
9. *State of Gujarat* v. *Shri Ambica Mills* 1974 (3) SCR 760. Herod ordering the death of all male children born on a particular day because one of them would some day bring about his downfall employed such a classification.
10. *Javed* v. *State of Haryana* (2003) 8 SCC 369.
11. *Ajoy Kumar Banerjee* v. *Union of India* 1984 (3) SCR 252.

Recently, the Supreme Court in *Cosmo Films*[12] has held that when a reform by way of new legislation is introduced, the doctrine of classification cannot be applied strictly and that some allowance for experimentation, to observe the effect of the law, is available to the executive or legislature. Speaking for the Court Justice S. Ravindra Bhat further held that **there is no constitutional compulsion that whilst framing a new law, or policies under a new legislation – particularly when an entirely different set of fiscal norms are created, overhauling the taxation structure, concessions hitherto granted or given should necessarily be continued in the same fashion as they were in the past. When a new set of laws are enacted, the legislature's effort is to on the one hand, assimilate- as far as practicable, the past regime. On the other hand, the object of the new law is creation of new rights and obligations, with new attendant conditions. Inevitably, this process is bound to lead to some disruption. Therefore, the exclusion of benefit of imports in anticipation of AAs, and requiring payment of duties, under Section 3(7) and (9) of the Customs Tariff Act, 1975, with the 'pre-import condition', cannot be characterized as arbitrary or unreasonable.**

5.7 Interpretation of Exemption Provisions

An exemption provision should be liberally construed or strictly construed? There is a large number of judicial decisions.

Income-tax

Ahmedabad Urban Development Authority[13]

The interpretation of Section 2(*15*) of the Income-tax Act, 1961, was involved in relation to charitable trusts which engage in activities that further objects of general public utility. The activities and cases of various kinds of charities, trusts, and organizations, including statutory corporations and bodies, regulatory bodies, non-statutory regulatory bodies, trade organizations and bodies, sports bodies and organizations, trusts, etc. were considered by the court, in *Ahmedabad Urban Development Corporation*[14]. The Supreme Court held that activities which are in the nature of trade, and carry on by a trust established for general public utility, have to specify certain parameters. The Court held that an assessee advancing general public utility cannot engage itself in any trade, commerce, or business, or provide service in relation thereto for any consideration ("cess, or fee, or any other consideration"). Generally, the charging of any

12. *Union of India* v. *Cosmo Films Limited* [Civil Appeal No. 290 of 2023 date of decision 28th April 2023]/[2023] 149 taxmann.com 473/72 GSTL 417/97 GST 544 (SC) [**In this case, the disruption is in the form of exporters needing to import inputs, pay the two duties, and claim refunds. Yet, this inconvenience is insufficient to trump the legislative choice of creating an altogether new fiscal legislation, and insisting that a section of assessees order their affairs, to be in accord with the new law.**]
13. *Asstt. CIT* v. *Ahmedabad Urban Development Authority* 2022 SCC Online SC 1461/[2022] 143 taxmann.com 278/[2023] 291 Taxman 11 (SC).
14. *Asstt. CIT* v. *Ahmedabad Urban Development Authority* 2022 SCC Online SC 1461/[2022] 143 taxmann.com 278/[2023] 291 Taxman 11 (SC).

amount towards consideration for such an activity (advancing general public utility), which is on a cost-basis or nominally above cost, cannot be considered to be "trade, commerce, or business" or any services in relation thereto. It is only when the charges are markedly or significantly above the cost incurred by the assessee in question, that they would fall within the mischief of "cess, or fee, or any other consideration" towards "trade, commerce or business".

New Noble Educational Society

In *Noble Education Society*[15], the Supreme Court interpreted the term "solely" in the context of exemption to charitable trust or institution under clause (*23C*) of section 10 of the Income-tax Act, 1961, and held that where the statute is clear and the words plain, the legislation has to be given effect in its own terms. The Court held that the plain and grammatical meaning of the term 'sole' or 'solely' however, is 'only' or 'exclusively'. The term 'solely' means to the exclusion of all others. Thus, a trust, university, or other institution imparting education, as the case may be, should necessarily have all its objects aimed at imparting or facilitating education.

Wipro

Wipro[16] is a recent decision of the Supreme Court. It was held that in a taxing statute, the provisions are to be read as they are and they are to be literally construed, more particularly in a case of exemption sought by an assessee. The Supreme Court observed that the High Court has committed a grave error in observing and holding that the requirement of furnishing a declaration under Section 10B(8)[17] of the IT Act is mandatory, but the time limit within which the declaration is to be filed is not mandatory but is directory. The same is erroneous and contrary to the unambiguous language contained in Section 10B(8) of the IT Act. We hold that for claiming the benefit under Section 10B(8) of the IT Act, the twin conditions of furnishing a declaration before the assessing officer and that too before the due date of filing the original return of income under section 139(1) are to be satisfied and both are mandatorily to be complied with.

Checkmate Services P. Ltd.

Recently[18], it has been held that **one of the rules of interpretation of a tax statute is that if a deduction or exemption is available on compliance with certain conditions, the conditions are to be strictly complied with.** This

15. *New Noble Educational Society* v. *Chief Commissioner of Income Tax* 2022 SCC OnLine SC 1458/[2022] 143 taxmann.com 276/[2023] 290 Taxman 206 (SC) decided on 19.10.2022.

16. *Principal Commissioner of Income Tax* v. *Wipro Limited* [Civil Appeal No. 1449 of 2022 (Arising out of SLP (Civil) No. 7620/2021) date of decision July 11, 2022]/[2022] 140 taxmann.com 223/288 Taxman 491 (SC).

17. "10B. (8) Notwithstanding anything contained in the foregoing provisions of this section, where the assessee, before the due date for furnishing the return of income under sub-section (1) of Section 139, furnishes to the Assessing Officer a declaration in writing that the provisions of this section may not be made applicable to him, the provisions of this section shall not apply to him for any of the relevant assessment year."

18. *Checkmate Services (P.) Ltd.* v. *Commissioner of Income Tax* [2022] 143 taxmann.com 178/ [2023] 290 Taxman 19 (SC).

rule is in line with the general principle that taxing statutes are to be construed strictly and that there is no room for equitable considerations. Thus, it is an essential condition for the deduction that such amounts are deposited on or before the due date. If such an interpretation were to be adopted, the non-obstante clause under Section 43B or anything contained in that provision would not absolve the assessee from its liability to deposit the employee's contribution on or before the due date as a condition for deduction.

GST

Krishi Upaj Mandi Samiti

Recently in *Krishi Upaj Mandi*[19], it was held that the exemption notification should be strictly construed and given a meaning according to legislative intendment. In this case, it was held that the Market committee, Alwar is liable to pay service tax and held that in a taxing statute, it is the plain language of the provision that has to be preferred, where language is plain and is capable of determining a defined meaning. Strict interpretation of the provision is to be accorded to each case on hand. Purposive interpretation can be given only when there is an ambiguity in the statutory provision or it results in absurdity.

Customs Act

Ambalal

Ambalal[20] is a recent decision. The Supreme Court made a distinction between exemptions which are to be strictly interpreted as opposed to beneficial exemptions having as their purpose - encouragement or promotion of certain activities and observed that it is settled law that the notification has to be read as a whole. If any of the conditions laid down in the notification is not fulfilled, the party is not entitled to the benefit of that notification. The rule regarding exemptions is that exemptions should generally be strictly interpreted but beneficial exemptions having their purpose as encouragement or promotion of certain activities should be liberally interpreted. This composite rule is not stated in any particular judgment in so many words. In fact, majority of judgments emphasise that exemptions are to be strictly interpreted while some of them insist that exemptions in fiscal statutes are to be liberally interpreted giving an apparent impression that they are contradictory to each other. But this is only apparent. A close scrutiny will reveal that there is no real contradiction amongst the judgments at all. The synthesis of the views is quite clearly that the general rule is strict interpretation while special rule in the case of beneficial and promotional exemption is a liberal interpretation. The two go very well with each other because they relate to two different sets of circumstances.

---

19. *Krishi Upaj Mandi Samiti* v. *Commissioner of Central Excise and Service Tax*, Alwar date of decision 23-02-2022/[2022] 135 taxmann.com 354/58 GSTL 129 (SC).

20. *Commr. of Customs* v. *M. Ambalal & Co.* (2011) 2 SCC 74.

Ambalal was followed in *CCE* v. *Favourite Industries*.[21] In *CCE* v. *Favourite*, the Court stated that the notification requires to be interpreted in the light of the words employed by it and not on any other basis. There cannot be any addition or subtraction from the notification for the reason the exemption notification requires to be strictly construed by the Courts. The wordings of the exemption notification have to be given its natural meaning, when the wordings are simple, clear, and unambiguous. Moreover, a liberal construction requires to be given to a beneficial notification.

Central Excise

Hari Chand Shri Gopal

In Hari Chand Shri Gopal[22], the constitution bench of the Supreme Court held that a provision especially a fiscal statute providing for an exemption, concession, or exception has to be construed strictly. The Court explained further that some of the provisions of an exemption notification may be directory in nature and some are of mandatory in nature. A distinction between provisions of the statute which are of substantive character and were built in with certain specific objectives of policy, on the one hand, and those which are merely procedural and technical in their nature, on the other, must be kept clearly distinguished.

The issue was whether a manufacturer is eligible to get the benefit of exemption from remission of excise duty on specified intermediate goods if captively consumed for the manufacture of final products on the ground that the records kept by it at the recipient end would indicate its "intended use" and "substantial compliance" of the procedure set out in Chapter X of the Central Excise Rules, 1944.

The Supreme Court held that the law is well settled that a person who claims exemption or concession has to establish that he is entitled to that exemption or concession. A provision providing for an exemption, concession or exception, as the case may be, has to be construed strictly with certain exceptions depending upon the settings on which the provision has been placed in the Statute and the object and purpose to be achieved. If exemption is available on complying with certain conditions, the conditions have to be complied with. The mandatory requirements of those conditions must be obeyed or fulfilled exactly, though at times, some latitude can be shown, if there is a failure to comply with some requirements which are directory in nature, the non-compliance of which would not affect the essence or substance of the notification granting exemption.

Notifications

If the words are plain and clear and directly convey the meaning, there is no need for any interpretation. In Wood Papers Ltd.[23], the Supreme Court held

21. (2012) 7 SCC 153 (see paragraph 42).
22. *Commissioner of Central Excise, New Delhi* v. *Hari Chand Shri Gopal* (2011) 1 SCC 236/[2005] 2005 taxmann.com. 1133 (SC).
23. *Union of India* v. *Wood Papers Ltd.* [1991] JT(1) 151 at 155.

that liberal and strict construction of an exemption provision is to be invoked at different stages of interpreting it. When the question is whether a subject falls in the notification or in the exemption clause then it being in nature of exception is to be construed strictly and against the subject but once ambiguity or doubt about applicability is lifted and the subject falls in the notification then full play should be given to it and it calls for a wider and liberal construction.

In Associated Cement[24], the Supreme Court held that when the question is whether a subject falls in the notification or in the exemption clause then it being in the nature of exception is to be construed strictly and against the subject but once ambiguity or doubt about applicability is lifted and the subject falls in the notification then full play should be given to it and it calls for a wider and liberal construction. Truly speaking, liberal and strict construction of an exemption provision is to be invoked at different stages of interpreting it. The primary reason for the strict construction of an exemption notification is that literally "exemption" is freedom from liability, tax, or duty. Fiscally it may assume varying shapes, specially, in a growing economy. In fact, an exemption provision is like an exception and on the normal principle of construction or interpretation of statutes it is construed strictly either because of legislative intention or on economic justification of inequitable burden of the progressive approach of fiscal provisions intended to augment State revenue.

In Wood papers[25], the Supreme Court held in fact an exemption provision is like an exception and on the normal principle of construction or interpretation of statutes it is construed strictly either because of legislative intention or on economic justification of inequitable burden or progressive approach of fiscal provisions intended to augment state revenue. But once exception or exemption becomes applicable no rule or principle requires it to be construed strictly. Truly, speaking liberal and strict construction of an exemption provision are to be invoked at different stages of interpreting it. When the question is whether a subject falls in the notification or in the exemption clause then it being in nature of exception is to be construed strictly and against the subject but once ambiguity or doubt about applicability is lifted and the subject falls in the notification then full play should be given to it and it calls for a wider and liberal construction.

In *Mangalore Chemicals*[26], the Supreme Court held that a distinction between the provisions of the statute which are of substantive character and were built-in with certain specific objectives of policy on the one hand, and those which are merely procedural and technical in their nature on the other must be kept clearly distinguished. The choice between a strict and a liberal construction arises only in case of doubt in regard to the intention of the Legislature manifest on the statutory language. Indeed, the need to resort to any interpretative

24. *Associated Cement Companies Ltd.* v. *State of Bihar* (2004) 7 SCC 642/[2004] 2004 taxmann.com 194 (SC).

25. *Union of India* v. *Wood Papers Ltd.* [1990] 4 SCC 256/[1991] 1991 taxmann.com 77 (SC).

26. *Mangalore Chemicals & Fertilizers Ltd.* v. *Dy. Commissioner of Commercial Taxes* [1992] Supp. (1) SCC 21.

process arises only where the meaning is not manifest on the plain words of the statute. If the words are plain and clear and directly convey the meaning, there is no need for any interpretation. The Court observed that Clause 3 of the notification leaves no discretion to the Deputy Commissioner to refuse the permission if the conditions are satisfied. The words are that he "will grant". Thus, the appellant had satisfied these conditions. Yet the permission was withheld--not for any valid and substantial reason but owing to certain extraneous things concerning some inter-departmental issues. Supreme Court referred to Lord Denning and Francis Bennon as under—

> "The answer to this is in the words of Lord Denning: "Now I know that a public authority cannot be estopped from doing its public duty, but I do think it can be estopped from relying on a technicality and this is a technicality" (See *Wells* v. *Minister of Housing and Local Government* [1967] 1 WLR 1000 at 1007).

Francis Bennion in his "Statutory Interpretation", 1984 edition, says at page 683: "Unnecessary technicality: Modern courts seek to cut down technicalities attendant upon a statutory procedure where these cannot be shown to be necessary to the fulfilment of the purposes of the legislation."

Supreme Court allowed the appeal and set aside the judgment of the High Court under appeal and directed the Deputy Commissioner of Sales Tax (Admn.) to grant permission for the said three years operative from the dates of the application to the adjustment of the refunds against the taxes due for the respective years. The demand notices were also quashed.

The constitution bench of five judges in Dilip Kumar and Company[27] considered and settled a question as to the interpretative rule to be applied where there is an ambiguity as to the applicability with reference to the entitlement of the assessee or the rate of tax to be applied. The core issue was whether in the event of an ambiguity in an exemption notification should the benefit of such ambiguity go to the subject/assessee or such ambiguity should be construed in favour of the revenue? The constitution bench found an unsatisfactory state of law as to the interpretation of exemption clauses. It was held that every taxing statute including, charging, computation, and exemption clause (at the threshold stage) should be interpreted strictly. Further, in case of ambiguity in a charging provision, the benefit must go in favour of the subject/assessee but in an exemption notification, the benefits of ambiguity must be strictly interpreted in favour of the revenue/state.

Very recently, the ratio of Dilip Kumar and Company was applied by the Supreme Court in Vile Parle Mandal[28]. It was held that it is for the assessee to show by the construction of the exemption clause/notification that it comes within the purview of the exemption. The assessee/citizen cannot rely on ambiguity or doubt to claim the benefit of exemption. The rationale is not to widen the

27. *Commissioner of Customs* v. *Dilip Kumar and Company* (2018) 9 SCC 1/[2018] 95 taxmann.com 327/69 GST 239 (SC).

28. *The State of Maharashtra* v. *Vile Parle Kelvani Mandal* [Civil Appeal No. 3327 decided by a bench of two judges dated July 07, 2022].

net at the stage of applicability. However, once the hurdle of the applicability is crossed, the notification is to be construed liberally.

Reconsideration of *Dilip Kumar and Company*[28a]

In Dilip Kumar and Company, the constitution bench of five judges held that exemption notification should be interpreted strictly; the burden of proving applicability would be on the assessee to show that his case comes within the parameters of the exemption clause or exemption notification. When there is ambiguity in the exemption notification which is subject to strict interpretation, the benefit of such ambiguity cannot be claimed by the subject/assessee and it must be interpreted in favour of the revenue.

The law laid down in Dilip Kumar and Company needs re-consideration for declaring the law that "the benefit of such ambiguity cannot be claimed by the subject/assessee and it must be interpreted in favour of the revenue." First, the notification is drafted by the department which is responsible for administering the law. Therefore, if there is any doubt or ambiguity in the notification the same should be corrected by amending the notification and not by laying down a legal proposition that the assessee/citizen cannot rely on ambiguity or doubt to claim the benefit of exemption. How an assessee or a citizen is responsible for drafting a notification that results in doubt or produces ambiguity? The second and more significant point is that the law settled by Dilip Kumar and Company goes against the principle of no taxation without clear words. This principle ought to be extended to exemption notifications. What are 'clear words' is to be ascertained upon normal principles: these do not confine the courts to a literal interpretation. There may, indeed, be considered the context and scheme of the relevant Act as a whole, and its purpose may, indeed should, be regarded[28b]. Thirdly, the issue involved related to the classification under the Customs Tariff Act. In M/S Reckitt Benckiser[28c], while interpreting an entry in the Kerala VAT the Supreme Court observed that while considering a particular entry the principles of classification which are fundamental to any matter relating to classification under the taxing statute are first, plain meaning to be given to the taxing provision; secondly, the burden to prove the classification in a particular entry is always on revenue, thirdly, any ambiguity has to be resolved in favour of the assessee and in case of reasonable doubt, the construction most beneficial to the assessee must be adopted. Further, the specific entry would override a residuary entry, and resort to residuary entry is to be taken as a last measure, only when by liberal construction the specific entry cannot cover the goods in question.

28a. *Commissioner of Customs* v. *Dilip Kumar and Company* (2018) 9 SCC 1/95 taxmann.com 327/69 GST 239 (SC).

28b. Lord Wilberforce in *Ramsay* [1982] AC 300, 323: *Inland Revenue Comrs* v. *Wesleyan and General Assurance Society* (1946) 30 TC 11, 16 per Lord Greene MR and: *Mangin* v *Inland Revenue Commr.* [1971] AC 739, 746 per Lord Donovan.

28c. *Reckitt Benckiser* v. *Commissioner of Commercial Taxes* [Civil Appeal No. 1335 of 2010 decided by a bench of two judges on April 10, 2023]/[2023] 5 Centax 151 (SC).

5.8 Tax Incentives

For granting incentives or concessional rates of tax the provisions are to be liberally construed.

In *Bajaj Tempo*[29], the question was whether the assessee was entitled to claim partial exemption from payment of tax under section 15C of the Income-tax Act of 1922 on Profits and gains derived from an industrial undertaking established in a building taken on lease used previously for other business. It was held that since a provision intended for promoting economic growth has to be interpreted liberally the restriction on it, too, has to be construed so as to advance the objective of the section and not to frustrate it. Thus, a provision granting incentives for promoting economic growth and development in taxing statutes should be liberally construed and restriction placed on it by way of exception should be construed in a reasonable and purposive manner so as to advance the objective of the provision.

In *Straw Board*[30], the Court held that in taxing statutes, provision for concessional rate of tax should be liberally construed. A liberal construction of an exemption provision means that the provision should be liberally construed in accordance with the object sought to be achieved if such provision is to grant an incentive for promoting economic growth or otherwise has some beneficial reason behind it.

Tata Cummins Ltd.[31] was concerned with the interpretation of a tax exemption notification for setting up an industry in a backward area. Supreme Court analyzed both the approaches of interpretation namely strict construction and liberal construction. A tax is a payment for raising general revenue. It is a burden. It is based on the principle of ability or capacity to pay. It is a manifestation of the taxing power of the State. An exemption from payment of tax under an enactment is an exemption from tax liability. Therefore, every such exemption notification has to be read strictly. On the other hand, when an assessee is promised a tax exemption for setting up an industry in the backward area as a term of the industrial policy, one has to read the implementing notifications in the context of the industrial policy. In such a case, the exemption notifications have to be read liberally keeping in mind the objects envisaged by the industrial policy and not in a strict sense as in the case of exemptions from tax liability under the taxing statute.

In *G.P. Ceramic*[32], the Supreme Court held that it is now a well-established principle of law that whereas eligibility criteria laid down in an exemption notification are required to be construed strictly, once it is found that the applicant satisfies the same, the exemption notification should be construed liberally.

29. *Bajaj Tempo Ltd.* v. *CIT* AIR 1992 SC 1622/1992 SCC (3).

30. *CIT* v. *Straw Board Mfg. Co. Ltd.* 1989 Supp (2) SCC 523.

31. *State of Jharkhand* v. *Tata Cummins Ltd.* (2006) 4 SCC 57/[2008] 2008 taxmann.com 1129 (SC).

32. *G.P. Ceramics Private Limited* v. *Commissioner, Trade Tax, Uttar Pradesh* (2009) 2 SCC 90.

5.9 Legitimate expectation

The doctrine of substantive legitimate expectation forms an integral part of both the common law as well as Indian jurisprudence. In Ram Pravesh Singh[33] Supreme Court explained the concept of legitimate expectation as a reasonable, logical, and valid expectation of certain benefit, relief, or remedy. However, the legitimacy of expectation is a question of fact and has to be determined after weighing the claimant's expectation against the larger public interest. Public interest serves as a limitation on the application of the doctrine of legitimate expectation. Courts have to determine whether the public interest is compelling and sufficient to outweigh the legitimate expectation of the claimant[34]. In the *State of Jharkhand* v. *Brahmaputra Metallics*[35], the issue was whether the respondent was entitled to claim a rebate or deduction on electricity duty under the Industrial Policy, 2012 for a period of five years from the commencement of production. Although the policy was announced in 2012, the exemption notification was issued in 2015 with prospective effect. Supreme Court observed that the representations made by the public authorities should be held to scrupulous standards because of the trust reposed by the citizens in the state. The state government made a solemn representation under its Industrial Policy, 2012 to provide exemption from payment of electricity duty to the claimants. However, the government failed to provide any justification for issuing the exemption notice after a delay of three years in 2015.The Court observed that the state is bound to act fairly and transparently while performing its public duties, and any deprivation of entitlement of private citizens and private business must be proportional to a requirement grounded in public interest.[36]

---

33. *Ram Pravesh Singh* v. *State of Bihar* (2006) 8 SCC 381.
34. *Sivanandan C T* v. *High Court of Kerala* [Writ Petition (Civil) No. 229 of 2017 decided by a Constitution Bench of Five Judges on July 12, 2023].
35. 2020 SCC OnLine SC 968 "41. .... Representations by public authorities need to be held to scrupulous standards, since citizens continue to live their lives based on the trust they repose in the State. In the commercial world also, certainty and consistency are essential to planning the affairs of business. When public authorities fail to adhere to their representations without providing an adequate reason to the citizens for this failure, it violates the trust reposed by citizens in the State. The generation of a business friendly climate for investment and trade is conditioned by the faith which can be reposed in government to fulfil the expectations which it generates."
36. *Ibid* "53. .... The state must discard the colonial notion that it is a sovereign handing out *doles* at its will. Its policies give rise to legitimate expectations that the state will act according to what it puts forth in the public realm. In all its actions, the State is bound to act fairly, in a transparent manner. This is an elementary requirement of the guarantee against arbitrary state action which Article 14 of the Constitution adopts. A deprivation of the entitlement of private citizens and private business must be proportional to a requirement grounded in public interest."

6 DTAA and International Taxation

6.1 Preliminary

Section 90[1] of the Income-tax Act, 1961, empowers the Central Government to enter into an agreement with foreign countries or specified territories for the purpose of granting reliefs, particularly in respect of double taxation. Under this power, the Central Government has entered into various treaties commonly known as Double Taxation Avoidance Agreements (DTAAs). Section 90 is specifically intended to enable and empower the Central Government to enter into a double taxation avoidance agreement. Double taxation, mostly arises, in the case of a non-resident. A non-resident is a person (natural and artificial). Different sets of provisions have been made for determining the residential status of an

1. 90. *Agreement with foreign countries or specified territories*.—(1) The Central Government may enter into an agreement with the Government of any country outside India or specified territory outside India,—

   (*a*) for the granting of relief in respect of—

   (*i*) income on which have been paid both income-tax under this Act and income-tax in that country or specified territory, as the case may be, or

   (*ii*) income-tax chargeable under this Act and under the corresponding law in force in that country or specified territory, as the case may be, to promote mutual economic relations, trade and investment, or

   (*b*) for the avoidance of double taxation of income under this Act and under the corresponding law in force in that country or specified territory, as the case may be without creating opportunities for non-taxation or reduced taxation through tax evasion or avoidance (including through treaty-shopping arrangements aimed at obtaining reliefs provided in the said agreement for the indirect benefit to residents of any other country or territory), or

   (*c*) for exchange of information for the prevention of evasion or avoidance of income-tax chargeable under this Act or under the corresponding law in force in that country or specified territory, as the case may be, or investigation of cases of such evasion or avoidance, or

   (*d*) for recovery of income-tax under this Act and under the corresponding law in force in that country or specified territory, as the case may be,

   and may, by notification in the Official Gazette, make such provisions as may be necessary for implementing the agreement.

   (2) Where the Central Government has entered into an agreement with the Government of any country outside India or specified territory outside India, as the case may be, under sub-section (1) for granting relief of tax, or as the case may be, avoidance of double taxation, then, in relation to the assessee to whom such agreement applies, the provisions of this Act shall apply to the extent they are more beneficial to that assessee.

individual and companies[2]. A non-resident has to pay income tax in India on income deemed to accrue or arise in India.[3]

Section 9 of the Income-tax Act, 1961 deals with cases of income which are deemed to accrue or arise in India. Sub-section (1) of section 9 creates a legal fiction that certain incomes shall be deemed to accrue or arise in India.

Clause (*i*) of sub-section (1) of section 9 provides a set of circumstances in which income accruing or arising, directly or indirectly, is taxable in India. Clause (*i*) of sub-section (1) of section 9 provides that all income accruing or arising, whether directly or indirectly, through or from any business connection in India, or through or from any property in India, or through or from any asset or source of income in India, or through the transfer of a capital asset situate in India shall be deemed to accrue or arise in India. This is a legal fiction created to tax income, which may or may not arise in India and would not have been taxable but for the deeming provision created by section 9. One of the parts of clause (*i*) of sub-section (1) of section 9 is that the income accruing or arising directly or indirectly through the transfer of a capital asset situated in India.

Section 9 codifies the **'source rule of taxation'**. In the 'source rule of taxation', the state where the actual economic nexus of income is situated has a right to tax the income. The place of residence of the entity deriving the income is not relevant. The 'source rule of taxation' is recognized by several countries. In the source rule of taxation, the source country has taxation rights. An issue of considerable significance giving retrospective effect to the amendment was settled by a parliament enactment,[4] most recently, is that of the taxability of gains arising from the transfer of assets located in India through the transfer of the shares of a foreign company.

---

2. Section 6 of the Income-tax Act, 1961 contains provisions relating to determination of residency of a person. The status of an individual, as to whether he is resident in India or a non-resident or not ordinarily resident, is dependent, *inter alia*, on the period for which the person is in India during a previous year or years preceding the previous year.
3. 5. *Scope of total income.* — (2) Subject to the provisions of this Act, the total income of any previous year of a person who is a non-resident includes all income from whatever source derived which—

   (*a*) is received or is deemed to be received in India in such year by or on behalf of such person ; or

   (*b*) accrues or arises or is deemed to accrue or arise to him in India during such year.

   Explanation 1.—Income accruing or arising outside India shall not be deemed to be received in India within the meaning of this section by reason only of the fact that it is taken into account in a balance sheet prepared in India.

   Explanation 2.—For the removal of doubts, it is hereby declared that income which has been included in the total income of a person on the basis that it has accrued or arisen or is deemed to have accrued or arisen to him shall not again be so included on the basis that it is received or deemed to be received by him in India.

   9. *Income deemed to accrue or arise in India.* — (1) The following incomes shall be deemed to accrue or arise in India –

   (*i*) all income accruing or arising, whether directly or indirectly, through or from any business connection in India, or through or from any property in India, or through or from any asset or source of income in India, or through the transfer of a capital asset situate in India.
4. The Taxation Laws (Amendment) Act, 2021.

However, in the area of international taxation, issues continue to come up. These issues come up before the constitutional courts, tribunal, and authority for advance rulings. However, most of the issues on tax-related barriers to cross-border trade and investment are addressed by adopting the OECD Model Tax Convention. The OECD Model Tax Convention helps to prevent tax evasion and avoidance.[5]

6.2 DTAA's

The DTAAs[6] between India and countries/parties have been entered into and notified. Each of these DTAAs is based on the OECD Model Tax Convention on Income and on Capital or the United Nations Model Double Taxation Convention between Developed and Developing Countries ["UN Model Convention"]. DTAAs are substantially similar, if not identical, in respect of the provisions concerning "business profits" and "royalties". The subject matter of each of the DTAAs is income tax payable in India and a foreign country. A question is often raised as to in case of conflict of the Income-tax Act, 1961 with the DTAA, which will prevail. *Explanation 4* to section 90 of the Income-tax Act, 1961 was inserted by the Finance Act, 2017. The said *Explanation* reads as under:

> "*Explanation 4*.—For the removal of doubts, it is hereby declared that where any term used in an agreement entered into under sub-section (1) is defined under the said agreement, the said term shall have the same meaning as assigned to it in the agreement; and where the term is not defined in the said agreement, but defined in the Act, it shall have the same meaning as assigned to it in the Act and explanation, if any, given to it by the Central Government."

Earlier, a circular[7] was issued to make clarification on whether the provisions of DTAA would prevail over general provisions contained in the Income-tax Act, 1961.

---

5. Transfer pricing guidelines and Base Erosion and Profit Sharing (BEPS) actions. See, https://www.oecd.org/tax/beps.

6. 1. Commonwealth of Australia, 2. Canada, 3. People's Republic of China 4. Republic of Cyprus 5. Republic of Finland 6. Republic of France 7. The Federal Republic of Germany 8. Hong Kong Special Administrative Region of the People's Republic of China 9. Republic of Ireland 10. Republic of Italy 11. Japan 12. Republic of Korea 13. Kingdom of Netherlands 14. Republic of Singapore 15. Kingdom of Sweden 16. India-Taipei Association in Taipei (Taiwan) 17. United States of America 18. United Kingdom of Great Britain and Northern Ireland.[DTAA with 99 foreign countries or jurisdictions have been entered into]

7. Circular No. 333 dated 2-4-1982. Specific provisions made in double taxation avoidance agreement - Whether it would prevail over general provisions contained in Income-tax Act 1. It has come to the notice of the Board that sometimes effect to the provisions of double taxation avoidance agreement is not given by the Assessing Officers when they find that the provisions of the agreement are not in conformity with the provisions of the Income-tax Act, 1961. 2. The correct legal position is that where a specific provision is made in the double taxation avoidance agreement, that provisions will prevail over the general provisions contained in the Income-tax Act. In fact that the double taxation avoidance agreements which have been entered into by the Central Government under section 90 of the Income-tax Act, also provide that the laws in force in either country will continue to govern the assessment and taxation of income in the respective countries except where provisions to the contrary have been made in the agreement. 3. Thus, where a double taxation avoidance agreement provides for a particular mode of computation of income, the same should be followed, irrespective of the provisions in the Income-tax Act. Where there is no specific provision in the agreement, it is basic law, *i.e.*, the Income-tax Act, that will govern the taxation of income.

The DTAAs that have been entered into by India with other Contracting States have to be interpreted liberally with a view to implementing the true intention of the parties. The principles adopted in the interpretation of treaties are not the same as those in the interpretation of statutory legislation.[8] Treaties are negotiated and entered into at a political level and have several considerations as their bases. In the Engineering Analysis Centre[9], Justice Nariman held that the OECD Commentary on Article 12 will continue to have persuasive value as to the interpretation of the term "royalties".

Once a DTAA applies, the provisions of the Income-tax Act, 1961 can only apply to the extent that they are more beneficial to the assessee and not otherwise. Further, by *Explanation 4*[10] to section 90 of the Income-tax Act, 1961 it has been clarified that where any term is defined in a DTAA, the definition contained in the DTAA is to be looked at. It is only where there is no such definition that the definition in the Income-tax Act, 1961 can then be applied.

6.3 Supreme Court on International Taxation

The issues in international taxation saw fierce legal battles on the taxability of the income of a non-resident. There are a number of cases. Azadi Bachao[11] (Indo-Mauritius) established legal principles followed by the courts in subsequent decisions. The effect of Vodafone[12] and Ishikawajma[13] was neutralised by the legislative amendments. On the interpretation of the term 'permanent establishment' (PE), DTAA prevailed over the Income-tax Act, 1961, in Morgan Stanley[14], UAE Exchange[15], and e-funds IT Solution[16]. The term 'royalty' has been explained and expounded by Justice Nariman in Engineering Analysis Centre

8. *Union of India* v. *Azadi Bachao Andolan* (2004) 10 SCC 1/[2003] 132 Taxman 373 (SC).
9. *Engineering Analysis Centre of Excellence Private Limited* v. *Commissioner of Income-tax* [Civil Appeal Nos. 8733-8734 of 2018 Decided on 2nd March, 2021]/[2021] 125 taxmann.com 42/281 Taxman 19 (SC).
10. *Explanation 4*.—For the removal of doubts, it is hereby declared that where any term used in an agreement entered into under sub-section (1) is defined under the said agreement, the said term shall have the same meaning as assigned to it in the agreement; and where the term is not defined in the said agreement, but defined in the Act, it shall have the same meaning as assigned to it in the Act and explanation, if any, given to it by the Central Government.
11. *Union of India* v. *Azadi Bachao Andolan* [2003] 263 ITR 706/132 Taxman 373 (SC).
12. *Vodafone International Holdings BV* v. *Union of India* (2012) 6 SCC 613/[2012] 17 taxmann.com 202/204 Taxman 408 (SC).
13. *Ishikawajma-Harima Heavy Industries Ltd.* v. *DIT* [2007] 288 ITR 408/158 Taxman 259 (SC).
14. *DIT (International Taxation)* v. *Morgan Stanley and Co. Inc.* [2007] 292 ITR 416/162 Taxman 165 (SC).
15. *Union of India* v. *U.A.E. Exchange Centre* [Civil Appeal No. 9775 OF 2011 decided on April 24th, 2020]/[2020] 116 taxmann.com 379/273 Taxman 122 (SC).
16. *ADIT* v. *E-Funds IT Solution Inc.* [2017] 399 ITR 34/86 taxmann.com 240/251 Taxman 280 (SC).

of Excellence Private Limited[17]. Other cases are Samsung Heavy Industries[18] and National Petroleum's Construction[19].

6.4 New Scheme of International Taxation

The gaps and mismatches in tax rules have been a concern of the international community. The gaps and mismatches in tax rules caused revenue loss because of the tax planning strategies of multinational corporations. These strategies which caused revenue loss include treaty abuse; base erosion and profit-shifting strategies by corporations. The profit-shifting strategies by corporations artificially shift profits to low or no-tax jurisdictions where there is little or no economic activity, resulting in negligible or no corporate tax being paid. Recently, India has signed and ratified the Multilateral Convention to Implement Tax Treaty-Related Measures to Prevent Base Erosion and Profit Shifting (commonly referred to as MLI). The MLI is an outcome of the G20-OECD project to tackle Base Erosion and Profit Shifting (the BEPS Project),

6.5 Amendments to the Income-tax Act, 1961

Recently, amendments have been made to the Income-tax Act, 1961 by the Finance Act, 2018 and the Finance Act, 2020. The statutory changes of section 9 and section 90 are given.

Statutory changes in section 9

Section 9 contains two sub-sections. Sub-section (1) of section 9 has clauses and explanations and provisos. *Explanation 1* is in the nature of exclusion. The income of a non-resident is not included in cases enumerated in *Explanation 1*. *Explanation 2* amplifies the term 'business connection'. *Explanation 2A* is about significant economic presence. The data transfer and soliciting of business systematically constitute a significant economic presence. *Explanation 4* and *Explanation 5* were added to neutralise the effect of Vodafone judgment. By insertion of *Explanation 6* the effect of *Explanations 4* and *5* have been softened. Thus, *Explanation 5*, shall be deemed to derive its value substantially from the assets (whether tangible or intangible) located in India, if, on the specified date, the value of such assets—(*i*) exceeds the amount of ten crore rupees; and (*ii*) represents at least fifty per cent of the value of all the assets owned by the company or entity, as the case may be.

Clause (*ii*) relates to salary earned in India. Clause (*iii*) relates to salary earned outside India by a citizen of India.

---

17. *Engineering Analysis Centre of Excellence Private Limited* v. *Commissioner of Income Tax* [Civil Appeal Nos. 8733-8734 of 2018 (date of decision March 2, 2021.) Three Judges Bench]/[2021] 125 taxmann.com 42/281 Taxman 19 (SC).

18. *DIT* v. *Samsung Heavy Industries* (2020) 7 SCC 347/[2020] 117 taxmann.com 870/272 Taxman 377 (SC).

19. *National Petroleum's Construction Company* v. *Deputy Commissioner of Income Tax* [Civil Appeal No. 4964 of 2022, dated 29th July, 2022. In view of the difference of opinion matter referred to three judges bench]/[2022] 140 taxmann.com 659/289 Taxman 87 (SC).

Statutory changes in section 90

Section 90 of the Income-tax Act, 1961 contains four sub-sections and four explanations. Sub-section (1) enables the Central Government to enter into an agreement with the Government of any country outside India or specified territory outside India for granting relief or for the avoidance of double taxation in respect of income subject to double taxation. A new sub-section (2A) enacts a *non-obstante* clause by stating that the provisions of Chapter X A of the Act shall apply to the assessee even if such provisions are not beneficial to him. Chapter X-A on General Ani-Avoidance rule has been inserted in the Income-tax Act, 1961 with effect from 1st April, 2016. Sub-sections (4) and (5) have been added in 2012. Sub-section (4) makes furnishing of a certificate mandatory. Sub-section (5) requires an assessee to provide such other documents and information as may be required by the tax officials.

It is a domestic requirement in India under sub-section (1) of section 90 of the Income-tax Act, 1961 that DTAA or amendment to DTAA are implemented after its notification in the Official Gazette. In *Azadi Bachao Andolan*[20] Hon'ble Supreme Court of India has observed that the DTAA provisions come into force on the date of issue of notification of such DTAA. Hon'ble Supreme Court also made it clear in the judgment that the beneficial provision of sub-section (2) of section 90 springs into operation once the notification is issued.

The rationale for the insertion of *Explanation 4* in section 90 was explained[21] as under—

> "Clarification with regard to the interpretation of 'terms' used in an agreement entered into under sections 90 and 90A.
>
> Under the existing provisions of Section 90 of the Act, power has been conferred upon the Central Government to enter into an agreement with the Government of any country outside India for granting relief in respect of income on which income tax has been paid both under the said Act and income-tax Act in that foreign country, avoidance of double taxation of income, exchange of information for the prevention of evasion or avoidance of income-tax or recovery of income-tax."

6.6 Section 90A

Similar provisions are provided in section 90A of the Act in the case of an agreement entered into by any specified association in India with any specified association in the specified territory outside India.

6.7 Terms used in the Agreement

Sections 90 and 90A of the Act provide that any 'term' used but not defined in Income-tax Act or in the agreement shall have the meaning assigned to it in the notification issued by the Central Government in the Official Gazette in this behalf, unless the context otherwise requires, provided the same is not inconsistent with the provisions of this Act or the agreement.

20. *Union of India* v. *Azadi Bachao Andolan* [2003] 263 ITR 706/132 Taxman 373 (SC).

21. Memorandum Explaining the provisions of the Finance Bill, 2020.

Sections 90 and 90A of the Act, provide that where any 'term' used in an agreement entered into under sub-section (1) of sections 90 and 90A of the Act, is defined under the said agreement, the said term shall be assigned the meaning as provided in the said agreement and where the term is not defined in the agreement, but is defined in the Act, it shall be assigned the meaning as definition in the Act or any explanation issued by the Central Government.

6.8 Interpretation of DTAA and MLI

A new architecture of international taxation has taken shape with detailed statutory changes and with the signing and ratification of MLI. The current interpretation of DTAA has been analysed by the authority of eminence from Canada. Brian J. Arnold in an inspiring and thought-provoking article titled 'The Interpretation of Tax Treaties: Looking to the Future[22] states as under:—

> "...the interpretation and application of the provisions of bilateral tax treaties by national courts could be significantly improved through the establishment of an international body to provide independent expert advisory opinions in tax treaty cases... it would be useful to consider establishing a process for experts to provide advisory opinions to national courts on cases involving the interpretation of tax treaty..."

Commenting on the approach of the national courts, in the Indian context of the Supreme Court, the reference is made of Azadi Bachao and Chettiar. Arnold argues as under—

> "*Union of India* v. *Azadi Bachao Andolan* (2003) 263 ITR 706/132 Taxman 373 (SC). The Supreme Court upheld an administrative circular indicating that a certificate of residence from Mauritius was sufficient to establish residence and beneficial ownership of a corporate shell in Mauritius under the India-Mauritius tax treaty, on the basis that treaty shopping was desirable for developing countries. The Court stated that "many principles in fiscal economy which, though at first blush might appear to be evil, are tolerated in a developing economy in the interest of long-term development. Deficit financing, for example, is one; treaty shopping is another."

In *Commissioner of Income Tax* v. *P.V.A.L. Kulandagan Chettiar*[22a] the Supreme Court held that a firm resident in India that derived income from Malaysia was not subject to Indian tax on the income despite the fact that article 7(2) of the treaty with Malaysia provided only that the income "may be taxed" in Malaysia. In effect, the court incorrectly interpreted the phrase "may be taxed" in Malaysia as meaning "shall only be taxed" in Malaysia."

6.9 CBDT Circular

Circular No. 3/2022 dated 3rd February 2022[23] provides Clarification regarding the Most-Favoured-Nation (MFN) clause in the Protocol to India's DTAAs with

22. Bulletin for International Taxation November/December 2021-The Interpretation of Tax Treaties: Looking to the Future- Brian J. Arnold* https://www.ibfd.org/ accessed on 9-6-2023.

22a. (2004) 267 ITR 654/137 Taxman 460 (SC).

23. Para 5. In view of the above, it is hereby clarified that the applicability of the MFN clause and benefit of the lower rate or restricted scope of source taxation rights in relation to certain

(*Contd. on p. 104*)

certain countries. The Protocol to India's Double Taxation Avoidance Agreements (DTAAs) with some of the countries, especially the European States and OECD members (The Netherlands, France, the Swiss Confederation, Sweden, Spain, and Hungary) contains a provision, referred to as the Most-Favoured-Nation (MFN) clause. Though each MFN clause in these DTAAs India limits its source taxation rights in relation to certain items of income (such as dividends, interest income, royalties, Fees for Technical Services, etc.) to a rate lower or a scope more restricted than the scope provided for those items of income in the DTAA with the first State, such beneficial treatment should also be extended to the first State.

Consequently, the CBDT issued clarifications on the applicability of the MFN clause, namely-: Unilateral decree/bulletin/publication do not represent shared understanding of the treaty partners on the applicability of the MFN clause; secondly, conditionality for the third State being a member of the OECD on the date of conclusion of the DTAA; Thirdly, application of concessional rates/ restricted scope from the date of entry into force of the DTAA with the third State and not from the date the third State becomes member of the OECD: Fourthly, Requirement of notification under section 90 of the Income-tax Act, 1961, and Fifthly, no selective import of concessional rates under MFN clause.

6.10 The Vienna Convention on the Law of Treaties

In the judgments of the Supreme Court purposive interpretation is more often used in the constitutional and statutory interpretation. The purposive interpretation of DTAA and MLI gets support from the Vienna Convention on the Law of Treaties. The Vienna Convention on the Law of Treaties establishes the rule of interpretation in Article 31, which establishes, *inter alia*, the object and purpose of a treaty and the latter's context as guidelines of interpretation. The text of articles 31, 32 and 33 of the Vienna Convention of the Law of treaties[24] is as under—

(*Contd. from p. 103*)

items of income (such as dividends, interest income, royalties, Fees for Technical Services, etc.) provided in India's DTAAs with the third States will be available to the first (OECD) State only when all the following conditions are met: (*i*) The second treaty (with the third State) is entered into after the signature/ Entry into Force (depending upon the language of the MFN clause) of the treaty between India and the first State; (*ii*) The second treaty is entered into between India and a State which is a member of the OECD at the time of signing the treaty with it; (*iii*) India limits its taxing rights in the second treaty in relation to rate or scope of taxation in respect of the relevant items of income; and (*iv*) A separate notification has been issued by India, importing the benefits of the second treaty into the treaty with the first State, as required by the provisions of sub-section (1) of Section 90 of the Income-tax Act, 1961. If all the conditions enumerated in Paragraph 5(*i*) to (*iv*) are satisfied, then the lower rate or restricted scope in the treaty with the third State is imported into the treaty with an OECD State having MFN clause from the date as per the provisions of the MFN clause in the DTAA, after following the due procedure under the Indian tax law. 6. Notwithstanding the clarification given in the above paragraphs, where in the case of a taxpayer there is any decision by any court on this issue favourable to such taxpayer this Circular will not affect the implementation of the court order in such case.

24. https://www.iilj.org/wp-content/uploads/2016/08/VCLT-Art.-31-33.pdf#:~:text=Article%2031General%20rule%20of%20interpretation%20A%20treaty%20shall,in%20the%20light%20of%20its%20object%20and%20purpose accessed on 9-6-2023.

"SECTION 3.

INTERPRETATION OF TREATIES

Article 31 General rule of interpretation

1. A treaty shall be interpreted in good faith in accordance with the ordinary meaning to be given to the terms of the treaty in their context and in the light of its object and purpose.
2. The context for the purpose of the interpretation of a treaty shall comprise, in addition to the text, including its preamble and annexes: (*a*) any agreement relating to the treaty which was made between all the parties in connection with the conclusion of the treaty; (*b*) any instrument which was made by one or more parties in connection with the conclusion of the treaty and accepted by the other parties as an instrument related to the treaty.
3. There shall be taken into account, together with the context: (*a*) any subsequent agreement between the parties regarding the interpretation of the treaty or the application of its provisions; (*b*) any subsequent practice in the application of the treaty which establishes the agreement of the parties regarding its interpretation; (*c*) any relevant rules of international law applicable in the relations between the parties.
4. A special meaning shall be given to a term if it is established that the parties so intended.

Article 32 Supplementary means of interpretation

Recourse may be had to supplementary means of interpretation, including the preparatory work of the treaty and the circumstances of its conclusion, in order to confirm the meaning resulting from the application of article 31, or to determine the meaning when the interpretation according to article 31: (*a*) leaves the meaning ambiguous or obscure; or (*b*) leads to a result which is manifestly absurd or unreasonable.

Article 33 Interpretation of treaties authenticated in two or more languages

1. When a treaty has been authenticated in two or more languages, the text is equally authoritative in each language, unless the treaty provides or the parties agree that, in case of divergence, a particular text shall prevail.
2. A version of the treaty in a language other than one of those in which the text was authenticated shall be considered an authentic text only if the treaty so provides or the parties so agree.
3. The terms of the treaty are presumed to have the same meaning in each authentic text.
4. Except where a particular text prevails in accordance with paragraph 1, when a comparison of the authentic texts discloses a difference of meaning which the application of articles 31 and 32 does not remove, the meaning which best reconciles the texts, having regard to the object and purpose of the treaty, shall be adopted.

6.11 Addy Judgment and Altra Energy Judgment

Recently, High Court of Australia in *Addy*[25] explained the rules of interpretation of a tax treaty. The Court observed that the principles of interpretation applicable to a tax treaty are well settled[26]. Although the text of the treaty is the starting point and has primacy in the interpretation process, it is mandatory "that courts look to the context, object and purpose of treaty provisions as well as the text ... consistent with the general principle that international instruments should be interpreted in a more liberal manner than would be adopted if the court was required to construe exclusively domestic legislation"[27]

Recently, Supreme court of Canada in *Altra Energy*[28] explained the role of OECD Model Treaty as a tool of interpretation of DTAA in these words: "Tax treaties do not themselves levy new taxes; they simply authorize the contracting parties to do so. Reciprocity is a fundamental principle underlying tax treaty, as they confer rights and impose obligations on each of the contracting states. **The objective of tax treaties, broadly stated, is to govern the interactions between national tax laws in order to facilitate cross-border trade and investment.** One of the most important operational goals is the elimination of double taxation, where the same source of income is taxed by two or more states without any relief. If left unchecked, double taxation risks creating barriers to international trade and investment, which are vital in a globalized economy. Thus, many substantive provisions of the **OECD Model Treaty**, a model for numerous bilateral tax treaties, are directed to achieving this goal and resolving conflicting claims between residence-based taxation and source-based taxation."

---

25. *Addy* v. *Commissioner of Taxation* [2021] HCA 34.

26. *Thiel* v. *Federal Commissioner of Taxation* (1990) 171 CLR 338 at 349, 356; Applicant A (1997) 190 CLR 225 at 251-256; *Bywater Investments* (2016) 260 CLR 169 at 227-228. See also *Lamesa Holdings* (1997) 77 FCR 597 at 604-605; *McDermott Industries (Aust) Pty Ltd.* v. *Commissioner of Taxation* (2005) 142 FCR 134 at 143; *SNF (Australia)* (2011) 193 FCR 149 at 184, 186; *Resource Capital Fund III LP* v. *Federal Commissioner of Taxation* (2013) 95 ATR 504 at 516-521; *Task Technology Pty. Ltd.* v. *Federal Commissioner of Taxation* (2014) 224 FCR 355 at 358; *Tech Mahindra Ltd* v. *Federal Commissioner of Taxation* (2015) 101 ATR 755 at 768-771.

27. *Applicant A* (1997) 190 CLR 225 at 255; see also 231, 240, 253-255. See also *Lamesa Holdings* (1997) 77 FCR 597 at 604-605; Vienna Convention on the Law of Treaties (1969), Art 31. The principles in the Vienna Convention apply even though that Convention has not been enacted as part of the law of Australia: see *Minister for Immigration and Multicultural and Indigenous Affairs* v. *QAAH* of 2004 (2006) 231 CLR 1 at 15.

28. *Canada* v. *Alta Energy Luxembourg S.A.R.L.* 2021 SCC 49.

7 Different Approaches to Interpretation

7.1 Basic principles of statutory interpretation

The basic principles of the statutory interpretation are not to be found in any statute. The basic principles of interpretation have developed through the decisions of the court. The principles which have evolved are sometime called rules, but it would be more accurate to describe them as different approaches to interpretation, on which at different periods of our legal history greater or lesser emphasis has been placed. Justice Holmes observed about the principle of interpretation in Boston Sand[1] as follows:

> "These are not in the real sense rule of law, but they are axioms of experience which may be applied by way of guidance in elucidation of language. They are valuable tools in the work of interpreting statute and other legal documents. They do not bind the interpreter; they only indicate to him what is linguistically possible in attributing a meaning to a particular word pattern."

Justin Dabner[2] in an illuminating article has stated as follows:

> "... the universal approach of common-law tax judges is to seek to resolve a case by identifying the true or correct meaning of the legislation: that is, to identify the intention of parliament from the words used in the statute... My thesis is that typically tax disputes arise because it is impossible to determine what Parliament intended from its words. We often observe Parliament respond to a judicial decision it does not like by enacting further legislation, that is, more words. But typically, this simply generates new issues for resolution and again the judiciary becomes involved. The result is that we see that legislation is spiralling out of control and judicial decision generating more uncertainty and complexity. The administration of, and compliance with, the system becomes a massive burden. Ultimately the public loses confidence in it and there is continuous demand for reform."

7.2 Principle of Interpretation

The principles of interpretation which have evolved are those based on the plain meaning of the words used and their grammatical meaning and those based on the intention or purpose of the legislature.

1. *Boston Sand and Gravel Company* v. *US 278, US 41* (1928)
2. Justin Dabner, An old methodology in a New World: A comment on our current system of Judicial decision making in Tax cases, Journal of Australian Law Teachers Association (2006) Vol. 2 No. 1.

7.3 Statutory Interpretation in the United Kingdom

The rules of interpretation laid down by the judges in the 19th Century were (*i*) literal rule, (*ii*) golden rule, and (*iii*) Mischief rule.

Literal rule

The dominant approach to the interpretation of tax legislation has been that the statutory language is to be construed literally and the ambiguities in taxing provisions were resolved in favour of the taxpayer.

The statement of Lord Cairns in Partington[3] case is as follows:

> "If the person sought to be taxed comes within the letter of the law he must be taxed, however the great the hardship may appear to the judicial mind to be. On the other hand, if the Crown, seeking to recover the tax, cannot bring the subject within the letter of the law, the subject is free, however apparently within the spirit of the law case might appear to be. In other words, if there be admissible in any statute, what is called equitable construction, certainly such construction is not admissible in a taxing statute where you simply adhere to the words of the Statute."

Strict construction required the courts to adhere to the letter of the law reflected in the words of the Statute notwithstanding the spirit of the law expressed in the scheme of the Act, the object of the Act or intention of the Parliament, or the consequences of the court's interpretation.

In Westminster[4], the cardinal principle which was laid down was that where a document or a transaction is genuine, the court cannot go behind it to find some supposed underlying substance. In this case, the Duke of Westminster entered into a deal with the gardener to pay the gardener in his employment a fixed sum per week for a period of 7 years or during the joint life of the parties. The question was whether the payments which the Duke made to his gardener in the form of annuity, but in substance remuneration for services were deductible in computation of his sur-tax liability.House Of Lords by a majority upheld the Dukes position that the sums were not payments of salary or wages. He was entitled to deduct them as annual payments.

Lord Tomlin said

> "It is said that in revenue cases there is a doctrine that the court may ignore the legal position and regards what is called the substance of the matter and the substance of the matter is that the annuitant was serving the Duke for something equal to its former salary or wages and that therefore while he so serving, the annuity must be treated as salary or wages.

Every man is entitled if he can so order his affairs so that the tax attaching under the appropriate act is less than it otherwise would be... this so-called doctrine of substance seems to me nothing more than an attempt to make a man pay notwithstanding that he has so ordered his affairs that the amount of tax sought from him is not legally claimable."

3. *Partington* v. *The Attorney General* (1869) LR 4 HL 100 at p 122.
4. *IRC* v. *Westminster* (1936)AC 1.

The decline of literal rule

In Ramsay[5] the facts involved an artificial, circular, self-cancelling transaction and whether the gain was a chargeable gain or allowable loss. Ramsay is concerned with the capital gain tax.

Company R had a large gain of 187, 977 pounds and wished to create an allowable loss which could be set against the gain and so offset its liability to tax. R bought a scheme from advisors on terms which made the amount of fee vary with the amount saved. Under the scheme, R bought shares in Company C and made two loans to Company C. Loans of an amount each 218, 75 pounds at 11% interest and payable at par after 30 years and 31 years, respectively. C was entitled to make early repayment and if either loan was repaid earlier before its maturity date, it had to be repaid at par or at its market value, whichever was higher.

R has the right to decrease the rate of interest on one loan, on one occasion only, provided there was a corresponding increase on the other loan. R exercised the right causing the rate on one loan 1 to drop to nil; raising thereby rate of interest on other loan 2 raised to 22 per cent. The loan 2 was sold by R at the market value price of 391, 481 pounds. Subsequently, C paid loan 1 at par as it was obliged to do. The value of shares in C dropped and the shares were sold by R at a loss of 175, 731 pounds.

R argued that while the loss on the shares should be recognised, the gains should not be recognised because a gain on debt as opposed to debt on security should not be recognised.

House of Lords treated a series of transactions as composite transactions and decided that there was no loss for capital gains tax. The Ramsay case liberated the construction of revenue statutes from being both literal and blinkered.

Peeper v. Hart[6]

In the UK situation changed after *Peeper* v. *Hart* as Lord Griffith observed:

> "The days have long passed when the court adopted a strict construction view of the interpretation which required them to adopt the literal meaning of the language."

The case of Peeper arose out of a benefit scheme for teachers employed at Malvern College where their sons would be educated at the school for one-fifth of the fees charged for other pupils. This concession was treated as an emolument for the purpose of income tax paid by the staff. The issue was whether the cash equivalent of this benefits should be determined by the marginal cost of educating one additional boy or a proportion of the overall costs of educating all of the pupils. The first method provided a smaller figure than the second and had been the practice of the Inland Revenue to use this for sometime. The Inland Revenue sought to use the second method. House of Lords by majority held that the marginal cost was the appropriate basis for calculation. In this case,

5. *Ramsay* v. *IRC* (1982) AC 300.
6. (1993) AC 593 (H.L.)

the statement of the Finance Secretary in the standing committee dealing with the situation at issue which supported the argument of the taxpayer was taken into account as it clearly resolved an ambiguity in the Finance Act, 1976 and as a consequence, it was found appropriate to use them as an aid to construction.

Golden rule

The golden rule permitted courts to avoid literal reading when it would lead to an absurdity or some injustice. This did not undermine Parliament but recognised that it would not have intended such a result.

The House of Lords in a tax case of the *Duke*[7] observed:

> "... in order to avoid imputing to Parliament an intention to produce an unreasonable result, we are entitled and indeed bound to discard the ordinary meaning of any provision and adopt some other meaning which will avoid that result".

Mischief rule

Mischief rule involves construing a statute when the meaning is not clear to cure defects which the statute sought to remedy. Despite the fact that the Mischief rule can be traced back to the 16th century far too much of statutory interpretation followed the literal rule.

On mischief rule, the House of Lords decision in *Inco-Europe*[8] is worth mentioning, which is as follows:

> " In Inco Europe, the main issue was whether the court of appeal has jurisdiction to hear an appeal of a decision made at arbitration. The relevant provision was section 18 of the Supreme Court Act, 1981 as amended by section 107 and schedule 3 of the Arbitration Act, 1996. The provision as amended stated plainly enough that no appeal shall lie to the court of appeal. Thus, a literal meaning would obviously dictate that no appeal would lie. However, the House of Lords and the Court of Appeal unanimously ruled that there was entitlement to appeal."

The conclusion was mainly drawn from the history of legislation in this field and the fact that there was no evidence of any intention to change the status for in this regard. Lord Nicholls in his judgment directly addressed this point.

Responding to the charge that the preferred intention was overly creative, he said:

> " I freely acknowledge that this interpretation of section 18(1)(*g*) involves reading words into paragraphs. It has long been established that the role of the courts in construing legislation is not confined to resolving ambiguities in statutory language. The court must be able to correct obvious drafting errors. In suitable cases in discharging its interpretative functions the court will add words, or omit words, or substitute words. some notable instances are given in Rupert's Cross statutory interpretation...."

In omitting or inserting words the judge is not really engaged in a hypothetical reconstruction of the intention of the drafter or the legislature, but is simply making as much sense as he can of the text of the statutory provision read in its appropriate context and within the limits of the judicial role.

7. *IRC* v. *Duke* (1963) 40 Tax Cases 6:30 at p. 648.
8. *Inco-Europe Limited* v. *First Choice* (2001) WLR 586.

Lord Nicholls went on to describe what he considered to be the proper limits of this aspect of the judicial role:

> "This power is confined to plain cases of drafting mistakes. The courts are ever mindful that their constitutional role in this field is interpretative. They must abstain from any course which might have the appearance of judicial legislation. A statute is expressed in language approved and enacted by the legislature. So, the courts exercise considerable caution before adding or omitting or substituting words. Before interpreting a statute in this way, the courts must be sure of three matters: (1) the intended purpose of the statute or provision in question; (2) that by inadvertence the draftsman and the parliament failed to give a fact to that purpose in the provision in question; (3) the substance of the provision Parliament would have made, had the error in the bill been noticed. The third of these conditions is of crucial importance. Otherwise, any attempt to determine the meaning of the enactment doesn't cross the boundary between construction and legislation.... in the present case, the three conditions are fulfilled."

New approaches in statutory interpretation

Purposive approach- This approach, a relation of the Mischief rule, has become the standard approach towards the interpretation of statute. Under the purposive approach, the words of the legislation are read in their fullest context, and with a view to giving effect to the purpose of the legislation.

In *Barclays Mercantile*[9], an Irish company, BGE had built a pipeline. They sold the pipeline to the taxpayers, BMBF 91.3 million pounds. BMBF leased the assets back to BGE which granted a sub-lease onwards to its British subsidiary. The question was whether BMBF was entitled to a capital allowance in respect of the amount spent 91.3 million pounds, as the said amount was spent to acquire an asset used in its business of finance leasing. House of Lords upheld the claim of Barclays.

In *Agassi*[10], the House of Lords held that endorsement earning was subject to UK tax law. The tax question involved in this case was how to construct sections 555 and 556 of the Income and Corporation Tax Act, 1988, which provide that entertainers and sportsperson, not residents in the United Kingdom, are subject to UK taxation in respect of profit or gains arising from commercial activities carried out by them in the UK.

In this case, Agassi, who was not a UK resident nor domiciled here, played a number of tournaments in the UK. Agassi owned a company, Agassi Enterprises which entered into sports sponsorship contracts with Nike Inc. and Head Sports Inc. incorporated in the USA. None of these companies were resident in the UK company nor any of them carried any trade in the UK. These companies made payment of 125, 908 pounds out of which 11, 640 pounds were related to tournaments played in UK.

---

9. *Barclays Mercantile Business Finance Limited* v. *Mawson* (2004) UKHL 51.
10. *Agassi* v. *Robinson* (2006) UKHL 23.

Revenue contended that Section 556(2) of the Income and Corporation Taxes Act applied which treats payment not made directly to an entertainer or a sportsperson but indirectly to an associated person as if they are made to the sportsperson him or herself. Agassi contended that section 556(2) had to be subject to Section 555(2) which exclude payments in respect of which there is a no obligation on the part of the payer to deduct tax. On plain language of section 556(2) it was held that Agassi was liable to tax in UK.

To sum up, the purposive approach consists of two steps. First, unambiguous legislation should be given its natural meaning. Second, legislation should be interpreted so as to give effect to its purposes derived from the text and scheme of the legislation as supported by Hansard where relevant.

7.4 Australia

The literal approach dominated in Australia till 1981. It means that the words of the legislation are given their normal meaning irrespective of the result. In *Consolidated Holdings*[11], the court observed: "... the task of statutory construction must begin with a consideration of the [statutory] text". So must the task of statutory construction end."

The High Court decision in *Cooper Brookes*[12] took a view that literal meaning could be departed from where the result was otherwise irrational. In such a situation the function of the court is to uphold the purpose of the legislation.

In *Peabody*,[13] the issue was whether section 26AAA of the Income-tax Amendment Act, 1936 was applicable. Section 26AAA operated to assess profit on the sale of property within 12 months of acquisition. The facts in this case were that Peabody was a beneficiary of a family trust. The Trustee rather than disposing of newly acquired shares the value of which was transferred to the parent company sold the oldest shares. These older shares were then sold for an enhanced tax-free gain. On a literal interpretation of the provisions of section 26AAA, this scheme was not caught.

In recent times, the context and purpose have been recognised in the interpretation. In *SZTAL*[14], the **importance of context** was emphasised in these words:

> "...The starting point for the ascertainment of the meaning of a statutory provision is the text of the statute whilst, at the same time, regard is had to its context and purpose. Context should be regarded at this first stage and not at some later stage and it should be regarded in its widest sense..."

11. *Commissioner of Taxation* v. *Consolidated Media Holdings Ltd*. (2012) 250 CLR 503. see also, *Project Blue Sky Inc* v. *Australian Broadcasting Authority* (1998) 194 CLR 355; *Certain Lloyd's Underwriters* v. *Cross* (2012) 248 CLR 378; *Alcan (NIT) Alumina Pty Ltd.* v. *Commissioner of Territory Revenue* (2009) 239 CLR 27; *Thiess* v. *Collector of Customs* (2014) 250 CLR 664; *Military Rehabilitation and Compensation Commission* v. *May* (2016) 257 CLR 468; *Probuild Constructions (Aust) Pty Ltd*. v. *Shade Systems Pty Ltd*. [2018] HCA 4.
12. (1981) 147 CLR 297
13. *FCT* v. *Peabody* (1994) 181 CLR 359.
14. *SZTAL* v. *Minister for Immigration and Border Protection* (2017) 347 ALR 405.

HP Mercantile[15] was concerned with the interpretation of the Goods and Services Tax Act. Justice Hill observed:

> "A more profitable approach to the question of construction is to consider both policy which is enshrined in division 11 and the legislative context, so far as that cast light upon the proper interpretation of sections 11- 15(2)(*a*)."

It is clear, both having regard to the modern principles of interpretation enunciated by the High Court in cases such as Bankstown Football Club[16] and Section 15AA of the Acts Interpretation Act, 1901 that the court will prefer an interpretation of Statute which give effect to the legislative purpose, as opposed to that which would not. This requires the court to identify that purpose, both by the language of the statute itself and also any extrinsic material which the court is authorised to take into account. In Thiess[17], the **importance of purpose was** emphasised in these words:

> "**Objective discernment of statutory purpose** is integral to contextual construction. The requirement of section 15AA of the *Acts Interpretation Act, 1901* (Cth) that "the interpretation that would best achieve the purpose or object of [an] Act (whether or not that purpose or object is expressly stated ...) is to be preferred to each other interpretation" is in that respect a particular statutory reflection of a general systemic principle."

7.5 Canada

The traditional approach to interpretation

Till recently, the approach to the interpretation of tax legislation in Canada was that of strict construction. It means that statutory language is to be construed literally, ambiguities in taxing provisions are to be settled in favour of the assessee. In Witthun[18], the board disallowed a medical expense deduction in respect of the cost of the full-time attendant for the taxpayer's bedridden wife, who could take for a few hours a day in a special rocking chair, on the basis that she was not necessarily confined by reason of illness, injury or affliction to a bed as required by section 27(1)(*c*)(*iv*) of the 1952 Act.

The Canadian Court applied the golden rule in Moldown[19]. In this case, section 13(1) limited the loss of a taxpayer from a farming business where his chief source of income for that particular year is neither farming nor a combination of farming and some other source of income.

15. (2005) 143 FCR 553.
16. *CIC Insurance* v. *Bankstown Football Club Ltd.* (1997).
17. *Thiess* v. *Collector of Customs* (2014) 250 CLR 664.
18. *Witthun* v. *MNR* (1957) DTC 174.
19. *Moldown* v. *Queen* (1977) CTC 310 (SCC).

Dickson J. observed:

> "Whether a source of income is a taxpayer's source of income, is both a relative and objective test. It is decidedly not a quantum measurement. A man who did farming all of his life does not cease to have his chief source of income from farming because he unexpectedly wins a lottery. The distinguishing features of the chief source of income are taxpayers reasonable expectations of income from his various revenue sources and his ordinary mode and habit of work. These may be tested by considering, *inter alia*, the source of income, the time spent, the capital committed, the profitability both actual and potential. A change in the taxpayer's mode and habit of work or reasonable expectations may signify a change in the chief source, but that is a question of fact in the circumstances."

In *Triple Holding*[20], the golden rule of interpretation was applied. The Minister had disallowed the taxpayer's claim for capital cost allowance on the basis that the building was constructed of steel frame and corrugated steel and not galvanized iron or corrugated iron as set out in clause 6 of Schedule B of the Income Tax Regulation.

The court accepted the evidence of a metallurgical engineer and said:

> ... it would be an absurdity on my part to follow the argument of the respondent that because the Income-tax Act uses these words galvanized iron and corrugated iron, the appellant who uses Steel frame and corrugated Steel is precluded from capital cost allowance allowed to him under clause 6.

New approaches to interpretation

Purposive interpretation - The purposive interpretation emphasizes the reasons for which the statutory text was enacted and the objective at which it aims, and interprets the text in the light of these reasons and objectives.

In *Bronfman Trust*[21], the taxpayer, the personal trust established by Samuel Bronfman for the benefit of his daughter and children borrowed a considerable sum of money to finance capital allocation to his daughter, incurring substantial interest expenses, which it sought to deduct in computing its income for each of the years 1970, 1971 and 1972. The Minister disallowed the deduction on the ground that the borrowed money was used to pay capital allocation to the beneficiaries, not for the purpose of earning income from a business or property as required by sub-paragraph 20. The question was whether the deduction required borrowed money to be used directly for the purpose of earning income or permitted qualifying indirect uses such as income-preserving purposes claimed by the taxpayer.

Dikson C.J. observed:

> "Parliament enacted section 20(1)(*c*)(*i*) ... in order to encourage the accumulation of capital which would produce taxable income. Not all borrowing expenses are deductible. Interest on borrowed money used to produce tax-exempt income is not

20. *Triple Holdings Ltd.* v. *MNR* (1981) CTC 2084.
21. *The Queen* v. *Bronfman Trust* (1987) 1 CTC 117 (SCC).

> deductible. Interest on borrowed money used to buy life insurance policies is not deductible. Interest on borrowing used for non-income earning purposes, such as personal consumption or the making of capital gains is similarly not deductible. The statutory deductions thus require a characterization of the use."

The court concluded that the taxpayer did not establish that its *bona fide* purpose was to earn income.

In *Newman*[22], the taxpayer, a lawyer practicing with Winnipeg firm, transferred his 128 57 14 shares in the firm management company (new Mac) valued at 120, 000 dollars to a newly incorporated holding company (Melru) in exchange for 12857 14 voting class G shares in Melru which also issued one common voting share to the taxpayer for $1 and 99 class F shares to taxpayer's wife, Ruby for $1 per share.

In 1982, Melru received $20,000 in dividends on the Newmac shares, where upon, Mrs. Newman, who had been elected sole director of Melru declared a dividend of 5000 dollars on the taxpayer's class G shares and 14, 800 dollars on her own class F shares. Upon receiving the dividends, Mrs. Neuman immediately loaned 14, 800 dollars to the taxpayer, receiving a demand promissory note as security. Mrs. Neuman died 1988 and the loan was never repaid.

Iacobucci J. held that section 56(2) did not apply to the dividend income received by Mrs. Neuman. Iacobucci J. employed a purposive interpretation of Section 56(2) observing that this provision strives to prevent tax avoidance through income splitting and this provision is a specific tax avoidance provision and not a journal provision against income is splitting.

Textual, contextual and purposive approach

Placer Dome[23] is regarded a landmark decision on tax interpretation. In this case, the issue involved was the meaning of the term 'hedging' in the Ontario Mining Tax Act. The Act imposes a tax on the profits of the mine operators. Profits is defined to mean proceeds less allowable deductions and proceeds is defined to include all consideration received or receivable from hedging and future sales of the output of the mine. 'Hedging' is defined to mean the fixing of a price output of a mine before delivery by means of a forward sale or future contract on a recognised commodity exchange or the purchase or sale forward of a foreign currency related directly to the output of a mine.

The question involved in this case was whether the term hedging was restricted to contracts requiring settlement by physical delivery of the output of a mine.

Supreme Court held that the meaning of the term hedging was ambiguous and that the broader definition was preferable, that is, link is not necessary between the financial transaction and output of the mine.

The decision also contains a summary of the general principles for the interpretation of the taxing statute which is as follows:

22. *Neuman* v. *Queen* (1998) 3 CTC 177 (SCC).

23. *Ontario (Ministry of Finance)* v. *Placer Dome Canada* (2006) SCC 20.

"21. In *Stubart Investment Limited* v. *The Queen* (1984) 1 SCR 536, this court rejected the strict approach to the construction of taxation statute and there held that the modern approach applies to taxation statute no less than it does to other statutes. That is the words of an Act are to be read in their entire context and in their grammatical and ordinary sense harmoniously with the scheme of the Act, the object of the Act and the intention of the Parliament(p 578): *British Columbia Limited* v. *Canada* (1999) 3 SCR 804 at p 50. However, because of the degree of precision and detail characteristics of many tax provisions, a greater emphasis has often been placed on textual interpretation where taxation statutes are concerned: *Canada Trustco Mortgage Co.* v. *Canada* (2005)2 SCR 601, 2005 SCC 54 at para 11. Taxpayers are entitled to rely on the clear meaning of taxation provisions in structuring their affairs. Where the words of a statute are precise and unambiguous those words will play a dominant role in the interpretative process.

22. On the other hand, where the words of a Statute give more than one reasonable interpretation, the ordinary meaning of words will play a lesser role, and greater recourse to the context and purpose of the Act may be necessary: Canada Trustco at para 10. Moreover, as McLachin C.J. noted in para 47, ' even where the meaning of particular provisions may not appear to be ambiguous at the first glance, statutory context and purpose may reveal or resolve latent ambiguity'. The Chief Justice went on to explain that in order to resolve explicit latent ambiguity in taxation legislation,' the courts must undertake a unified textual, contextual and purposive approach to statutory interpretation.'

23. The interpretative approach is thus informed by the level of precision and clarity with which a taxing provision is drafted. Where such provision admits of no ambiguity in its meaning or its application to the facts, it must simply be applied. Reference to the purpose of the provision cannot be used to create an unexpressed exception to clear language."

In Shell Canada[23a], it was observed that where a provision admits of more than one reasonable interpretation, greater emphasis must be placed on the context, scheme and purpose of the Act. Thus, legislative purpose may not be used to supplant clear statutory language, but to arrive at the most plausible interpretation of an ambiguous statutory provision.

Recently, in *Dean Knight*[24] the **transactions went against the rationale of section 111(5) of the Income Tax Act and amounted to abusive tax avoidance.** Dean Knight complied with the literal text of section 111(5) of the Act, the transaction was held abusive as it frustrates its rationale. The rationale behind section 111(5) of the Act is to prevent corporations from being acquired by unrelated parties in order to deduct their unused losses against income from another business for the benefit of new shareholders. The court held as under-

"The use of a provision's text, context, and purpose to determine the rationale differs from traditional statutory interpretation. Since in a GAAR analysis, the search is for the rationale that underlies the words, considering the provision's text, context and purpose ensures that the intrinsic and extrinsic evidence used to discern that rationale remains tied to the provision itself. Considering a provision's text involves asking how it sheds light on what the provision was designed to achieve since the

23a. *Shell Canada Ltd.* v. *Canada* (1999) 3 SCR 622.

24. *Deans Knight Income Corp.* v. *Canada* 2023 SCC 16.

language and structure of the provision can be evocative of Parliament's underlying concerns. Courts must also consider the provision's context, with a focus on the relationship between the provision alleged to have been abused and the particular scheme within which it operates. Understanding the provision's purpose is central to the GAAR analysis, and legislative history and extrinsic evidence provide insight into the rationale for specific provisions".

7.6 India

Tax laws provide a useful set of cases for exploring the interpretative approaches of the judiciary in India. Some general observations made by the courts are first mentioned before analysing the different approaches.

It is the function of the legislature to say what shall be the law and it is for the court to say that what the law is. The court has to interpret a law so as to apply to the facts before it. Interpretation cannot be in a vacuum or in relation to hypothetical facts. Interpretation or construction means that the court has to ascertain the facts and then interpret the law to apply to such facts. [25]A general observation equally important is that when the language is plain and unambiguous and admits of only one meaning no question of construction of statutes arises, for the statute speaks for itself[26]. The principle that fiscal statute should be construed literally does not rule out the application of the principle of reasonable construction. This was stated while interpreting section 40A(7) of the Income-tax Act, 1961 in *Sajjan Mills*.[27]

Very recently, in *Apex Laboratories*[28], the Supreme Court held that Interpretation of law has two essential purposes: one is to clarify to the people governed by it, the meaning of the letter of the law; the other is to shed light and give shape to the intent of the lawmaker. And, in this process, the courts' responsibility lies in discerning the social purpose which the specific provision subserves.

Literal interpretation

In *Polestar*[29], Justice Bhagwati observed that the rule of literal construction is firmly established. The statutory enactment must ordinarily be construed according to the plain natural meaning and that no words are to be added or modified unless it is really necessary to do so in order to prevent a provision from being unintelligible, absurd, unreasonable, unworkable, or totally irreconcilable with the rest of the statute. In the Polestar, the question of law relating to the interpretation of section 5(2)(*a*)(*ii*) of the Bengal Finance (Sales Tax) Act, 1941, as applied to the Union Territory of Delhi, involved was whether the expression 'resale' in the aforesaid section and the second proviso means anywhere without

25. *National Insurance Co. Ltd.* v. *Laxmi Narayan Dhut* (2007) 3 SCC 700 at p 716.
26. *Orient Paper & Industries Ltd.* v. *State of M.P.* (2006) 12 SCC 468.
27. *Shree Sajjan Mills Ltd.* v. *CIT* (1985) 156 ITR 585/23 Taxman 37 (SC).
28. *Apex Laboratories (P.) Ltd.* v. *Deputy Commissioner of Income Tax* [Special Leave Petition (Civil) No. 23207 of 2019 decided on 22-2-2022]/[2022] 135 taxmann.com 286/286 Taxman 200 (SC).
29. *Polestar Electronic (P) Ltd.* v. *Addl. Commissioner* (1978) 41 STC 408(SC)/AIR 1978 SC 897.

any geographical limitation or it is confined only to resale inside Delhi. The court held that we do not, in the circumstances, see any cogent and compelling reason for reading the words 'inside the Union Territory of Delhi' after resale in the aforesaid section and the proviso.

If the language is plain, the court is to apply regardless of the result in order to find out the plain and literal meaning, the background, the context, and the purpose have to be looked into.[30]

Plain meaning rule

In *Baldev Singh*,[31] it was observed that time and again Supreme Court has laid down that legislative intent has to be ascertained according to the plain language used in the enactment and the basic rule of statutory construction should be preferred which advances the purpose and object of legislation not which leads to anomalies, injustices, or absurdities... the golden rule of interpretation is that when the words of the legislation are plain and unambiguous, effect must be given to them. The basic principle on which this rule is based is that since the words must have spoken as clearly to legislatures, as to judges, it may be safely presumed that the legislature intended what the words plainly say.

The legislative intent of the enactment may be gathered from several sources which are:—

(*a*) from the statute itself;

(*b*) from the Preamble to the statute;

(*c*) from the statement of objects and reasons;

(*d*) from the legislative debates;

(*e*) report of the committee is and commissions which preceded the legislation; and

(*f*) from all legitimate and admissible sources from where they may be allowed.

For ascertaining the plain meaning certain tests were laid down by the constitution bench of the Supreme Court in *Mathuraram Agarwal*[32] held that in a taxing Act, it is not possible to assume any intention or governing purpose of the Statute more than what is stated in plain language. It is not the economic results sought to be obtained by making the provision which is relevant in interpreting a fiscal statute. Equally impermissible is an interpretation which does not follow from the plain, unambiguous , language of the statute. Words cannot be added or substituted so as to give meaning to the statute which will

30. See, *Kanai Lal Sur* v. *Paramnidhi Sadhukhan* AIR 1957 SC 907, 910; *Lt. col Pritipal Singh* v. *Union of India* AIR 1982 SC 1413, 1419; *Atma Ram Mittal* v. *Ishwar Singh Punia* AIR 1988 SC 2031, 2034; *The Member-Secretary, Andhra Pradesh State Board for Prevention and Control of Water Pollution* v. *A.P. Rayons Ltd.* AIR 1989 SC 611; *Commissioner of Wealth-tax* v. *Smt. Hashmatunnisa Begum AIR* 1989 SC 1024, 1029.

31. *Baldev Singh Bajwa* v. *Monish Soni* (2005) 12 SCC 778.

32. *Mathuraram Agrawal* v. *State of Madhya Pradesh* AIR 2000 SC 109.

serve the spirit and intention of the legislature. The statute should clearly and unambiguously convey the three components of the tax law *i.e.* the subject of the tax; the person who is liable to pay the tax and the rate at which the tax is to be paid. If there is any ambiguity regarding any of the ingredients in a taxation statute then there is a no tax in law. Then it is for the legislature to do the needful in the matter.

In the *Mathuraram* case, the proviso to clause (*b*) of sub-section (2) of section 127A of the Madhya Pradesh Municipality Act, 1961 was struck down as *ultra vires* being contrary to the charging section as the rate of tax applied to such properties was not indicated. In this case the municipality aggregated the annual value of all the buildings and levied property tax on the deemed annual letting value so aggregated.

in Govind Singh[33], the court observed that when the words of a statute are clear, plain, or unambiguous *i.e.*, they are reasonably susceptible to only one meaning, the courts are bound to give effect to that meaning irrespective of consequences. The intention of the legislation is primarily to be gathered from the language used, which means that attention should be paid to what has been said as also to what has not been said.

Recently, in *Noble Education Society*[34] the term 'solely' used in section 10(23C) was given plain meaning. Thus, a trust, university or other institution imparting education, as the case may be, should necessarily have all its objects aimed at imparting or facilitating education. Having regard to the plain and unambiguous terms of the statute and the substantive provisions which deal with exemption, there cannot be any other interpretation.

Strict construction

The difference between literal interpretation and strict construction has been pointed out in *Dilip Kumar and Company*[35]. The strict interpretation does not encompass strict literalism in its fold. The strict interpretation does not encompass such literalism, which leads to absurdity and go against legislative intent. However, there is not much difference as strict interpretation of a statute involves literal or plain meaning test.

In *A. V. Fernandez*[36], the Supreme Court stated that If the revenue satisfies the court that the case falls strictly within the provisions of the law, the subject can be taxed. If, on the other hand, the case is not covered within the four corners of the provisions of the taxing statute, no tax can be imposed by inference or by analogy or by trying to probe into the intention of the legislature and by considering what was the substance of the matter.

33. *State of Jharkhand* v. *Govind Singh* (2005) 10 SCC 437 (SC).

34. *New Noble Educational Society* v. *Chief Commissioner of Income Tax* [C.A. No. 3795/2014 (date of decision 19 October, 2022)]/[2022] 143 taxmann.com 276/[2023] 290 Taxman 206 (SC).

35. *Commissioner of Customs* v. *Dilip Kumar and Company* (2018) 9 SCC 1/[2018] 95 taxmann.com 327/69 GST 239 (SC).

36. *A.V. Fernandez* v. *State of Kerala* [1957] 8 STC 561 (SC).

In *Provident Investment Co*[37]., the Supreme Court held that the transaction between a company and the purchaser of shares of two companies was by way of relinquishment of the Managing agency of the assessee company and therefore the provisions of section 12B of the Income-tax Act, 1922, as they stood at that time, but not attracted and assessee was not chargeable to tax in respect of any capital gain made by him. It is useful to look at section 12B which was as under:

> "12B. (1) The tax shall be payable by the assessee under the head capital gain in respect of any profits or gain arising from the sale, exchange or transfer of a capital asset effected after 31st March, 1946; and such profits and gains shall be deemed to be income of the previous year in which the sale, exchange or transfer took place."

The court must look squarely at the words of the statute and interpret them. It must interpret a taxing statute in the light of what is clearly expressed. It cannot imply anything which is not expressed. It cannot import provisions in the statutes so as to supply any assumed deficiency. In interpreting a taxing statute, equitable considerations are entirely out of place. Nor can taxing statutes be interpreted on any presumptions or assumptions.[38]

The rule of strict construction applies a fortiori to provisions which create an artificial and vicarious liability to tax.

In *National Taj Traders*[39], the Supreme Court observed that the principle that the fiscal statute should be strictly construed is applicable only to charging provision or a provision imposing penalty and not to those parts of the statute which contain machinery provisions.

In *Associated Cement*[40] the Supreme Court observed that charging sections are construed strictly, the machinery provisions are not generally subject to rigorous construction. Thus, a distinction has to be made by the court while interpreting the provisions of a taxing statute between charging provisions which impose a tax, and machinery provision which provides the machinery for quantification of the tax and levying and collection of tax so imposed. While charging sections are construed strictly the machinery provisions are not generally subject to rigorous construction.

A taxing statute should be strictly construed and the machinery provisions must be so construed to effectuate the object and purpose of the statute and the exemption provisions must be construed strictly and by a strict interpretation[41].

However, strict interpretation' does not encompass such literalism, which leads to absurdity and goes against the legislative intent.[42]

---

37. *CIT* v. *Provident Investment Co. Ltd.* (1957) 32 ITR 190 (SC).
38. *Commissioner of Sales Tax, Uttar Pradesh* v. *The Modi Sugar Mills Ltd.* 1961 (2) SCR 189.
39. *CIT* v. *National Taj Traders* AIR 1980 SC 485.
40. *Associated Cement Co. Ltd.* v. *Commercial Tax Officer* AIR 1981 SC 1887.
41. *Commissioner of Income Tax-III* v. *Calcutta Knitwears, Ludhiana* (2014) 6 SCC 444.
42. *Commissioner of Customs (Import), Mumbai* v. *Dilip Kumar & Co.* (2018) 9 SCC 1/[2018] 95 taxmann.com 127/69 GST 239 (SC).

In *Ajmera Housing*[43], the Supreme Court held that a taxing statute is to be construed strictly. In a taxing Act, one has to look merely at what is said in the relevant provision. There is no presumption as to a tax. Nothing is to be read, nothing is to be implied. There is no room for any intendment. There is no equity in a tax statute. Thus, in interpreting a taxing statute, the Court must look squarely at the words of the statute and interpret them. Considerations of hardship, injustice, and equity are entirely out of place in interpreting a taxing statute.

In *Standard Chartered*[44], Justice Balakrishnan (as his lordship then was) observed:

> "... the distinction between a strict construction and a more free one has disappeared in modern times and now mostly the question is what is the true construction of the statute."

In *Shardindu*[45] it was argued that when an Act is silent, then the vacuum can be filled up by the court. It was submitted that the present contingency was never visualised by the draftsman that if the incumbent is charge-sheeted then what is the remedy in that contingency? It was submitted that the lacuna be filled up by the court. Repelling the contention, the court observed that lacunae could be filled in where it is found that the Act does not provide any method or the Act is silent. From the scheme of the Act and the rules, it is apparent that the appointment of the chairperson of the National Council of Teacher Education is a tenure post for a period of four years or till he attained the age of 65 years. Thus, the tenure of the respondent could only be terminated in terms of sections 5 and 6 of the Act.

In *Rakesh Wadhawan's*[46] the Supreme Court stated that a statute can never be exhaustive. The legislature is incapable of contemplating all possible situations which may arise in future litigation and myriad circumstances. The scope is there always for the courts to interpret the law with pragmatism consistently with the demands of varying situations. The construction placed by the court on the statutory provisions has to be meaningful. The legislative intent has to be found out and effectuated.

Casus omissus

The doctrine of Casus Omissus is a judicial technique of interpretation. A casus omissus cannot be supplied by the court. Thus, a statute may not be extended to meet a case for which provision has clearly and undoubtedly not been made. This dictum was followed by the Supreme Court in *Parson Tools*[47]. The Supreme Court refused to import the provisions of section 14(2) of the Limitation Act into

43. *Ajmera Housing Corporation* v. *Commissioner of Income-tax* 2010 (8) SCC 739/[2010] 193 Taxman 193 (SC).
44. *Standard Chartered Bank* v. *Directorate of Enforcement* (2005) 4 SCC 530/[2005] 60 SCL 217 (SC).
45. *Union of India* v. *Shardindu* (2007) 6 SCC 276.
46. *Rakesh Wadhawan* v. *Jagdamba Industrial Corporation* (2002) 5 SCC 440.
47. *CST* v. *Parson Tools and Plants* AIR 1975 SC 1039.

Section 10(3B) of the UP-Sales Tax Act. The court observed that if the legislature wilfully omits to incorporate something of an analogous law in a subsequent statute... the language of which is otherwise plain and unambiguous, the court is not competent to supply the omission by ingrafting on it or introducing in it, under the guise of interpretation by analogy or implication, something what it thinks to be a general principle of justice and equity.

In *National Taj Traders*[48], the court observed that a *casus omissus* cannot be supplied by the court except in the case of clear necessity and when the reason for it is found in the four corners of the statute itself but at the same time a *casus omissus* should not readily be inferred and for that purpose, all the parts of a statute or section must be construed ... with reference to the context and other clauses thereof so that the construction to be put on a particular provision makes a consistent enactment of the whole statute.

In *C.A. Abraham*[48a] the court observed that in interpreting a fiscal statute, the court cannot proceed to make good deficiencies, if there be any, the court must interpret the statute as it stands and in case of doubt in a manner favourable to the taxpayer.

Golden rule- This rule is a modification of the literal rule. If literal construction leads to absurdity or repugnancy then external aids to construction can be resorted. [49]Recently, in *Apex Laboratory*[50], the strict or narrow construction of *Explanation* I to section 37(1) of the Income-Tax Act, 1961 would have allowed a deduction to pharmaceutical companies on freebies given to doctors. On a narrow construction, acceptance of freebies is punishable by the MCI. but not covered in the expression any purpose which is an offence or which is prohibited by law. Justice S. Ravindra Bhat observed that the well-established principle of interpretation of taxing statutes - that they need to be interpreted strictly - cannot be sustained when it results in an absurdity contrary to the intentions of the Parliament. It was further observed that ... a narrow interpretation of *Explanation* 1 to Section 37(1) defeats the purpose for which it was inserted, *i.e.*, to disallow an assessee from claiming a tax benefit for its participation in an illegal activity. Though the memorandum to the Finance Bill, 1998 elucidated the ambit of *Explanation* 1 to include "protection money, extortion, hafta, bribes, etc..", yet, *ipso facto*, by no means is the embargo envisaged restricted to those examples. It is but logical that when acceptance of freebies is punishable by the MCI (the range of penalties and sanctions extending to the ban imposed on the medical practitioner), pharmaceutical companies cannot be granted the tax benefit for providing such freebies, and thereby (actively and with full knowledge) enabling the commission of the act which attracts such opprobri-

---

48. *CIT* v. *National Taj Trader AIR* 1980 SC 485.

48a. *C.A Abraham* v. *ITO* (1961) 41 ITR 425 (SC)

49. *Modji Jaitha & Co.* v. *Khandesh Spinning and Weaving Mills Co. Ltd.* AIR 1950 FC 83, 116; *Jugalkishore Saraf* v. *Raw Cotton Co. Ltd.* AIR 1955 SC 376. The golden rule was given by in *Kehar Singh* v. *State (Dehi Admn.)* AIR 1988 SC 1883, 1945; *Administrator, Municipal Corporation* v. *Dattatraya Dahekar* AIR 1992 SC 1846-1848.

50. *Apex Laboratories Pvt. Ltd.* v. *Deputy Commissioner of Income Tax*, Large Tax Payer Unit - II [Special Leave Petition (Civil) No. 23207 of 2019 date of decision February 22, 2022]/[2022] 135 taxmann.com 286/286 Taxman 200 (SC).

um. Thus, pharmaceutical companies' gifting freebies to doctors, etc. is clearly "prohibited by law", and not allowed to be claimed as a deduction under Section 37(1). Doing so would wholly undermine public policy.

Where the language is ambiguous or capable of more than one meaning, then the court has to adopt that interpretation which favours the assessee. In *Vegetable Product*[51], the court had to consider the interpretation of the term ' the amount of tax, if any payable by him' occurring in section 271(1)(*a*)(*i*) of the Income-tax Act, 1961. The two views of the above term were advanced. According to one view does the term mean the amount of tax assessed under section 143 of the Act or it means the amount of tax payable under section 156 of the Act? The court observed that the word assessed is a term often used in several provisions of the Act. The quantification of the tax payable is always referred to in the Act as tax assessed. The tax payable is not the same thing as the tax assessed. The tax payable is the amount for which the demand notice is issued under section 156. In determining the tax payable, the tax already paid has to be deducted. Hence, there can be no doubt that the expression 'the amount of tax, if any, payable by him' refers to the tax payable under the demand notice.

The Supreme Court while interpreting section 245D(6) of the Income-tax Act, 1961 in *Om Prakash Mittal*[52] observed that an approach which will make provision workable rather than otiose is to be adopted by the court. In this case, a prayer was made by the Commissioner to declare the settlement order passed by the Settlement Commission to be void and to withdraw benefits and immunities granted to the assessee. The Supreme Court held that merely because section 245-I provides that the order of the commission is conclusive it does not take away the power of the commission to decide whether the settlement order has been obtained by fraud or misrepresentation of facts. The court observed that the commission had really missed the true scope of section 245D(6). If the commissioner was able to establish that the earlier order was obtained because of misrepresentation of facts, it is certainly open to the commission to decide that issue.

Where the plain literal interpretation of statutory provision produces a manifestly unjust result which could never have been intended by the Legislature, the court may modify the language used by the legislature so as to achieve the intention of the legislature and produce a rational construction. These prepositions were laid down by the Supreme Court in *J.H.Gotla*[53]. In this case, the court interpreted section 16(3) of the Indian Income-tax Act, 1922 by holding that in the clubbing provisions whereby the share of minor children and wife is included in the income of the assessee the income is to be regarded as the business income derived from business carried on by the assessee and in that view of the matter the assessee is entitled to set off his losses carry forward from the previous year.

---

51. *CIT* v. *Vegetable Product Ltd.* (1973) 88 ITR 192 (S.C.).
52. *CIT* v. *Om Prakash Mittal* (2005) 2 SCC 751/[2005] 143 Taxman 373 (SC).
53. *CIT* v. *JH Gotla* AIR 1985 SC 1698.

In National Taj Traders[54], the literal rule was not followed. In this case, the issue involved the interpretation of section 33B(2)(*b*) which prescribed the period of limitation on revisional powers of the Commissioner by providing that no order shall be made under sub-section (1) after the expiry of two years from the date of the orders sought to be revised by the Commissioner and a literal construction of section 33B(2)(*b*) also suggests that the bar of limitation imposed thereby was absolute in the sense that it applies to every kind of order to be made sub-section (1) and no distinction was made between *suo motu* order and an order that might be made by him pursuant to a direction given by any appellate or other higher authority but the question is whether such literal construction should be accorded to that provision?

The court took the view that literal construction would lead to a manifestly absurd because in a given case, like the present one, where the appellate authority *i.e.* the Tribunal has found the ITO order to be erroneous as being prejudicial to the interests of the revenue and the Commissioner's order unsustainable as being in violation of the principles of the natural justice and how the appellate authority exercised its applied power? It further held:

> "The words of section 33B(2)(*b*) will be applicable to *suo motu* orders of the Commissioner in revision and not to orders made by him in pursuant to a direction or order passed by the Appellate Tribunal under sub-section (4) or by any other higher authority. Such construction will be in consonance with the principles that all parts of the section should be construed together and every clause thereof should be construed with reference to the context and other clauses thereof so that the construction put on that particular provision makes a consistent enactment of the whole statute."

Strict compliance of conditions for deductions - One of the rules of interpretation of a tax statute is that if a deduction or exemption is available on compliance with certain conditions the conditions are to be strictly complied with. This rule is in line with the general principle that taxing statutes are to be construed strictly and that there is no room for equitable considerations.[55] Thus deductions are to be granted only when the conditions which govern them are strictly complied with.

The choice between a strict and a liberal construction - In *Mangalore Chemicals and Fertilisers Ltd.* v. *Deputy Commissioner of Commercial Taxes*[55a] the Supreme Court observed that the choice between a strict and a liberal construction arises only in case of doubt in regard to the intention of the legislature manifest on the statutory language. Indeed, the need to resort to any interpretative process arises only where the meaning is not manifest in the plain words of the statute. If the words are plain and clear and directly convey the meaning, there is no need for any interpretation.

---

54. *CIT* v. *National Taj Traders* AIR 1980 SC 485.

55. *Eagle Flask Industries Ltd.* v. *Commissioner of Central Excise* 2004 Supp (4) SCR 35.

55a. 1991 (55) ELT 437 (SC).

Purposive interpretation

Courts rely on various forms of evidence to locate the meaning of the text. These are statutory text; legislative intent; agency interpretation and judicial precedents. There are many purposes. Immediate purposes, general purposes, objective purposes, and subjective purposes. An eminent scholar Aaron Barak in Purposive Interpretation in Law (2005) states that subjective purposes are those which can be attributed specifically to the legislature enacting the law; while objective purposes are those which one can assume were the goals of a rational thinking legislature.

Justice SB Sinha in *Jeet Singh Bist* case[55b] has observed that it is not the mere blackletter in law which guides the interpretation but the goal which is embodied by that particular body of law, which may be termed the rationality of law. Purposive interpretation, lately, has gained considerable currency, which is relevant for the sake of maximizing the efficiency with respect to the point behind the rule.

The above observations which may have appropriateness in constitutional interpretation but is required to be seen more cautiously in the interpretation of an Act of Parliament. These observations made in 2008 by the author, require consideration. Now, it is almost established that purposive interpretation is a better approach to interpreting statutory enactments including the Constitution.

In *Southern Coalfield*[56], the purposive rule was applied. The issue for determination was whether the workshop in question could be said to be situated within the precincts of mine. Notification number 63/95 dated 16 March 1995 exempted all goods manufactured in the mine. Mine shall have meaning as assigned to it in section 2(1)(*g*) of the Mines Act. The workshop was declared mine by a notification under Section 82 of the Mines Act. In the present case, the court found that the word ' precincts' is not a word of clear import which has a single clear-cut meaning. The word 'precincts' does not have a single meaning rather it has several meanings. It was held that the purposive rule should be applied. The word precincts have to be given a wider meaning. In other words, we have to interpret the word precincts in the exemption notification to mean the surrounding region or area. The courts have to interpret the notification so as to include a workshop within the definition of mine for the purpose of grant of exemption as that would encourage the mining industry.

The legislature often uses open texture language which is susceptible to varying interpretation. For example, section 260A is open textual and does not specify the High Court before which an appeal under section 260A of the Act would lie. Should it be the High Court of the State in which the ITAT is physically located or the High Court of the State in which the assessee is residing and/or doing its business or the High Court where the Assessing Officer who assessed the assessee is located? Recently, the Supreme Court stated that a judicial remedy

55b. (2007) 6 SCC 586.

56. *Southern Eastern Coalfields Limited* v. *CCE* (2006) 6 SCC 340/[2006] 2006 taxmann.com 1792 (SC).

must be effective, independent and at the same time certain. Certainty of forum would involve unequivocal vesting of jurisdiction to adjudicate and determine the dispute in a named forum. The Supreme Court held that the appellate jurisdiction of a High Court under Section 260A is exercisable by a High Court within whose territorial jurisdiction the assessing officer is located[57].

Contextual interpretation

In *Apex Laboratory*[58], freebies to medical practitioners were disallowed under section 37 of the Income-tax Act, 1961. Justice S. Ravindra Bhat observed that a narrow interpretation of *Explanation* 1 to Section 37(1) defeats the purpose for which it was inserted, *i.e.*, to disallow an assessee from claiming a tax benefit for its participation in an illegal activity... Thus, pharmaceutical companies' gifting freebies to doctors, etc. is clearly "prohibited by law", and not allowed to be claimed as a deduction under Section 37(1). Doing so would wholly undermine public policy. The well-established principle of interpretation of taxing statutes - that they need to be interpreted strictly - cannot sustain when it results in an absurdity contrary to the intentions of the Parliament.... the incentives (or "freebies") given by Apex, to the doctors, had a direct result of exposing the recipients to the odium of sanctions, leading to a ban on their practice of medicine. Those sanctions are mandated by law, as they are embodied in the Code of Conduct and ethics, which are normative, and have legally binding effects. The Supreme Court referred to the memorandum explaining the provisions of the Finance Bill and stated that though the memorandum to the Finance Bill, 1998 elucidated the ambit of *Explanation 1* to include "protection money, extortion, hafta, bribes, etc.", yet, *ipso facto*, by no means is the embargo envisaged restricted to those examples. The object of all the rules of interpretation is to give effect to the object of the enactment having regard to the language used. While a literal construction may be the general rule in construing taxing enactments, it does not mean that it should be adopted even if it leads to a discriminatory or incongruous result. Interpretation of statutes cannot be a mechanical exercise.[59]

In *M/s. Mitsubishi Corporation*[60], the issue involved related to the liability of an assessee to pay interest on short payment of advance tax due to default of the payer in not deducting tax at the time of payment, under the provisions of the Income-tax Act, 1961. The Supreme Court rejected the contention of the revenue that Section 234B should be read in isolation without reference to the other provisions of Chapter XVII. The dispute related to the interpretation of the words "would be deductible or collectible" in Section 209(1)(*d*) of the

57. *Pr. Commissioner of Income Tax* v. *ABC Papers Ltd.* [Civil Appeal No. 4252 of 2022 *three judges bench* decided on August 18, 2022]/[2022] 141 taxmann.com 332/289 Taxman 150 (SC).

58. *Apex Laboratories Pvt. Ltd.* v. *Deputy Commissioner of Income Tax* [Special Leave Petition (Civil) No. 23207 of 2019 decided on 22-2-2022]/[2022] 135 taxmann.com 286/286 Taxman 200 (SC).

59. *C.W.S. (India) Ltd.* v. *CIT* 1994 Supp. (2) SCC 296.

60. *Director of Income Tax, New Delhi* v. *Mitsubishi Corporation* [Civil Appeal No. 1262 of 2016 decided by a bench of two judges on, September 17, 2021]/[2021] 130 taxmann.com 276/283 Taxman 273 (SC).

Act. The dispute was resolved by referring to the proviso to Section 209(1)(*d*), which was inserted by the Finance Act, 2012. The proviso makes it clear that the assessee cannot reduce the amounts of income tax paid to it by the payer without deduction while computing liability for advance tax. The memorandum explaining the provisions of the Finance Bill, 2012 provides the necessary context that the amendment was warranted due to the judgments of courts, interpreting Section 209(1)(*d*) of the Act to permit computation of advance tax by the assessee by reducing the amount of income-tax which is deductible or collectible during the financial year. If the construction of the words "would be deductible or collectible" as placed by the Revenue is accepted, the amendment made to Section 209(1)(*d*) by insertion of the proviso would be meaningless and an exercise in futility. Therefore. to give the intended effect to the proviso, Section 209(1)(*d*) of the Act has to be understood to entitle the assessee, for all assessments prior to the financial year 2012-13, to reduce the amount of income tax which would be deductible or collectible, in the computation of its advance tax liability, notwithstanding the fact that the assessee has received the full amount without deduction.

Recent Cases in UK and India (GST and Income tax)

Recent cases in U.K.

The approach of UK courts in other cases is as under—

In Hancock[61], the Supreme Court agreed with the Court of Appeal that although the wording of the carve out could be read literally in favour of the taxpayers, that result would be contrary to Parliament's intention. Therefore, the appellant's claim for relief failed. Instead, they were entitled to rollover relief deferring tax to redemption. In the appeal before the Supreme Court, Mr. and Mrs. Hancock showed that the redemption of the loan notes issued to them in connection with the sale of their shares in their company, Blubeckers Ltd., fell outside the charge to Capital Gains Tax ("CGT") by virtue of the exemption in section 115 of the Taxation of Chargeable Gains Act, 1992 ("TCGA") for disposals of "qualifying corporate bonds" ("QCBs"). TCGA confers "rollover relief" on the disposal of securities as part of a reorganisation, *i.e.*, it brings securities issued as consideration into charge for CGT purposes but defers the tax until their subsequent realisation. This is less favourable to the taxpayer than the exemption in TCGA, section 115. The roll-over provisions constitute a carve-out from the exemption in TCGA, section 115.

In UBS[62] the issue concerned with composite transactions designed to avoid the payment of income tax on bankers' bonuses. UBS AG, a well-known bank, devised an employee bonus scheme. The scheme involved the carrying out of a number of pre-ordained steps according to a detailed time-table. UBS agreed

61. *Hancock and another* v. *Commissioners for Her Majesty's Revenue and Customs* [2019] UKSC 24.

62. *UBS AG* v. *Commissioners for Her Majesty's Revenue and Customs* [2016] UKSC 13.

which of its employees were to be awarded a discretionary bonus. In this case, the issue was whether, in section 423(1) of the Income Tax (Earnings and Pensions) Act, 2003, the words "any contract, agreement, arrangement or condition which makes provision to which any of sub-sections (2) to (4) applies" should be construed as referring to "provision" with a genuine business or commercial purpose. The Supreme Court held that the reference in section 423(1) to "any contract, agreement, arrangement or condition which makes provision to which any of sub-sections (2) to (4) applies" is to be construed as being limited to provision having a business or commercial purpose, and not to commercially irrelevant conditions whose only purpose is the obtaining of the exemption. Ordinarily, the award to an employee of shares in a company by reason of his employment gives rise under ordinary tax rules to a charge to income tax on the market value of the shares at that time, even where the shares are subject to a condition or restriction affecting their value. Section 425(2) confers an exemption from income tax in respect of the acquisition of employment-related securities where they are restricted securities by virtue of section 423(2) at the time of the acquisition and will cease to be restricted securities by virtue of that provision within the next five years.

Birmingham City Council[63] emphasised that ordinary meaning is used for interpreting a definition clause. Although successor is a defined expression, the ordinary meaning of the word is part of the material which can be used to construe the definition. In this case, the House of Lords was construing section 88(1) of the Housing Act, 1985. The issue was whether the events to which section 88(1) refers are events in relation to tenancies which have become secure tenancies and also to events which happened earlier. House of Lords held that the events to which section 88(1) refers are events in relation to tenancies which have become secure tenancies and not to events which happened earlier. In support of this construction, the House of Lords relied on three indications. First, the general presumption against retrospectivity. One does not expect rights conferred by the statute to be destroyed by events which took place before it was passed. Secondly, the word "successor" most naturally means successor to a secure tenancy. Although successor is a defined expression, the ordinary meaning of the word is part of the material which can be used to construe the definition. Thirdly, there is the absence of any rational purpose in giving the definitions a retrospective effect.

The issue in the Airtours Holidays[63a] case was whether PwC supplied services to Airtours Holidays. Thus, whether the payments made by Airtours were simply third-party consideration for services provided by PwC exclusively to the Banks, or whether they were at the same time consideration for services provided to Airtours itself. The majority[64] held that where the person who pays the supplier is not entitled under the contractual documentation to receive any services

63. *Birmingham City Council* v. *Walker* [2007] UKHL 22.

63a. *Airtours Holidays Transport Limited* v. *Commissioners for Her Majesty's Revenue and Customs* [2016] UKSC 21.

64. Lord Neuberger (with whom Lord Mance and Lord Hodge agree).

from the supplier, then, unless the documentation does not reflect the economic reality, the payer has no right to reclaim by way of input tax the VAT in respect of the payment to the supplier. It was also observed that decisions about the application of the VAT system are highly dependent upon the factual situations involved. A small modification of the facts can render the legal solution in one case inapplicable to another. In view of dissenting judges[65], the contractual position is generally the most useful starting point for the VAT analysis. It is inappropriate to resolve the appeal on a narrow legalistic approach to the construction of the Contract, particularly where the distinction between services to Airtours and services to the Institutions is unlikely to have been seen as of any practical significance to the parties.

The issue in WHA Ltd.[65a] was whether there is a supply of repair services for the purposes of WHA's business by the garages to WHA, as well as or instead of a supply of services to the insured, on which WHA may claim a deduction of input tax. The Supreme Court held that there is no supply of repair services by the garages to WHA. Thus, when determining the relevant supply in which a taxable person engages, regard must be had to all the circumstances in which the transaction in question takes place. In the appeal, WHA does not bear the burden of the VAT paid to the garage: it pays the garage out of the float provided by discount, and its profit or loss is unaffected by the VAT.

Recent cases in India

GST Law

Parliament and the State Legislatures have the power to make laws governing goods and services tax. The tax is on the supply of goods and services. It will include both sales and consignments. While "sale" is for consideration, "consignments" are in the nature of branch transfers. The input tax credit would be available for GST paid on both sales as well as consignments in the course of inter-State trade. The expression "reverse charge" denotes the liability of the recipient of the supply of goods or services or both to pay tax instead of the supplier. The term "recipient" has been defined with reference to three situations (i) when consideration is payable for the supply of goods or services or both; (ii) when no consideration is payable for the supply of goods; and (iii) when no consideration is payable for the supply of services. In the first situation, the recipient is the person by whom consideration is payable. In the second situation, the recipient is the person to whom (a) the goods are delivered or made available; or (b) possession or the use of the goods is given or made available. The rates of GST are to be recommended by the GST Council depending on various factors such as economic conditions, revenue buoyancy, etc. At the same time, every effort would be made by the GST Council to ensure that the rate of GST is reasonable. Further, there may be certain demerit goods such as tobacco, or luxury goods, that may, if the GST Council so decides, attract a higher rate of GST.

65. Lord Carnworth and Lord Clarke.

65a. *WHA Limited and another* v. *Her Majesty's Revenue and Customs* [2013] UKSC 24.

Since the advent of the GST regime in 2017, the Supreme Court of India has delivered a number of landmark judgments. Some of them are discussed below.

Skill Lotto Solutions[66] is a landmark judgment on the definition of the expression 'goods. In this case, the levy of GST on lotteries was held constitutional. The Supreme Court reiterated that a tax law may be challenged under Article 32 of the Constitution. The Supreme Court looked into the definition of the expression 'goods' in the Constitution of India and in the Sales of the Goods Act besides looking into the definition as given the Central Goods and Services Tax Act. The inclusion of only one actionable claim namely, 'lottery' in the definition was held reasonable. Thus, the Supreme Court held that the definition of goods under section 2(*52*) of the Act, 2017 does not violate any constitutional provision nor it is in conflict with the definition of goods given under Article 366(12).

VKC Footsteps India Pvt Ltd.[67] is a landmark judgment on refund of tax. VKC Footsteps involved the interpretation of the expression "inputs" in section 54(3)(*ii*) of the CGST Act and the definition of "Net ITC" in the amended rule 89(5). Section 54(3) provides for a claim of refund of unutilised ITC. Supreme Court looked at the structure of section 54(3). The main part of section 54(3)(*i*) permits: (*i*) a claim; (*ii*) in the nature of refund; (*iii*) of any unutilized ITC; and (*iv*) at the end of the tax period. The Supreme Court pointed out that the use of the word 'any' in the main clause of section 54(3) uses the expression "any unutilised ITC". On the other hand, the expression 'any' is conspicuous by its absence in all three provisos. Another difference in the language of the main provision and of the proviso pointed out by the Supreme Court is that the main clause of section 54(3) uses the expression "a registered person may claim refund" while on the other hand, the three provisos have employed a restrictive expression or a negative expression, that is, "no refund of unutilized ITC shall be allowed". Thus, the Supreme Court interpreted the provisos under section 54(3) as restrictions and not as qualifications. The expression 'qualifications' is to be understood as eligibility requirements.

The Supreme Court while rejecting the claim of refund on unutilised inputs on services observed that Parliament has rightly used the expression 'unutilised ITC' both in the main clause and in the first proviso to deal with zero-rated supplies and restricted refund to those arising out of 'inputs' when it comes to an inverted structure. Parliament could not have used the expression 'inputs' in the main clause and first proviso as this would act as a disability to zero-rated supplies where Parliament intended to grant a refund arising out of both input goods and input services. Parliament has therefore appropriately employed the expression 'unutilized ITC' in the main clause and the first proviso and has used the limited expression 'inputs' in sub-clause (*ii*) to the first proviso in the inverted structure. In view of the Supreme Court, the refund of tax can be regulated by a law. This right is not a constitutionally protected right.

---

66. *Skill Lotto Solutions* v. *Union of India* (2021) 15 SCC 667 (SC).

67. *Union of India* v. *VKC Footsteps India (P) Ltd.* (2022) 2 SCC 603/[2021] 130 taxmann.com 193/52 GSTL 513 (SC).

VKS Footsteps reiterated some well-established legal prepositions. Firstly, The refund of taxes is neither a fundamental right nor a constitutional right. The Constitution only guarantees that the levy should be legal and that the collection should be in accordance with law. There is no constitutional right to refund. Refund is always a matter of a statutory prescription and can be regulated by the statute subject to conditions and limitations. Secondly, the legislature is entitled to the widest latitude when it identifies categories of classification, and unless things constituting the same class are treated differently without a rationale, the provision cannot be declared as unconstitutional. Thirdly, Exemptions, concessions, and exceptions have to be treated at par and must be strictly construed. Fourthly, A legislative amendment which reflects a policy choice is not subject to judicial review. Fifthly, A proviso may not be only an exception but may constitute a restriction on the operation of the main statutory provision.

Mohit Minerals[68] is a landmark decision of the Supreme Court on GST. Besides adjudicating the issue before it the Supreme Court reiterated well-settled prepositions of taxation law, such as cannons of taxation, and extra-territorial operation of tax law, and explained the nature of the decision of the GST Council and problems in the working of the GST regime.

The four cannons of taxation law are (*i*) The taxable event; (*ii*) The person on whom the levy is imposed; (*iii*) The rate at which the levy is imposed; and (*iv*) The measure or the value to which the rate will be applied. These are also essential legislative functions. On the extra-territoriality of the taxation law, the Supreme Court reiterated that the power of Parliament to legislate over events occurring extra-territorially. The only requirement imposed by the Court is that such an event must have a real connection to India. On the problems in the implementation of the GST, the Supreme Court reproduced the observations of the Gujarat High Court that the difficulty which is being experienced today in the proper implementation of the GST is because of the erroneous misconception of law, or rather, erroneous assumption on the part of the delegated legislation that service tax is an independent levy as it was prior to the GST and it go vivisect the transaction of supply to levy more taxes on certain components completely overlooking or forgetting the basic concept of composite supply introduced in the GST legislation and the very idea of levying the GST. *Prima facie*, it appears that while issuing the impugned notification, the delegated legislature had in mind the provision of the Finance Act, 1994, rather than keeping in mind the object of bringing the GST by making the Constitutional (101st) Amendment Act, 2016 to merge all taxes levied on the goods and services to one tax known as the GST. On the binding nature of the GST Council, the Supreme Court held that the recommendations of the GST Council are not binding on the Union and States.

The issue for consideration in Mohit Minerals was whether imported goods procured on a CIF basis constitute an inter-state supply or is it an extra-terri-

68. *Union of India* v. *Mohit Minerals (P.) Ltd.* [2022] 138 taxmann.com 331/61 GSTL 257/ 92 GST 101 (SC).

torial tax? And if so, whether the importer of goods can be considered as the recipient of the service of shipping in CIF contracts?

The IGST Act confers the powers on the Central Government, in consultation with the GST Council, to designate imports as a supply of services under section 5(3) of the IGST. The second issue is whether the importer can be considered as the recipient of such supply, liable to pay tax on a reverse charge basis. Thirdly, the Court had to determine if the Central Government, in consultation with the GST Council, has the powers to designate the importer as a recipient of service under 5(4) of the IGST Act, when goods are imported on a CIF basis. The Supreme Court considered the Preamble to the IGST Act and the scheme of Chapter IV and Chapter IX of the IGST Act. Section 5(3) of the IGST Act provides the Government the power to specify categories of supply of goods or services or both on which tax shall be paid on a reverse charge basis by the recipient. The Government is to exercise this power on the recommendation of the GST Council.

While striking down a part of the notification the Supreme Court observed that having paid the IGST on the amount of freight which is included in the value of the imported goods, the impugned notifications levying tax again as a supply of service, without any express sanction by the statute, are illegal and liable to be struck down. The nature of the CIF Contract was explained by the Supreme Court by observing that In a CIF contract, the supply of goods is accompanied by the supply of services of transportation and insurance, the responsibility for which lies on the seller (the foreign exporter in this case). The supply of service of transportation by the foreign shipper forms a part of the bundle of supplies between the foreign exporter and the Indian importer, on which the IGST is payable under section 5(1) of the IGST Act read with section 20 of the IGST Act, Section 8 and section 2(30) of the CGST Act. To levy the IGST on the supply of the service component of the transaction would contradict the principle enshrined in Section 8 and be in violation of the scheme of the GST legislation. Based on this reason, we are of the opinion that while the impugned notifications are validly issued under section 5(3) and 5(4) of the IGST Act, it would be in violation of section 8 of the CGST Act and the overall scheme of the GST legislation.

Delhi International Airport was served a notice for the payment of GST on UDF levy. The Supreme Court held that UDF is a statutory levy. The activities performed by the sovereign/public authorities under the provision of law are in the nature of statutory obligations. If such authority performs a service, which is not in the nature of statutory activity and the same is undertaken for a consideration not in the nature of statutory fee/levy, then in such cases, service tax would be leviable, if the activity undertaken falls within the ambit of a taxable service. In this case, the revenue's appeals failed and were dismissed[69].

69. *Central GST Delhi* v. *Delhi International Airport Ltd.* [Civil Appeal No(s). 8996 of 2019 two judge's bench decision dated 19th May 2023]/(2023) 152 taxmann.com 324 (SC)/[2023] 6 Centax 199 (SC).

Radha Krishan Industries[70] is a landmark judgment on the power of the provisional attachment under the State GST Act. The Supreme reiterated that the High Court's power under Article 226 of the Constitution is a very wide power and in suitable cases, adequate relief is to be given to a petitioner. On the power of the provisional attachment, the Supreme Court held that the power to order a provisional attachment of the property of the taxable person including a bank account is draconian in nature and the conditions which are prescribed by the statute for a valid exercise of the power must be strictly fulfilled. The exercise of the power to order a provisional attachment must be preceded by the formation of an opinion by the Commissioner that it is necessary so to do for the purpose of protecting the interest of the government revenue. Before ordering a provisional attachment, the Commissioner must form an opinion on the basis of tangible material that the assessee is likely to defeat the demand, if any, and that therefore, it is necessary so to do for the purpose of protecting the interest of the government revenue. The expression "necessary so to do for protecting the government revenue" implicates that the interests of the government revenue cannot be protected without ordering a provisional attachment. The formation of an opinion by the Commissioner under section 83(1) must be based on tangible material bearing on the necessity of ordering a provisional attachment for the purpose of protecting the interest of the government revenue.

Quick Heal Technology[71] is an important decision on the taxability of anti-virus software prior to the GST regime. The expression 'goods' has been given a meaning in the taxation laws different from its ordinary meaning under the Sales of Goods Act 1930. The test to determine whether a property is 'goods' for the purpose of sales tax, is not confined to whether the goods are tangible or intangible, or incorporeal. The correct test would be to determine whether an item is capable of abstraction, consumption, and use and whether it can be transmitted, delivered, stored, possessed, etc. The Supreme Court held that the software put in the CD is goods and hence service tax cannot be levied.

Recent cases of Income tax

Strict construction

The principle that provisions and exemptions under taxation statutes are to be strictly interpreted in accordance with legislative intent is well settled. The principle that provisions and exemptions under taxation statutes are to be strictly interpreted in accordance with legislative intent without any addition or subtraction was upheld In Arcelor Mittal[72] and Augustan Textile[73]. In M/S. D.N. Singh[74] section 69A of the Income-tax Act, 1961 was construed strictly and

70. *Radha Krishan Industries* v. *State of H.P.* (2021) 6 SCC 771.

71. *Commissioner of Service Tax* v. *Quick Heal Technologies Ltd.* (2023) 5 SCC 469.

72. *State of Gujarat* v. *Arcelor Mittal Nippon Steel India Ltd.* (2022) SCC OnLine SC 76.

73. *Augustan Textile Colours Ltd.* v. *Director of Industries* [Civil Appeal No. 2830/2022]/(2022) 6 SCC 626/[2022] 137 taxmann.com 166/172 SCL 191 (SC).

74. *D.N. Singh* v. *Commissioner of Income Tax* [Civil Appeal Nos. 3738-3739 of 2023 Two judges bench decision dated 16th May 2023].

it was held that bitumen does not fall in the term any other valuable article in section 69A of the Income-tax Act, 1961. In his concurring opinion, Justice Hrishikesh Roy observed that for purposes of interpreting section 69A of the Income-tax Act, 1961- the ordinary and literal meaning should be opted as the words in the statute are clear and unambiguous. The provision does not need any addition or subtraction and stands on its own legs. The phrase 'valuable article' would simply mean an item 'worth a great deal of money'. It cannot mean, as is said in the impugned order, to include 'any article of value'. Therefore, in the context of section 69A, unexplained valuable article has to be high-priced item which are procured to hide income, to avoid tax liability. To adopt a wide interpretation for the phrase- 'valuable article' and thereby include within its scope any sundry article of whatever value, is found to be unjustified. It needs to be also reiterated that, ordinarily, fiscal laws including taxation statutes, are to be strictly interpreted and tax must not be imposed through analogy, inference, or by extension of phrases used by the legislature. For purpose of section 69A of the Income-tax Act, it is therefore declared that- an 'article' shall be considered 'valuable' if the concerned article is a high-priced article commanding a premium price. As a corollary, an ordinary 'article' cannot be bracketed in the same category as the other high priced articles like bullion, gold, jewellery mentioned in section 69A by attributing high value to the run-of-the-mill article, only on the strength of its bulk quantity. To put it in another way, it is not the ownership of huge volume of some low-cost ordinary article but the precious gold and the like, that would attract the implication of deemed income under section 69A.

In AMD Industries[75], it was held that an exemption notification/exemption provision, the same is required to be construed literally and the person claiming the exemption must satisfy all the conditions of exemption provision. In this case, *Explanation* 5 to section 4A(5) of the UP Trade Act, which grants exemption from payment of trade tax to units, which had undertaken 'diversification' in their units on or after 31.03.1995 has been interpreted literally to mean diversification and not modernisation of units.

In Augustan Textile Colours Limited[76], it was held that, the 2004 government order of the Kerala Government granting tax exemptions should be read as a whole and in absence of any time line being prescribed, such a time line in the G.O. cannot be imported from the 1994 government order following the strict and literal rule of construction.

True interpretation

In US Technologies[77], the question involved the meaning and scope of the words 'fails to deduct'. The levy of penalty on the failure to deduct TDS is provided

75. *AMD Industries Limited (Earlier known as Ashoka Metal Décor Pvt. Ltd.)* v. *Commissioner of Trade Tax Lucknow* [Civil Appeal No. 108 of 2013]/(2023) 4 SCC 231/2 Centax 126 (SC).

76. *Augustan Textile Colours Limited* v. *Director of Industries* [Civil Appeal No. 2830 of 2022]/(2022) 6 SCC 626/137 taxmann.com 166/172 SCL 191 (SC).

77. *US Technologies* v. *CIT* [Civil Appeal No. 7934 of 2021 dated 10th April 2023]/[2023] 149 taxmann.com 144/293 Taxman 27 (SC).

in section 271C of the Income-tax Act, 1961. In this case, the assessee made a belated or delayed payment of the TDS. Supreme Court analysed sections 201 and 271 and 276B of the Income-tax Act,1961, and held that on the true interpretation of section 271C, there shall not be any penalty under section 271C on mere delay in remittance of the TDS after deducting the same by the concerned assessee. Supreme Court observed that the penal provisions are required to be construed strictly and literally.

In Vile Parle Kelvani Mandal[78], the question was whether the charitable institutions registered under the provisions of the Maharashtra Public Trust Act, 1950 are entitled to exemption from the payment of the electricity duty under the Maharashtra Electricity Duty Act, 2016. It was held that on the true interpretation of section 3(2)(*iii*) of the Maharashtra Electricity Duty Act, 2016 where the words used are plain and simple and are capable of only one meaning there is no exemption provided to the charitable institutions from the payment of electricity duty.

Expenditure includes loss also

Section 37 of the Income-tax Act, 1961 allows business expenditure as an allowable deduction. An important question has been whether business loss suffered because of an illegal activity is an allowable deduction or not. Recently, in Prakash Chand Lunia[79] Supreme Court held that the word 'any expenditure' mentioned in section 37 of the Act takes in its sweep loss occasioned in the course of business, being incidental to it. However, in terms of *Explanation*, 1 to section 37 of the Act any loss incurred by way of an expenditure by an assessee for any purpose which is an offence or which is prohibited by law is not deductible and an expenditure/loss incurred for any purpose which is an offence shall not be deemed to have been incurred for the purpose of business or profession or incidental to it, and hence, no deduction can be made. A penalty or a confiscation is a proceeding in rem, and therefore, a loss in pursuance to the same is not available for deduction regardless of the nature of business, as a penalty or confiscation cannot be said to be incidental to any business.

Exercise of discretionary power by the Settlement Commission

Kotak Mahindra Bank Limited[80], Supreme Court observed that any judicial, *quasi judicial*, or administrative authority must while exercising discretion, direct itself properly in law and consider all the facts and material that it is bound to consider while excluding from consideration irrelevant aspects of

---

78. *The State of Maharashtra* v. *Vile Parle Kelvani Mandal* [Civil Appeal No. 3327 decided by a bench of two judges dated July 07, 2022].

79. *CIT* v. *Prakash Chand Lunia (D) Thr. Lrs* [Civil Appeal Nos. 7689-90 of 2022 decided by a Two Judges Bench dated April 24, 2023]/[2023] 149 taxmann.com 416/293 Taxman 229 (SC). The silver bars confiscated by the customs authorities was not allowed as business loss and consequently, value allowing the same as business loss was held unsustainable.

80. *Kotak Mahindra Bank Limited* v. *Commissioner of Income Tax*, [Civil Appeal No. 9720 of 2014 Two Judge's Bench decision decided on 25th September, 2023]/[2023] 154 taxmann.com 545/295 Taxman 588 (SC).

the matter. A constitutional court (under Article 32, article 136, or Article 226 of the Constitution) may not interfere with an order of the Commission, passed in the exercise of its discretionary powers, except on the ground that the order contravenes provisions of the Act or has caused prejudice to the opposite party. Interference may also be open on the grounds of fraud, bias, or malice. A word of caution has been given by the Supreme Court that having regard to the legislative intent, frequent interference with the orders or proceedings of the Settlement Commission should be avoided. Thus, the scope of interference is very limited and narrow for judicial review of the Settlement Commission's orders, passed in the exercise of its discretionary powers. The Supreme Court declared the law by observing that the High Court should not scrutinize an order or proceeding of a Settlement Commission as an appellate court. Unsettling reasoned orders of the Settlement Commission may erode the confidence of the *bona fide* assessees, thereby leading to a multiplicity of litigation where settlement is possible. This larger picture has to be borne in mind.

Deduction under section 80P Income-tax Act, 1961

In KSCARDB[81], the controversy was whether the KSCARDB is a co-operative bank and if so, it would be covered within the scope and meaning of sub-section (4) of Section 80P and therefore, would not be eligible for the benefit of deduction as provided therein. It was held that the apex cooperative society is not a cooperative bank and hence is entitled to deduction under section 80P. It was held that Section 80P of the Act is a benevolent provision which is enacted by Parliament in order to encourage and promote the growth of the cooperative sector in the economic life of the country. Therefore, such a provision has to be read liberally, reasonably, and in favour of the assessee with a view to effectuate the object of the Legislature and not to defeat it. Therefore, all those cooperative societies which fall within the purview of section 80P of the Act are entitled to a deduction in respect of any income referred to in sub-section (2) of section 80P. Supreme Court took note of the marginal note of section 80P, the scheme of section 80P, and the definition in the Banking Regulation Act, 1948.

Section 80-IB Income-tax Act, 1961

M/s. Saraf Exports[82] the issue was whether the assessee is entitled to the deduction under section 80-IB of the Income-tax Act, 1961 with respect to the receipts under the Duty Drawback Scheme and on the transfer of Duty Entitlement Pass Book Scheme. Section 80-IB provides for deductions in respect of profits and gains from certain 'industrial undertakings' other than infrastructure development undertakings. The language used in section 80-IB with regard to calculating the deduction is that the deduction would be applicable on "any profits and gains 'derived from' any business referred to in..." included in the

81. *Kerala State Co-operative Agricultural and Rural Development Bank Ltd.* v. *Assessing Officer, Trivandrum* [Civil Appeal No(s).10069 of 2016 a Two Judges Bench decided on 14th September, 2023]/[2023] 154 taxmann.com 305/295 Taxman 675 (SC).

82. *Saraf Exports* v. *CIT* [Civil Appeal No. 4822 of 2022 decided by a Two-Judges' Bench on 10th April 2023]/[2023] 149 taxmann.com 145/293 Taxman 280 (SC).

gross total income of the assessee. Supreme Court held that the assessee shall not be entitled to the deductions under section 80-IB as such income cannot be said to be an income "derived from" industrial undertaking.

Surplus funds of clubs

In Secundrabad Club[83], a long-standing issue was settled by the Supreme Court whether the deposit of surplus funds by the appellant Clubs by way of bank deposits in various banks is liable to be taxed in the hands of the Clubs or, whether, the principle of mutuality would apply and the interest earned from the deposits would not be subject to tax under the provisions of the Income-tax Act, 1961. Supreme Court held that the interest income earned on fixed deposits made in the banks by the appellant Clubs has to be treated like any other income from other sources within the meaning of section 2(*24*) of the Income-tax Act, 1961.

The Secundrabad Club decision is a landmark judgment, particularly for explaining in detail what part of a judgment is binding. There have been a large number of writings on how to determine the ratio decidendi of a case. It is not everything said by a judge when giving judgment that constitutes a precedent. The only thing in a judge's decision binding a party is the principle upon which the case is decided and for this reason, it is important to analyse a decision and isolate from it the ratio decidendi. Even a dissenting opinion is important since the dissenting judgment refers to a principle of general application, not refuted by the majority. Every decision contains three basic ingredients: "(*i*) findings of material facts, direct and inferential. An inferential finding of facts is the inference which the Judge draws from the direct or perceptible facts; (*ii*) statements of the principles of law applicable to the legal problems disclosed by the facts; and (iii) judgment based on the combined effect of (*i*) and (*ii*) above." For the purposes of the parties themselves and their privies, ingredient (*iii*) is the material element in the decision for it determines finally their rights and liabilities in relation to the subject matter of the action. It is the judgment that estops the parties from reopening the dispute. However, for the purpose of the doctrine of precedents, ingredient (*ii*) is the vital element in the decision. This indeed is the *ratio decidendi*.

83. *Secundrabad Club* v. *CIT* [Civil Appeal No. 5195 of 2012 dated August 17, 2023, Nagarathna] 2023 INSC 736.

8 Tax Evasion, Tax Avoidance and Tax Mitigation

8.1 Tax evasion

Tax evasion denotes all those activities which are responsible for the person not paying tax that the existing law charges upon him. Such non-payment of tax may be because of failure to make his return or by making of deliberately fraudulent return or non-payment of tax at the proper time. Various steps have been taken from time to time to check evasion of tax. To prevent evasion of tax, it is necessary that each taxpayer is assessed properly and tax is properly paid by him. Coercive steps are taken to prevent evasion of tax. These include imposition of fines, interest, penalty, and prosecution.

The penalty of 100% provided under section 271(1)(*c*) of the Income-tax Act was challenged as unconstitutional in the case of Rahim Bhai[1]. The assessee challenged the said provision as violative of Article 14 of the Constitution as there was no classification though there was a difference between various types of tax evasion. The challenge was rejected by the Gujarat High Court in these words:

... the object of the Legislature in levying penalty is to provide deterrence against tax evasion and to put a stop to a practice which the Legislature considers to be against the public interest... The object of the Legislature in enacting the impugned provision is not to provide for confiscation but to provide a penalty for concealment of income and that too by providing a deterrent penalty.

The nature of penalty in tax law came up for consideration in *Sukhpal Singh*[2]. In this case, section 10(3) of the Uttar Pradesh Motor Vehicles Taxation Act,1997 was challenged as being discriminatory. The Allahabad High Court held the provision unconstitutional. Reversing the decision, the Supreme Court observed:

> "... we are of the view that the High Court had erred in striking down section 10(3) as *ultra vires* Article 14 and Article 19(*g*) of the Constitution. Penalty is a slippery word and it has to be understood in the context in which it is used in a given statute. Penalty may be a subject matter of a breach of statutory duty or it may be a subject matter of complaint. In ordinary parlance, the proceedings may cover penalties for avoidance of civil liability which do not constitute offences against the state. This distinction is responsible for any enactment intended to protect public revenue.

1. *Rahimbhai Karimbhai Nagriwala* v. *B.B. Patel* (1974) 97 ITR 660 (Gujarat).
2. *State of UP* v. *Sukhpal Singh Bal* (2005) 7 SCC 615.

> Thus, all penalties do not flow from an offence as is commonly understood but all offences lead to a penalty. Whereas the former is a penalty which flows from disregard of statutory provisions, the latter is entailed where there is *mens rea* and is made the subject- matter of adjudication. In our view, the penalty under section 10(3) of the Act is compensatory. It is levied for breach of statutory duty for non-payment of tax under the Act. Section 10(3) is enacted to protect public revenue. It is enacted as a deterrent for tax evasion. If statutory dues of the government are paid, there is no question of imposition of a heavy penalty. Everything which is incidental to the main purpose of a power is contained within the power itself. The power to impose a penalty is for the purpose of vindicating the main power which is conferred by the statute in question. Deterrence is the main theme or object behind the imposition of penalty under section 10(3)."

In view of the nature and character of a penal provision, it must be construed strictly regardless of the hardship it may put on the taxpayer or on the department. The principle of strict construction is to be applied in case the provisions is quasi-criminal in character. It is not applicable if the penalty is civil in nature.

In the *Gujarat Agency*[3], the Supreme Court held that the nature of the proceeding has to be examined having regard to the context under which the liability is created. If the liability reveals the civil liability only to ensure compliance through a coercive manner, then it is a civil liability without any criminal implication. But as soon as criminal liability is imposed by reason of default in compliance with statutory provisions the proceeding can be taken to be quasi criminal in nature.

Penal interest can be charged on delayed payment of tax only when the statute specifically so provides.[4]

8.2 Tax Interpretation and GAAR

The question of substance over form has consistently arisen in the implementation of taxation laws. Most countries have codified the "substance over form" doctrine in the form of a General Anti Avoidance Rule (GAAR) though specific anti-tax avoidance provisions exist in the tax laws of most of the common law countries.

USA

The courts in the USA have developed a variety of robust judicial doctrines to counter abusive avoidance schemes. These doctrines include the business purpose doctrine, the substance over form doctrine, the step transaction doctrine, and the assignment of income doctrine. Although distinct, these doctrines are closely related and generally reflect a willingness of the American Court to grapple with business and commercial realities in the tax arena.

3. *Gujarat Travancore Agency* v. *CIT* (1989) 177 ITR 455/44 Taxman 278 (SC).
4. *CIT* v. *Anjum M.H. Ghaswala* (2001) 252 ITR 1/119 Taxman 352 (SC).

UK

In the United Kingdom, there have been provisions, some narrow and others broad, to counter tax avoidance. Before 1970, judges used to regard tax avoidance with neutrality but that attitude has changed now. In *Ormond*[5], Lord Buckmaster said that the imposition of tax must be in plain terms. The rule was expressed by Lord Atkinson as under:

> " It is established that one is bound, in construing revenue Acts, to give fair and reasonable construction to their language without leaning to one side or the other, that no tax can be imposed on a subject by an Act of Parliament without words clearly showing an intention to lay the burden upon him, that the words of a statute must be adhered to, and that so called equitable construction of them are not permissible."

In the *Duke of Westminster*[6], Lord Tomlin observed:

> " It is said that in revenue cases there is a doctrine and that the courts may ignore the legal position and regard what is called the substance of the matter.... every man is entitled to order his affairs so that the tax attaching under the appropriate Acts is less than it otherwise would be. If he succeeds in ordering them so as to secure this result, then, however unappreciative the commissioner of Inland revenue or his fellow taxpayer may be of his ingenuity, cannot be compelled to pay an increased tax. This so-called doctrine of the substance seems to me to be nothing more than an attempt to make a man pay notwithstanding that he has so ordered his affairs that the amount of tax sought from him is not legally claimable."

The shift in the approach of the court started with Ramsay[7]. **Until the case of Ramsay, the interpretation of fiscal legislation was based predominantly on a linguistic analysis.** The facts in Ramsay involved an artificial, circular, self-cancelling transaction that could be used to create a non-taxable gain and a tax relievable loss. In this case, House of Lords adopted a new approach of the composite transaction doctrine. The court abandoned the old approach of treating every transaction which had an individual legal identity (such as payment of money, transfer of property, creation of debt, etc.) as having its own separate tax consequences.

The new approach of the composite transaction helped the court in finding out the real commercial characterization of the facts. The thrust of the new approach was to decide the genuineness of the transaction. The new approach became known as the **Ramsay doctrine,** holding that the court was entitled to look at the whole and composite transaction and to conclude that the taxpayer had not suffered a loss or had not made a non-taxable gain.

Burmah Oil[8] followed Ramsay. In this case, Lord Diplock observed as follows:

Lord Tomlin of quoted dictum in Westminster tells us a little or nothing as to what methods of ordering one's affairs will be recognised by the court as effective

5. *Ormond Investment Company* v. *Betts* (1928) AC 143.
6. *IRC* v. *Duke of Westminster* (1936) AC 1.
7. *W T Ramsay Ltd.* v. *IRC* [1981] AC 300 (HL).
8. *IRC* v. *Burmah Oil Co. Ltd.* [1982] STC 30.

to lessen the tax that would otherwise attached to them if business transactions were conducted in straight forward way... The kinds of tax-avoiding schemes that have occupied the attention of the court in recent years involve interconnected transactions between artificial persons, and limited companies, without minds of their own but directed by a single mastermind.

Equally important are the observations of Lord Steyn in *McGukian*[9] which are as follows:

While Lord Tomlin observations in the Duke of Westminster case still points to a material consideration, namely the general liberty of the citizens to arrange his financial affairs as he thinks fits, they have ceased to be canonical as to the consequences of a tax avoidance scheme.

Ramsay principles were formulated by the revenue in *Westmoreland Investment*[10] in the following terms:

when a court is asked—

(*a*) to apply a statutory provision on which the taxpayer relies for the sake of establishing some tax advantage;

(*b*) in circumstances where the transaction said to give rise to the tax advantage is, all forms part of, some pre-ordained, circular, self-cancelling transaction;

(*c*) which transaction though accepted as perfectly genuine (*i.e.*, not impeach as a sham) was undertaken for no commercial purpose other than the obtaining of tax advantage in question,

then, unless there is a something in the statutory provisions concerned to indicate that this rule should not be applied there is a rule of construction that condition laid down in the statute for the obtaining of tax advantages has not been satisfied.

The facts of the case were that Westmoreland was a company that owed 17 million pounds including 40 million pounds arrears of interest on loan from Pension Fund. The Pension Fund shareholders lent the money to Westmoreland, which passed it back as payment of interest. The facts thus disclosed a preordained series of transactions carried out in order to secure the payment of interest and a tax advantage in that Westmoreland had an allowable loss.

House of Lords acknowledged that the Ramsay approach is no more than a useful aid and the paramount question is of interpretation of the particular statutory provision and its application to the facts of the case and there was no room for revenues broadly formulated principle.

Scottish Provident[11] is another important case. Scottish Provident involved the transaction of cross-options by creating an untaxed profit prior to their intro-

9. *CIR* v. *McGukian* (1997) 1 WLR 991.

10. *MacNivern* v. *Westmoreland Investment Limited* (2001) STC 237/(2001) UKHL 6.

11. *Inland revenue* v. *Scottish Provident Institution* (2004) UKHL 52.

duction and an allowable loss after their introduction. House Of Lords defeated the transaction through the interpretation of the expression 'debt contract' having regard to the reality of the transaction.

Barclay[12] involved the interpretation of the Capital Allowance Act, 1990. The issue was whether in finance leasing the relevant expenditure is that incurred to acquire plant and machinery for the purpose of leasing in course of trade. The revenue attack on Barclay transaction was not based on the provisions of the capital allowance act but on judicial anti avoidance doctrine of Ramsay. The transaction in Barclay was a circular transaction. Barclay bought a gas pipeline from the Iris Gas board and leased it back to a subsidiary of Gas Board and took a bank guarantee from Barclay. The Iris Gas board guaranteed its subsidiary obligation to Barclay and deposited the sales proceeds with Barclay subsidiary as security. The usual schedule of final payment was to be ensured and Barclay would be paid as any secured lender would be expected to be paid.

In Barclay, the House of Lords held that a taxing statute is to be applied by reference to the ordinary principles of statutory construction, *i.e.* by giving the provision a purposive construction in order to identify its requirements and then deciding whether the actual transaction answers to the statutory description.

In *UBS*[13], Lord Reed stated the issue as under:

> "In our society, a great deal of intellectual effort is devoted to tax avoidance... The present appeals are concerned with composite transactions designed to avoid the payment of income tax on bankers' bonuses."

Later on, Lord Reed observed:

> "In our society, a great deal of intellectual effort is devoted to tax avoidance. **Taxing statutes generally draw their life-blood from real world transactions with real world economic effects ...**, the reference in section 423(1) of the **Income Tax (Earnings and Pensions) Act, 2003** to "any contract, agreement, arrangement or condition which makes provision to which any of sub-sections (2) to (4) applies" is to be construed as being limited to provision having a business or commercial purpose, and not to commercially irrelevant conditions whose only purpose is the obtaining of the exemption... Where schemes involve intermediate transactions inserted for the sole purpose of tax avoidance, it is quite likely that a purposive interpretation will result in such steps being disregarded for fiscal purposes."

GAAR in U.K.

Part V of the Finance Act, 2013 introduced the new "General Anti-Abuse Rule" designed in terms to counteract tax arrangements deemed to be "abusive". Tax arrangements are defined by reference to whether "having regard to all the circumstances, it would be reasonable to conclude that the obtaining of a tax advantage is the main purpose, or one of the main purposes, of the arrangements". "Abusive" is defined by reference to whether the arrangements are "a reasonable course of action in relation to the relevant tax provisions", having regard to all the circumstances including (*inter alia*) whether it uses "one or

---

12. *Barclays Mercantile Business Finance Ltd.* v. *Mawson* [2004] UKHL 51/[2005] 1 AC 684.
13. *UBS AG* v. *Commissioners for Her Majesty's Revenue and Customs* [2016] UKSC 13.

more contrived or abnormal steps", and "whether the arrangements are intended to exploit any shortcomings in those provisions".

Canada

GAAR provisions are contained in section 245 of the Income-tax Act, 1985. GAAR superimposed a prohibition on abusive tax avoidance, with the effect that the literal application of provisions of the Act may be seen as abusive in light of their context and purpose. GAAR applies both to the abuse of provisions found in the Act and to the abuse of provisions found in a tax treaty.

There are a number of cases. **In Loblaw Financing**[14] it was observed that statutory interpretation entails discerning legislative intent by examining statutory text in its entire context and in its grammatical and ordinary sense, in harmony with the statute's scheme and objects" **(*Michel* v. *Graydon*, 2020 SCC 24, at para 21).**

In *Alta Enery*[15], the question was whether allowing Alta Luxembourg the benefit of the exemption would be a misuse or an abuse of the provisions. On GAAR principles the Court observed as under:

> "First and foremost, tax avoidance is not tax evasion, and there is no suggestion by either party that the transaction in this case was evasive. In addition, tax avoidance should not be conflated with abuse. Even if a transaction was designed for a tax avoidance purpose and not for a *bona fide* non-tax purpose, such as an economic or commercial purpose, it does not mean that it is necessarily abusive within the meaning of the GAAR (Canada Trustco, at paras. 36 and 57; see also Lipson, at para. 38). The purpose of a transaction is relevant mainly to characterize it as either an avoidance transaction or a *bona fide* transaction and, specifically, to assess the abusive nature of the transaction. In their factual analysis, courts may consider whether an avoidance transaction was "motivated by any economic, commercial, family or other non-tax purpose" (Canada Trustco, at para. 58). However, a finding that a *bona fide* non-tax purpose is lacking, taken alone, should not be considered conclusive evidence of abusive tax avoidance."

Very recently, in *Deans Knight*[16], the Supreme Court of Canada dealt with a case involving a complex series of transactions circumventing the text of section 111(5) of the Income-tax Act,1985. Rowe J. speaking on behalf of majority observed:

> **"The use of a provision's text, context, and purpose to determine the rationale differs from traditional statutory interpretation.** Since in a GAAR analysis, the search is for the rationale that underlies the words, considering the provision's text, context and purpose ensures that the intrinsic and extrinsic evidence used to discern that rationale remains tied to the provision itself... "The object, spirit and purpose of a provision must be worded as a description of its rationale. A court is not repeating the test for the provision or crafting a new, secondary test; rather, the object, spirit and purpose is a concise description of the rationale underlying the provision, such as why relief is being provided, the conduct that Parliament sought to encourage, or the result or mischief that Parliament sought to prevent... **Understanding the provision's purpose is central to the GAAR analysis, and**

14. *Canada* v. *Loblaw Financial Holdings Inc.* 2021 SCC 51.
15. *Canada* v. *Alta Energy Luxembourg S.A.R.L.* 2021 SCC 49.
16. *Deans Knight Income Corp.* v. *Canada* 2023 SCC 16.

> **legislative history and extrinsic evidence provide insight into the rationale for specific provisions.**

Côté J in dissenting opinion observed:

> "The GAAR requires a careful balance between the interest of the taxpayer in minimizing his or her taxes through technically legitimate means and the legislative interest in ensuring the integrity of the income tax system. The majority's approach to determining the object, spirit and purpose of s. 111(5) fails to account for the central principle that the GAAR does not and cannot override Parliament's specific intent regarding particular provisions of the Act. **The GAAR analysis rests on the same interpretive approach employed by the Court in all questions of statutory interpretation, and is little more than a specialized form of statutory interpretation to determine Parliament's intent.** It should not be assumed that the GAAR plays a role in every transaction and in every context. There is agreement with the majority that there is no bar to applying the GAAR in situations where the Act specifies precise conditions that must be met to achieve a particular result, as with a specific anti avoidance rule; however, a provision's text can sometimes be conclusive and fully explain its underlying rationale."

India

Tax avoidance is the legal utilisation of the provisions of the tax laws in such a manner so as to minimise his tax liability. The tax laws however contain specific provision to counter the tax avoidance. In the Indian context, judicial decisions have varied. While some courts in certain circumstances had held that legal form of transactions can be dispensed with and the real substance of transaction can be considered while applying the taxation laws, others have held that the form is to be given sanctity. The existence of anti-avoidance principles is based on various judicial pronouncements. There are some specific anti-avoidance provisions but general anti-avoidance has been dealt only through judicial decisions in specific cases. Tax avoidance postulates that the assessee is in receipt of the amount which is really his income but on which avoids payment of tax by some artifice or device.

Raman and Mcdowell are to important decisions of the Supreme Court. In *Raman*[17], it was held that the avoidance of tax by so arranging commercial affairs that charge of tax is diminished is not prohibited. A taxpayer may resort to a device to divert the income before it accrues or arises to him. Effectiveness of device depends not upon consideration of morality, but on the operation of the Income-tax Act. In Raman case, the assessee was a firm, whose two partners were managers of two HUF. The goods were sold by the firm to HUF and in turn HUF sold them at a higher price and in this way, profits were made by HUF which would could have been made by the firm. The court held that it was not the income of the firm.

In *McDowell*[18], landmark judgment of the Supreme Court, the observations in Raman's case, were disapproved by the Supreme Court, in these words:

> ... tax planning may be legitimate provided it is within the law. Colourable devices cannot be part of tax planning. It is wrong to encourage or entertain the belief that

17. *CIT* v. *A Raman* & Co. (1968) 67 ITR 11 (SC).
18. *McDowell & Co. Ltd.* v. *Commercial Tax Officer* [1985] 154 ITR 148/22 Taxman 11 (SC).

it is honourable to avoid the payment of tax by resorting to dubious methods. It is the obligation of every citizen to pay tax honestly without resorting to subterfuges.

The reference to McDowell and tax avoidance was explained by Justice Sabyasachi *Mukherjee*[19] in these words:

> "...It is true that tax avoidance in an under-developed developing economy should not be encouraged on practical as well as ideological grounds. One would wish, as noted by Reddy, J. that one could get the enthusiasm of Justice Holmes that taxes are the price of civilization and one would like to pay that price to buy civilization. But the question which many ordinary tax-payers very often in a country of shortages with ostentatious consumption and deprivation for the large masses ask, is does he with taxes buy civilization or does he facilitate the wastes and ostentatiousness of the few. Unless wastes and ostentatiousness in Government's spendings are avoided or eschewed, no amount of moral sermons would change people's attitude to tax avoidance."

In Playworld Electronics[20], Justice Sabyasachi Mukherjee observed:

> "While it is true, as observed by Chinnappa Reddy, J. in *McDowell and Co. Ltd.* v. *Commercial Tax Officer*, too much to expect the legislature to intervene and take care of every device and scheme to avoid taxation and it is up to the court sometimes to take stock to determine the nature of the new and sophisticated legal devices to avoid tax and to expose the devices for what they really are and to refuse to give judicial' benediction, it is necessary to remember as observed by Lord Reid in *Greenberg* v. *IRC* [1971] 47 TC 240 (HL) that one must find out the true nature of the transaction. It is unsafe to make bad laws out of hard facts and one should avoid subverting the rule of law."

The decision in McDowell was explained by the high courts of Madras, Gujarat and Calcutta.

In *Minal's*[21] case, the Gujarat High Court did not approve the transaction in question after looking into the substance of the transaction. The court disagreed with the argument of the respondent that the observation of the Supreme Court in McDowell being obiter in nature need not be followed. The Gujarat High Court observed that obiter of the supreme court is entitled considerable weight as observed by the supreme court in Vazir Sultan[22].

In *Valliappan*[23], the Madras High Court did not agree with the argument that section 171(9) of the Income-tax Act should be upheld as a measure to prevent tax evasion. The court held

... we have gone through carefully the judgment in McDowell. That decision cannot in our view, be read as laying down that every attempt of tax planning is illegitimate and must be ignored or that every transaction or arrangement which is perfectly permissible under the law which has the effect of reducing the tax burden of the assessee, must be looked upon with disfavour ... it is only colourable devices adopted for evading the tax liability will have to be ignored.

---

19. *CWT* v. *Arvind Narottam* (1988) 4 SCC 113/[1988] 39 Taxman 368 (SC).
20. *Union of India* v. *Playworld Electronics (P.)* (1989) 3 SCC 181.
21. *CIT* v. *Smt. Minal Rameshchandra* (1987) 167 ITR 507/30 Taxman 282 (Gujarat).
22. *CIT* v. *Wazir Sultan and Sons* (1959) 36 ITR 175 (SC).
23. *MV Valliappan* v. *ITO* (1988) 170 ITR 238/37 Taxman 46 (Madras).

It appears to us on careful reading of that decision that legitimate transaction which does not amount to a dubious device is not hit even by the new approach adopted by the English courts. This is clear from the separate judgment of Rangnath Mishra J in McDowell which is as follows:

> "Tax planning may be legitimate provided it is within the framework of law. Colourable devices cannot be part of tax planning and it is wrong to encourage or entertain the belief that it is honourable to avoid the payment of tax by resorting to dubious methods. It is the obligation of every citizen to pay the taxes honestly without resorting to subterfuges."

In *Preeti Rungta*[24], the Calcutta High Court said that observations of the Supreme Court in McDowell do not amount to a direction to the court to ignore the provisions of law and embark upon an enquiry within the regulatory framework of the statute and decide an issue of tax evasion according to the court's personnel ideas of right or wrong.

Recently, in *South Indian Bank Ltd.*[25], Justice Hrishikesh Roy, observed:

> "...Echoing what was said by the 18th century economist[26], it needs to be observed here that in taxation regime, there is no room for presumption and nothing can be taken to be implied. **The tax an individual or a corporate is required to pay, is a matter of planning for a tax payer and the Government should endeavour to keep it convenient and simple to achieve maximization of compliance.** Just as the Government does not wish for avoidance of tax equally it is the responsibility of the regime to design a tax system for which a subject can budget and plan. If proper balance is achieved between these, unnecessary litigation can be avoided without compromising on generation of revenue."

What is significant in South India Bank is the recognition of tax planning by a taxpayer and advise to the government to design a tax system for which a subject can budget and plan. If proper balance is achieved between these, unnecessary litigation can be avoided without compromising on the generation of revenue.

The cost of litigation to the economy was highlighted and explained in the statement of objects and reasons to the Direct Tax Vivad se Vishwas Bill, 2020[27]. *SOR*[28] states as under:

---

24. *Preeti Rungta* v. *ITO* (1995) 154 ITR 594 (Calcutta).

25. *South Indian Bank Ltd.* v. *Commissioner of Income Tax* [Civil Appeal No. 9606 of 2011 date of decision 22 September 2021]/[2020] 130 taxmann.com 178/283 Taxman 178 (SC), Two Judges Bench.

26. *Ibid*. 29. In the above context, the following saying of Adam Smith in his seminal work – The Wealth of Nations may aptly be quoted: "The tax which each individual is bound to pay ought to be certain and not arbitrary. The time of payment, the manner of payment, the quantity to be paid ought all to be clear and plain to the contributor and to every other person."

27. Introduced on The 1st February, 2020. Enacted as Direct Tax Vivad se Vishwas Act, 2020.

28. Over the years, the pendency of appeals filed by taxpayers as well as Government has increased due to the fact that the number of appeals that are filed is much higher than the number of appeals that are disposed. As a result, a huge amount of disputed tax arrears is locked-up in these appeals. As on the 30th November, 2019, the amount of disputed direct tax arrears **is ₹ 9.32 lakh crores.** Considering that the actual direct tax collection in the financial year 2018-19 was ₹ 11.37 lakh crores, the disputed tax arrears constitute nearly one year direct tax collection.

"Tax disputes consume copious amounts of time, energy, and resources both on the part of the Government as well as taxpayers. Moreover, they also deprive the Government of the timely collection of revenue. Therefore, there is an urgent need to provide for the resolution of pending tax disputes. This will not only benefit the Government by generating timely revenue but also the taxpayers who will be able to deploy the time, energy and resources saved by opting for such dispute resolution towards their business activities."

8.3 Statutory framework on tax avoidance

In the Income-tax Bill,1961, Chapter X titled 'Special provisions relating to avoidance of tax' contained three clauses. These were titled 'Income from transaction with a non-resident, how computed in certain cases (clause 92); 'Avoidance of income-tax by transactions resulting in transfer to non-resident (clause 93)'; 'Avoidance of tax by certain transactions in securities'(clause 94). Now, the chapter titled 'Special provisions relating to avoidance of tax' contains 18 sections covering transfer pricing, Avoidance of income-tax by transactions resulting in transfer of income to non-residents[29], Avoidance of tax by certain transactions in securities[30], Special measures in respect of transactions with

29. 93. *Avoidance of income-tax by transactions resulting in transfer of income to non-residents.* — (1) Where there is a transfer of assets by virtue or in consequence whereof, either alone or in conjunction with associated operations, any income becomes payable to a non-resident, the following provisions shall apply.—

(*a*) where any person has, by means of any such transfer, either alone or in conjunction with associated operations, acquired any rights by virtue of which he has, within the meaning of this section, power to enjoy, whether forthwith or in the future, any income of a non-resident person which, if it were income of the first-mentioned person, would be chargeable to income-tax, that income shall, whether it would or would not have been chargeable to income-tax apart from the provisions of this section, be deemed to be income of the first-mentioned person for all the purposes of this Act;

(*b*) where, whether before or after any such transfer, any such first-mentioned person receives or is entitled to receive any capital sum the payment whereof is in any way connected with the transfer or any associated operations, then any income which, by virtue or in consequence of the transfer, either alone or in conjunction with associated operations, has become the income of a non-resident shall, whether it would or would not have been chargeable to income-tax apart from the provisions of this section, be deemed to be the income of the first-mentioned person for all the purposes of this Act.

Explanation.—The provisions of this sub-section shall apply also in relation to transfers of assets and associated operations carried out before the commencement of this Act.

30. 94. *Avoidance of tax by certain transactions in securities*—(1) Where the owner of any securities (in this sub-section and in sub-section (2) referred to as "the owner") sells or transfers those securities, and buys back or reacquires the securities, then, if the result of the transaction is that any interest becoming payable in respect of the securities is receivable otherwise than by the owner, the interest payable as aforesaid shall, whether it would or would not have been chargeable to income-tax apart from the provisions of this sub-section, be deemed, for all the purposes of this Act, to be the income of the owner and not to be the income of any other person.

Explanation.—The references in this sub-section to buying back or reacquiring the securities shall be deemed to include references to buying or acquiring similar securities, so, however, that where similar securities are bought or acquired, the owner shall be under no greater liability to income-tax than he would have been under if the original securities had been bought back or reacquired.

persons located in notified jurisdictional area[31], and Limitation on interest deduction in certain cases[32].

Under section 92, where a business is carried on between resident and non-resident and because of a close connection between them, the resident is receiving profit or less than the ordinary profits, in such cases the income tax officer, shall determine the amount of profits which may reasonably be deemed to have been derived therefrom and into such amount in the total income of the resident.

Section 93 brings to tax the income of the residents that Income which he has power to enjoy without having the ownership of the property which is the source of income. This happens when a resident transfer to a non -resident any asset but retains for himself (resident) power to enjoy immediately or in future the income arising to non-resident out of the transferred asset.

Chapter X containing special provisions relating to avoidance of tax substituted section 92 by the Finance Act, 2001 by sections 92 to 92F. Again, by the Finance Act, 2002, section 92 was substituted. Sections 92 to 92F (as originally enacted) relate to computation of income from international transaction having arm's length price.

---

31. 94A. *Special measures in respect of transactions with persons located in notified jurisdictional area*—(1) The Central Government may, having regard to the lack of effective exchange of information with any country or territory outside India, specify by notification in the Official Gazette such country or territory as a notified jurisdictional area in relation to transactions entered into by any assessee.

    (2) Notwithstanding anything to the contrary contained in this Act, if an assessee enters into a transaction where one of the parties to the transaction is a person located in a notified jurisdictional area, then—

    (*i*) all the parties to the transaction shall be deemed to be associated enterprises within the meaning of section 92A;

    (*ii*) any transaction in the nature of purchase, sale or lease of tangible or intangible property or provision of service or lending or borrowing money or any other transaction having a bearing on the profits, income, losses or assets of the assessee including a mutual agreement or arrangement for allocation or apportionment of, or any contribution to, any cost or expense incurred or to be incurred in connection with a benefit, service or facility provided or to be provided by or to the assessee shall be deemed to be an international transaction within the meaning of section 92B,

    and the provisions of sections 92, 92A, 92B, 92C [except the second proviso to sub-section (2)], 92CA, 92CB, 92D, 92E and 92F shall apply accordingly.

32. 94B. *Limitation on interest deduction in certain cases*—(1) Notwithstanding anything contained in this Act, where an Indian company, or a permanent establishment of a foreign company in India, being the borrower, incurs any expenditure by way of interest or of similar nature exceeding one crore rupees which is deductible in computing income chargeable under the head "Profits and gains of business or profession" in respect of any debt issued by a non-resident, being an associated enterprise of such borrower, the interest shall not be deductible in computation of income under the said head to the extent that it arises from excess interest, as specified in sub-section (2):

    Provided that where the debt is issued by a lender which is not associated but an associated enterprise either provides an implicit or explicit guarantee to such lender or deposits a corresponding and matching amount of funds with the lender, such debt shall be deemed to have been issued by an associated enterprise.

The special provisions, as contained in Chapter X, are in addition to other provisions of the Income-tax Act, 1961 where by the attribution rules are applied to prevent avoidance of tax. Where a statutory provision is designed to prevent the avoidance of tax through income splitting by deeming any income or loss from property transferred or loaned to a spouse or minor child or property transferred to that of the transferor or of the lender and not of the recipient.

For example, section 64 of the Income-tax Act, 1961. These provisions are, in fact, the product of repeated legislative responses to judicial decisions in which courts traditional adherence to strict construction ignored the purpose of the rule to prevent tax avoidance through income splitting.

8.4 Transfer pricing provisions

Special provisions for avoidance of tax were inserted in the year 2001. **The purpose of Transfer pricing regulations is to prevent shifting of profits outside India.** The statutory provisions are contained in the Income-tax Act, 1961 and the Income-tax Rules,1962. These provisions lay down the legal framework which is to be followed when in an international transaction of goods, services, and intangible the transfer price is to be charged by the assessee from its associate enterprise. It is the duty of the assessee to ensure that the price charged is at arm's length. The first step in the determination of arm's length price is to analyse the specific characteristics of the controlled transactions whether it relates to transfer of goods, services, or intangibles. Intangible all the characteristics of the control transactions which are likely to affect its open market value must be taken into account. In case of goods, these characteristics include physical features of the property, its quality, reliability, and availability. This is necessary for location of similar or nearly similar characteristics of uncontrolled transactions.

How and in what manner comparable are to be selected is a difficult exercise. Does any such exercise is likely to affect the rights of the parties to the transaction, it is necessary that the statutory powers are exercised in judicial manner. The scheme requires that the assessing officer in an appropriate case, may refer the matter to the Transfer pricing officer. In case of dispute, the matter may be referred to a dispute resolution panel. There is a provision of an appeal to the Income tax appellate Tribunal. Only on a substantial question of law, the matter may go to the High Court. Against the decision of the High Court an appeal lies to the supreme court under article 136.

The statutory rules deal the procedural matters which are of binding in nature. The power has been delegated by declaring the policy of the law and by laying down the standards for guidance of those on whom the power to execute the law is conferred. Supreme Court in Morgan Stanley[32a] considered the transfer pricing provisions of the Income-tax Act and avoidance of double taxation treaty. Against the order of the Authority of Advance Ruling, the matter came up before the supreme court. The court observed:

32a. *Director of Income Tax* v. *Morgan Stanley & Co.* (2007) 162 Taxman 165 (SC)

"It is relevant to mention that a payer is required to compute arm's length price for a transactions using one of the five methods stipulated in the Income-tax Rules. Rule 10C(1) of Income-tax Rules defines the most appropriate method as the method which is the best suited to the facts and circumstances of each particular international transaction. As per rule 10C(2) the most appropriate method has to be selected having regard to number of factors which are enumerated therein. The arm's length price has to be computed by the application of methods mentioned in section 92C of the Income-tax Act.

The object behind enactment of transfer pricing regulations is to prevent shifting of profits outside India. A foreign enterprise is liable to be taxed in India on so much of its business profit as is attributable to the PE in India. The quantum of taxable income is to be determined in accordance with the provisions of the Income-tax Act. All provisions of Income-tax Act are applicable including provisions relating to depreciation, investment losses, deductible expenses, carry forward and set off losses, etc."

In the interpretation of transfer pricing provisions, OECD Commentary will have persuasive value and can be referred for guidance to determining a particular issue.[33]

On the question as to when an appeal lies to the High Court against the decision of the Income-tax appellate Tribunal, the Supreme court has clarified the law, removing ambiguity as to the interpretation. In *SAP Labs*[34], Justice M.R. Shah, observed:

"para 7 while determining the arm's length price, the Tribunal has to follow the guidelines stipulated under Chapter X of the IT Act, namely, Sections 92, 92A to 92CA, 92D, 92E and 92F of the Act and Rules 10A to 10E of the Rules. Any determination of the arm's length price under Chapter X *de hors* the relevant provisions of the guidelines, referred to hereinabove, can be considered as perverse and it may be considered as a substantial question of law as perversity itself can be said to be a substantial question of law. Therefore, there cannot be any absolute proposition of law that in all cases where the Tribunal has determined the arm's length price the same is final and cannot be the subject matter of scrutiny by the High Court in an appeal under Section 260A of the IT Act. When the determination of the arm's length price is challenged before the High Court, it is always open for the High Court to consider and examine whether the arm's length price has been determined while taking into consideration the relevant guidelines under the Act and the Rules. Even the High Court can also examine the question of comparability of two companies or selection of filters and examine whether the same is done judiciously and on the basis of the relevant material/evidence on record. The High Court can also examine whether the comparable transactions have been taken into consideration properly or not, i.e., to the extent non comparable transactions are considered as comparable transactions or not. Therefore, the view taken by the Karnataka High Court in the case of Softbrands India (P) Ltd. that in the transfer pricing matters, the determination of the arm's length price by the Tribunal is final and cannot be subject matter of scrutiny under Section 260A of the IT Act cannot be accepted."

---

33. *Engineering Analysis Centre of Excellence Pvt. Ltd.* v. *Commissioner of Income-tax* [2021] 125 taxmann.com 42/281 Taxman 19/432 ITR 471 (SC).

34. *SAP Labs India Private Limited* v. *Income-tax Officer*, [Civil Appeal No. 8463 of 2022 date of decision 19th April, 2023 (two Judge's Bench)]/[2023] 149 taxmann.com 327/293 Taxman 263 (SC).

Stating the law in clear terms, Justice M.R. Shah explained as under:

> "Thus, in each case, the High Court should examine whether the guidelines laid down in the Act and the Rules are followed while determining the arm's length price... in an appeal challenging the determination of the arm's length price, it is always open for the High Court to examine in each case whether while determining the arm's length price, the guidelines laid down under the Act and the Rules, referred to hereinabove, are followed or not and whether the determination of the arm's length price and the findings recorded by the Tribunal while determining the arm's length price are perverse or not."

8.5 GAAR

The basis of the GAAR is to prevent the abuse of tax provisions. A long debate preceded its introduction by the Finance Act, 2012[35]. The main purpose of the GAAR scheme is to prevent the taxpayer from obtaining a tax benefit through impermissible means. The main features of GAAR has been explained in the memorandum explain the provisions of the Finance Bill, 2012 (later enacted as the Finance Act, 2012) as under:—

A. The main feature of such a regime are (*i*) An arrangement whose main purpose or one of the main purposes is to obtain a tax benefit and which also satisfies at least one of the four tests, can be declared as an "impermissible avoidance arrangements". (*ii*) The four tests referred to in (*i*) are– (*a*) The arrangement creates rights and obligations, which are not normally created between parties dealing at arm's length. (*b*) It results in misuse or abuse of provisions of tax laws. (*c*) It lacks commercial substance or is deemed to lack commercial substance. (*d*) Is carried out in a manner, which is normally not employed for *bona fide* purpose. (*iii*) It shall be presumed that obtaining of tax benefit is the main purpose of an arrangement unless otherwise proved by the taxpayer. (*iv*) An arrangement will be deemed to lack commercial substance if – (*a*) the substance or effect of the arrangement as a whole, is inconsistent with, or differs significantly from, the form of its individual steps or a part; or (*b*) it involves or includes - (*i*) round trip financing; (*ii*) an accommodating party ; (*iii*) elements that have effect of offsetting or cancelling each other; or (*iv*) a transaction which is conducted through one or more persons and disguises the value, location, source, ownership or control of fund which is subject matter of such transaction; or (*c*) it involves the location of an asset or of a transaction or of the place of residence of any party which would not have been so located for any substantial, commercial purpose other than obtaining tax benefit for a party. (*v*) It is also provided that certain circumstances like period of existence of arrangement, taxes arising from arrangement, exit route, shall not be taken into account while determining 'lack of commercial substance' test for an arrangement. (*vi*) Once the arrangement is held to be an impermissible avoidance arrangement then the consequences of the arrangement in relation to tax or benefit under a tax treaty can be determined by keeping in view the circumstances of

35. The Forty-ninth Report of the Parliamentary Standing Committee on Finance on the Direct Tax Code Bill, 2010. (March, 2012).

the case, however, some of the illustrative steps are:- (*a*) disregarding or combining any step of the arrangement. (*b*) ignoring the arrangement for the purpose of taxation law (*c*) disregarding or combining any party to the arrangement. (*d*) reallocating expenses and income between the parties to the arrangement. (*e*) relocating place of residence of a party, or location of a transaction or situs of an asset to a place other than provided in the arrangement. (*f*) considering or looking through the arrangement by disregarding any corporate structure. (*g*) re-characterizing equity into debt, capital into revenue etc. (*vii*) These provisions can be used in addition to or in conjunction with other anti-avoidance provisions or provisions for determination of tax liability, which are provided in the taxation law. (*viii*) For effective application in cross border transaction and to prevent treaty abuse a limited treaty override is also provided.

B. The procedure for invoking GAAR is proposed as under:- (*i*) It is proposed that the Assessing Officer shall make a reference to the Commissioner for invoking GAAR and on receipt of reference the Commissioner shall hear the taxpayer and if he is not satisfied by the reply of taxpayer and is of the opinion that GAAR provisions are to be invoked, he shall refer the matter to an Approving Panel. In case the assessee does not object or reply, the Commissioner shall make determination as to whether the arrangement is an impermissible avoidance arrangement or not. (*ii*) The Approving Panel has to dispose of the reference within a period of six months from the end of the month in which the reference was received from the Commissioner (*iii*) The Approving Panel shall either declare an arrangement to be impermissible or declare it not to be so after examining material and getting further inquiry to be made. (*iv*) The Assessing Officer (AO) will determine consequences of such a positive declaration of arrangement as impermissible avoidance arrangement. (*v*) The final order in case any consequence of GAAR is determined shall be passed by AO only after approval by Commissioner and, thereafter, first appeal against such order shall lie to the Appellate Tribunal. (*vi*) The period taken by the proceedings before Commissioner and Approving Panel shall be excluded from time limitation for completion of assessment. (*vii*) The Approving Panel shall be set up by the Board and would comprise of officers of rank of Commissioner and above. The panel will have a minimum of three members. The procedure and working of Panel shall be administered through subordinate legislation. In addition to the above, it is provided that the Board shall prescribe a scheme for regulating the condition and manner of application of these provisions."

In the Finance Act, 2012 provided the date of 1st April, 2013 the commencement of GAAR provisions. The commencement of the provision of GAAR was deferred by one year[36]. Also, certain clarifications[37] were issued by the Central

36. In order to provide more time to both taxpayers and the tax administration to address the issues arising from GAAR provisions so that there is clarity and certainty in the matter, it is proposed to defer the applicability of the GAAR provisions, proposed in Chapter X-A and section 144BA of the Act, by one year so that they would now apply to income chargeable to tax in respect of assessment year 2014-15 and subsequent years.

37. Dated 27-01-2017.

Board of Direct Taxes in 2017. Finally, GAAR provisions have come into force from the assessment year 2018-19[38].

GAAR empowers the Tax Authorities to deal effectively with, and guard against, schemes that are designed primarily for avoiding tax. GAAR applies to any arrangement that is considered an Impermissible Avoidance Arrangement (IAA). The overall scheme of GAAR provisions[39] (Sec. 95 to Sec. 102) contained in Chapter X-A of the Act consists of two limbs: (*i*) determination of the existence of an Impermissible Avoidance Arrangement (IAA) resulting into tax benefit, and (*ii*) determination of the tax consequences, including denial of tax benefit, of an Impermissible Avoidance Arrangement (IAA). Sec. 96 of the Act provides that unless the main purpose of an arrangement is to obtain a tax benefit, the arrangement cannot be declared as an Impermissible Avoidance Arrangement. GAAR Advisory Panel of independent experts appointed by the Commissioners to give guidance on the application of the principles in particular cases. On an appeal, the Tax Tribunal is obliged to take account of their guidance.

For the application of GAAR, it is necessary to determine whether tax benefit arises from the transaction or not. Secondly, the *bona fide* purpose of the transaction is to be determined. Lastly, whether the tax avoidance transaction is abusive or not that is to be seen. A transaction is considered to be abusive if the transaction results directly or indirectly in a misuse of the provisions of the tax law. A transaction could be commercial transaction or a family arrangement or an investment transaction.

8.6 Tax mitigation

Tax mitigation

Tax mitigation has come to be recognised. It is different from tax avoidance. In a Privy Council decision from New Zealand, in *Challenge Corporation*[40], Lord Templeman said:

> "The material distinction in the present case is between tax mitigation and tax avoidance. A tax payer has always been free to mitigate his liability to tax. In the oft-quoted words of Lords Tomlin, every man is entitled if he can so order his affairs so that the tax attaching under the appropriate acts is less than otherwise it would be."

The *Willoughby* case[41] is significant in succinctly putting up tax mitigation in these words:

> "The hallmark of tax mitigation, on one hand, is that the taxpayer takes advantage of a fiscally attractive option accorded to him by the tax legislation and genuinely suffers the economic consequences that Parliament intended to be suffered by those taking advantage of the option.

38. The Finance Act, 2015.
39. Section 95 to Section 102.
40. (1987) Appeal Cases 155.
41. (1997) 1 WLR 1071.

> The main of object is, for the purposes of the section, the avoidance of tax. No commercial man in his senses is going to carry out commercial transactions except upon the footing of paying smallest amount of tax involved."

It is part of a choice, that is, choosing between two alternatives- if one is carrying out a commercial or a family or an investment transaction, choosing the most tax efficient- is not tax avoidance.

In *Shell Canada*[42], where the company had the need to borrow US hundred million. Instead of borrowing US dollars they took out a Kiwi loan. They borrowed New Zealand dollars, switched them into US dollars and then when they have to repay the loan, switched it back. At the time the New Zealand rate of interest was almost twice that on US dollar so they claimed almost twice as much interest deduction. On conversation of the currency, they made capital gain because the New Zealand dollar had been deflating during the period of the loan. But the gain was not fully taxed. A classical situation of two ways of carrying out a commercial transaction, one of them more efficient. The Supreme Court of Canada overruling the Federal court said that was not avoidance. That seems to be quite fundamental: choice doctrines should be regarded as indicating mitigation and not avoidance.

Tax mitigation is, therefore, a behaviour which without amounting to tax avoidance serves to attract less liability than otherwise might have arisen.

42. *Shell Canada Ltd.* v. *Canada* (1999) 3 SCR 622.

Aids to interpretation

9.1 General

There are several additional aids that courts may take to help in interpreting statutes. These are internal and external aids to interpretation, general presumptions, and maxims. The guide to legislative intention can be derived from rules *i.e.*, common law rules or all statutory rules which have binding force; principles derived from the legal policy which are mainly persuasive and; presumptions based on the nature of legislation and general linguistic cannons applicable to any piece of prose.

9.2 Internal aids

Internal aids to interpretation are contained within the body of the enactment. These are the preamble, headings, marginal notes, punctuation, etc. In recent years, Preamble has been given in the enactments which implement the international conventions. For example, the Prevention of Money Laundering Act, 2003.

9.3 External aids to interpretation

Materials that are considered to be external to the words of the enactment are referred to as external aids to the statutory interpretation. These include dictionaries; statute *pari materia*; interpretation Acts; prior state of the law and legislative history. Legislative history refers to the material that contains the history, that is, the account of the events that occurred during the conception, preparation, and passing of the enactment.

Parliamentary debates - The exclusionary rule which prohibits references to parliamentary material departed from India in tax cases, namely in *KP Varghese*[1] and *Susheela Rani*[2]. The position as it has been in other countries is being given as follows:

USA - In the United States of America, the use of parliamentary history was made in Holy Trinity Church[2a]. The exclusionary rule was formally repudiated

1. *K.P. Varghese* v. *Income-tax Officer* AIR 1981 SC 1922.
2. *Smt. Sushila Rani* v. *CIT* (2002) 2 SCC 697/[2002] 121 Taxman 343 (SC).

2a. *Church of Holy Trinity* v. *United States* 143 US 457 (1892).

in the year 1940 in the American Trucking Association[2b]. Thus, since the new deal, the US Supreme Court has freely consulted legislative history in informing itself about Congress's intent surrounding the statute. In an excellent article[3], A Flood of Light? comments on the Interpretation Act, 2005, Dr. SP Donald and Kennedy quoting from Eskridge and Scalia stated:

> "In general, the use of parliamentary history is not unusual statutory interpretation includes consideration of the common law, legislative history, and agency interpretations even when the statutory tax has an apparent plain meaning... but these... usually do not trump over a clear text."

However, overuse of such material led Scalia J of the United States Supreme Court to disregard congressional debates in a number of cases.

9.4 General presumptions

The general presumptions which apply to statutory interpretation are:—

1. Statutes are presumed to be constitutional, thus the laws are to be interpreted so as to avoid constitutional problems;
2. The presumption is that the tax statutes are to be construed strictly, that is, they are to be interpreted narrowly and in favour of the taxpayer;
3. Statutes are not to have retrospective effect;
4. Statutes are not to have extraterritorial effect;
5. Presumption against implied exceptions- it means that exemptions are not to be assumed;
6. Presumption against implied repeal;
7. Presumption against irrationality and injustice;
8. Rules against lenity;
9. All words in a statute have meaning and those meanings are updated with the change of time.

9.5 Presumption of constitutionality

Central Acts

In RK Garg, [4]the constitutionality of the issue of Special Bearer Bonds was challenged as being violative of Article 14 of the Constitution. The Supreme Court observed that there is always a presumption in favour of the constitutionality of a statute. The burden lies upon a person who challenges the constitutionality to show that there has been a clear violation of the constitutional provisions.

2b. *United States* v. *American Trucking Association* 310 US 534 (1940).

3. Juridical Studies Journal, Volume 6:1 (2006).

4. *RK Garg* v. *Union of India* AIR 1981 SC 2138.

Stamp duty

"Indisputably, there exists a presumption as regards the constitutionality of a statute. The rule of presumption in favour of constitutionality, however, only shifts the burden of proof and rests it on the shoulders of the person who attacks it. It is for the person to show that there has been a clear transgression of constitutional principles (see, *Chiranjit Lal Chaudhari*). But this rule is subject to the limitation that it is operative only till the time it becomes clear and beyond reasonable doubt that the legislature has crossed its limits. This rule in its application as principles of construction means that if two meanings are possible then the court will reject the one which renders it unconstitutional and accept the other upholding the validity of impugned legislation."

The above observations of the Supreme Court were made in Basant Nahata[5]. The court referred to *Elphinstone Spinning Company Limited*[5a] and said that the principle of presumption is not absolute rule but it is also subject to limitations. Its application in interpretation can only be applied to resolve a conflict when two interpretations are possible and not when there is only one leading to the conclusion that the delegated legislation is unguided and excessive. If the provisions are unconstitutional a mere presumption that decides the burden of proof cannot save them.

Entertainment Tax

Significant observations were made by the Supreme Court in Aashirwad films[6]. In this case, a notification levying different rates of entertainment tax was in question. The rate of tax on Telugu films was fixed at 10% whereas on non-Telugu films the rate of tax was fixed at 24%. It was contended that the purported classification only on the basis of language without anything more and having regard to the different rates of tax was *ex facie* arbitrary. The Court observed that the objectives in a statute may have a wide range. But the entire matter should also be considered from a social angle. In any case, it cannot be the object of any statute to be socially divisive in which event it may fall foul of the broad constitutional scheme enshrined under Article 19 and Article 21 and the Preamble of the Constitution. It is important to read the object of a taxation statute on the touchstone of social values as mentioned in the Constitution. An adverse conclusion can be drawn if a particular statute goes against such values. It is one thing to say that the taxation statute does not further social good, but quite another when it disturbs the social fabric. The court may take adverse address note in respect to statute falling in the latter category.

Municipal taxation

Another important case is the Bidhan Nagar Welfare Association[7]. In this case, the validity of certain provisions of the West Bengal Central Valuation Board

5. *State of Rajasthan* v. *Basant Nahata* (2005) 12 SCC 77.

5a. *Union of India* v. *Elphinstone Spg. and Wvg. Co. Ltd.* (2001) 4 SCC 139; AIR 2001 SC 724.

6. *Aashirwad Films* v. *Union of India* (2007) 6 SCC 624.

7. *Bidhan Nagar (Salt Lake) Welfare Association* v. *Central Valuation Board* (2007) 6 SCC 668.

(Amendment) Act, 1994 was in question. The Supreme Court observed that in the present case the proviso appended to Section 9(1) of the West Bengal Central Valuation Board Act, 1978, made the situation worse inasmuch as before taking recourse to review provision a pre-deposit is to be made in terms thereof.

A statute which provides for civil consequences must conform to the test of reasonableness, fairness, and non-arbitrariness. The court observed further that in a democracy, the people are supreme and all authorities must function for public welfare. Excessive increase in the tax burden on the public is not solely for public welfare... the 1978 Act or even the amending Act has not provided for any guidelines. When a statute does not provide for procedural fairness at may be *ultra vires*.

Motor Vehicles Taxation

In Paramjit Bhasin[8], the notification issued by various state governments permitting the carriage of excess weight after compounding was challenged by the petitioners. The court held that any notification which runs counter to the clear import of section 194 of the Motor Vehicles Act, 1988 has no validity.

On the taxation of motor vehicles, some of the recent cases which came up before the Supreme Court are Natwar Parikh, MB Kishore, Krishnappan and Hardev Motors,Sukhpal, and Goel Bus Service.

In Hardev Motors[9], the issue arose regarding the constitutional validity of entry IV(g) of Schedule I of the Madhya Pradesh Motor Karadhan Adhiniyam, 1991 read with *Explanation* 7 of the First Schedule. The court found the provision unconstitutional.

In Krishnappan[10], the question of the validity of lifetime tax on motor vehicles came up before the Supreme Court. While upholding the constitutional validity, the court observed that when an economic activity is to be valued it is open to the lawmaker to take into account various factors including the paying capacity of the user, the value of the vehicle, the economic life of the vehicle, etc. Lastly in the present case, for the vehicle registered before 1st July, 1988, the option between annual and one-time tax is retained.

In Sukhpal[11] Justice Kapadia speaking for the Bench held that section 10(3)[12] of U.P. Motor Vehicles Taxation Act, 1997, which provided for charging of such tax or additional tax along with penalty where transport vehicles were found plying in Uttar Pradesh without payment of tax or additional tax under the said Act to be valid as being regulatory and compensatory.

8. *Paramjit Bhasin* v. *Union of India* (2005) 12 SCC 642.
9. *Hardev Motors* v. *State of MP* (2006) 8 SCC 613.
10. *State of Tamil Nadu* v. *Krishnappan* (2005) 4 SCC 53.
11. *State of U.P* v. *Sukhpal Singh Bal* (2005) 7 SCC 615.
12. Section 10(3) was enacted to protect public revenue and as a deterrent for tax evasion. Deterrence was the main theme and object behind the imposition of penalty under Section 10(3) as such would be regulatory in nature.

Very recently, in **Goel Bus Service**[13], the High Court[14] of Himachal Pradesh declared sub-section (3)[15] of Section 3A of the Himachal Pradesh Motor Vehicles Taxation Act, 1972 as *ultra vires*. On appeal to the Supreme Court, speaking for the Court Justice Vikram Nath held that Section 3A(3) of the 1972 Act was within the legislative competence of the State Legislature, and lumpsum tax could be levied. Krishnappan was followed in Goel Bus Service.

In *MB Kishore*[16], the power to levy additional tax was struck down as section 9 of the Andhra Pradesh Motor Vehicles Taxation Act, 1963, confers power on the state government only to exempt or reduce the rate of tax. The Court held that Section 9 gives the government power to issue a notification granting exemption, making a reduction in the rate. But it specifically prohibits an enhancement in the rate of tax payable. Section 9 only permits the cancellation of exemption or the reduction which has been granted. Thus, at the highest, what the government could have provided was that if there was a violation of the G.O. then the normal tax, payable under the said Act, would become payable. In this case, what is sought to the required is more than the normal tax which would be payable in respect of the limited stage carriage. The High Court has, therefore, correctly held that there was no power to levy additional tax. In fact, the law prohibits an enhancement of the tax.

9.6 The presumption that statutes do not have a retrospective effect

The principle that no one should be penalized by retroactive law is expressed by the Latin maxims which means that no crime can be committed and no punishment can be imposed except under a prior penal law. Freedom from the retrospective operation of criminal law has been recognized as a fundamental element of democratic rights and the same has been recognised in Article 15 of the International Convention on Civil and Political Rights. Article 15 reads as under-

> "No one shall be held guilty of any criminal offense on account of any act or omission which did not constitute a criminal offense, under national or international law, at the time it was committed."

The Constitutions of countries such as India and United States of America prohibit retrospective legislation.

---

13. *State of Himachal Pradesh* v. *Goel Bus Service*, [Civil Appeal No (s). 5534-5594 of 2011 date of decision January 13, 2023. (Three Judge's Bench)].
14. The High Court was of the opinion that the tax imposed by Section 3A(3) was in the nature of penalty and for which the State Legislature had no power to make laws.
15. (3) Where a transport vehicle is plied without a valid permit or in any manner not authorised by the permit to be plied, there shall be levied, charged and paid to the State Government further special road tax in addition to the tax payable under sub-section (1), on such vehicles at the rates as may be specified by the State Government, by notification, but not exceeding the rates specified in column (3) of Schedule III of this Act.
16. *Deputy Transport Commissioner* v. *MB Kishore* (2005) 11 SCC 541.

Tax legislation is not a promise and taxpayers have no vested right in the Internal Revenue Code. In the USA, in Welch case[17] Justice Stone explained as under:

> "Taxation is neither penalty imposed on the taxpayer nor a liability which he assumes by contract. It is but a way of apportioning the cost of government among those who in some measures are privileged to enjoy its benefits and must bear its burdens. Since no citizen enjoys immunity from that burden, its retroactive position does not necessarily infringe due process...."

Justice of Connor, concurring in the judgment observed:

> "Retroactive application of revenue measures is rationally related to the legitimate government purpose of raising revenue. In enacting revenue measures, retroactivity allows the legislative body, in the revision of tax laws, to distribute the increased cost of government among its taxpayers in the light of the present need for revenue and with knowledge of the sources and amount of the various classes of taxable income during the taxable period preceding revision."

In *Carlton*[18], it was held that retroactive application of the Federal Estate Tax Statute to Carlton's 1986 transactions does not violate due process. Justice Scalia, concurring in the judgment observed:

> "The picking and choosing among various rights to be accorded "substantive due process" protection is alone enough to arouse suspicion; but the categorical and inexplicable exclusion "of so-called "economic rights" (even though the Due Process Clause explicitly applies to "property") unquestionably involves policymaking rather than neutral legal analysis. I would follow the text of the Constitution, which sets forth certain substantive rights that cannot be taken away, and adds, beyond that, a right to due process when life, liberty, or property is to be taken away."

India

It is a fundamental rule of law that no statutes shall be construed to have respective operation unless such a construction appears very clearly in the terms of the Acts or arises by necessary implication. Retrospective effect cannot be given to a subordinate legislation unless the parent Act permits.

In *Raghbir Singh*[19], it was propounded that close attention must be paid to the language of the statutory provision for determining the scope of retrospectivity intended by the parliament.

Retrospective tax legislation is permissible as no one has a right to the continuity of law. However, the validity of retrospective tax law can be challenged if the same is unreasonable and violative of Articles 14 and 19 of the Constitution. A law cannot be held to be unreasonable merely because it operates retrospectively. The Supreme Court in *RC Tobacco*[20] observed that the retrospective operation of the fiscal statute would have to be found to be duly oppressive and confiscatory before it can be held to be so unreasonable as to violate constitutional norms.

---

17. *Welch* v. *Henry* (1938) 305 US at pp. 146-147.
18. *United States* v. *Carlton* 512 U.S. 26, 30-31 (1994).
19. *Union of India* v. *Raghubir Singh* (1989) 2 SCC 754/[1988] 1988 taxmann.com 1324 (SC).
20. *RC Tobacco Private Limited* v. *Union of India* (2005) 7 SCC 754.

Where for instance it appears that the taxing statute is plainly discriminatory or provides no procedural machinery for assessment and levy of tax or that it is confiscatory, Courts would be justified in striking down the impugned statute as unconstitutional. In such cases, the character of the material provisions of the impugned statute is such that the court would feel justified in taking the view that in substance, the taxing statute is a cloak adopted by the legislature for achieving its confiscatory purposes (see *Rai Ram Krishna* v. *State of Bihar* AIR 1963 SC 1667)".

Liability to pay service tax by the broadcaster came up before the Supreme Court in Star India Limited[21]. The service of broadcasting was introduced in the Finance Act, 1994 as a taxable service with effect from 16-7-2001 by the Finance Act, 2001. The appellant disputed its liability to make any payment of service tax on the ground that it did not, in fact, broadcast. The commissioner held against the appellant. The appellant appealed before the Commissioner (Appeals). While the appeal was pending, the Finance Act, 2001 was amended by the Finance Act, 2002. The effect of the amendment was to make an agent such as the appellant a broadcaster. Before the Supreme Court, an issue arose regarding the payment of interest. Repelling the contention of the appellant, the Supreme Court held:

> "In any event, it is clear from the language of the validation clause, that the liability was extended not by way of clarification but by way of amendment to the Finance Act with retrospective effect. It is well established that while it is permissible to retrospectively legislate, such retrospectivity is normally not permissible to create an offence retrospectively. There were clearly judgments, decrees, or orders of the courts and Tribunals or other authorities, which were required to be neutralized by the validation clause ... liability to pay interest would only arise on default and is really in the nature of quasi-punishment. Tax liability although created retrospectively could not entail the punishment of payment of interest with retrospective effect.
>
> A validating legislation enacted with retrospective effect was challenged in Gujarat Ambuja[22]. In this case, sections 116 and 117 of the Finance Act, 2000 and section 158 of the Finance Act, 2003 sought to overcome the decision of the Supreme Court in Laghu Udyog Bharati[23]. In Gujarat Ambuja, the supreme court held that the charging section itself has been amended so as to make the provisions of the Act and rules compatible, the criticism of the earlier law upheld by this court can no longer be availed of. There is thus no question of the Finance Act, 2000 overruling the decision of this court in Laghu Udyog Bharati as the law itself has been changed. A legislature is competent to remove infirmities retrospectively and make any imposition of tax declared illegal, and valid. This has been the uniform approach of this Court. Such exercise in validation must of course also be legislatively competent and legally sustainable." (see also, Prithvi Cotton Mills[24])

---

21. *Star India Limited* v. *CCE Mumbai* (2005) 7 SCC 203/[2006] 150 Taxman 128 (SC).
22. *Gujarat Ambuja* v. *Union of India* (2005) 4 SCC 214/[2005] 144 Taxman 512 (SC).
23. *Laghu Udyog Bharati* v. *Union of India* (1999) 6 SCC 418/[1999] 105 Taxman 630 (SC), the Supreme Court struck down rule 2(1)(*d*)(*xii*) and (*xvii*) to of the Service Tax Rules 1994 as amended in 1997.
24. *Shri Prithvi Cotton Mills Limited* v. *Broach Borough Municipality* (1969) 2 SCC 283.

In a landmark judgment of recent times, *Vatika Township*[25], speaking on behalf of the constitution bench of five judges, Justice AK Sikri observed that the rule against retrospective operation is a fundamental rule of law that no statute shall be construed to have a retrospective operation unless such a construction appears very clearly in the terms of the Act, or arises by necessary and distinct implication. Dogmatically framed, the rule is no more than a presumption and thus could be displaced by outweighing factors.

Justice AK Sikri explained the general principles of retrospectivity by stating that

of the various rules guiding how legislation has to be interpreted, one established rule is that unless a contrary intention appears, legislation is presumed not to be intended to have a retrospective operation. The idea behind the rule is that a current law should govern current activities. Law passed today cannot apply to the events of the past. If we do something today, we do it keeping in view the law of today and in force and not tomorrow's backward adjustment of it. Our belief in the nature of the law is founded on the bedrock that every human being is entitled to arrange his affairs by relying on the existing law and should not find that his plans have been retrospectively upset. This principle of law is known as *lex prospicit non respicit* : law looks forward not backward.

9.7 Presumption in regard to exemption provisions

An exemption from payment of tax under an enactment is an exemption from tax liability. Therefore, every exemption provision has to be read strictly.

An exemption provision is to be construed strictly or liberally and has often come up for consideration before the courts. In *Tata Cuumins*[26], it was observed that a tax is a payment for raising general revenue. It is a burden. It is based on the principle of ability or capacity to pay. It is a manifestation of the taxing power of the state. Exemption from payment of tax under an enactment is an exemption from tax liability. Therefore, every such exemption notification has to be read strictly. The court observed further that when an assessee is promised with tax exemption for setting up an industry in the backward area as a term of industrial policy, we have to read implementing notifications in the context of the industrial policy. In such a case. The exemption notifications have to be read liberally keeping in mind objects envisaged and by the industrial policy and not in a strict sense as in the case of exemption from tax liability under the taxing statute.

A constitution bench decision in *Union of India* v. *Commercial Tax Officer*[27] is an important decision to the effect that exemption provisions are to be construed strictly, though there was dissent from Justice Sinha.

---

25. *Commissioner of Income Tax (Central)-I, New Delhi* v. *Vatika Township Private Limited* (2015) 1 SCC 1 [Five Judge's Bench]
26. *State of Jharkhand* v. *Tata Cummins Limited* (2006) 4 SCC 57/[2008] 2008 taxmann.com 1129 (SC).
27. AIR 1956 SC 202.

Section 5 of the Bengal Finance (Sales Tax) Act, 1941, in section 2(*a*)(*iii*) exempted sales to the Indian stores department, the supply department of the Government of India, and any Railway or water transport administration. Sale to other departments was not exempted. With effect from 29th August, 1947, the Department of Industry and Supply was redesignated as the Ministry of Industry and Supply. It was argued that exemption was granted by the Bengal Finance (Sales Tax) Act, 1941 to departments by name. It was not given to sales to the Government of India in all its departments.

Justice SK Das, speaking on behalf of the majority observed

> "... to extend the benefit of statutory exemption to the sales made to the newly created department of industries and supplies, of goods not required for war purposes but, say, for meeting international obligations will necessarily widen the scope of the exemption and impose greater loss of revenue on the State of West Bengal then what the Act by its language intent to do. At any rate, the Bengal Finance (Sales Tax) Act, 1941 by providing for the deduction of the sales to two named departments from the taxable turnover certainly created these two departments as distinct entities. The exemption is the creation of a statute and must be construed strictly and cannot be extended to sales to other departments".

Justice Sinha, in his dissent, observed

> "... it is well settled that the provisions of a statute have to be construed with reference to the state of affairs as they existed at the time statute was passed. In my view, the terms of Section 5(2)(*a*)(*iii*) show that it was an exemption granted to a particular function of the Government of India described by a certain name ... sometimes the language of a statute has to be construed in a modified form in order to give effect to the real intentions of the legislature, where the language is only of a descriptive nature language and not a definitive one".

Exemption from tax has to be created explicitly. In *Falkom Tyres*[28] v. *State of Karnataka*, the provisions of the Karnataka Tax on Entry of Goods Act, 1979 came up for interpretation. The appellant, the manufacturer of tyres, used rubber as the main input in the manufacture of tyres. The issue for consideration was though rubber was included in the definition but it was not in section 3 and the second schedule of the Act. Supreme Court held that if the legislature intended to create an exception for rubber also it could have done so.

In Petron Engineering[29], while interpreting the expression 'foreign enterprise' for the purposes of Section 80-O of the Income-Tax Act, 1961 the court held that it is true that an exemption provision should be liberally construed but this does not mean that such liberal construction should be made doing violence to the plain meaning of such exemption provision. Thus, to construe 'foreign enterprise' in section 80-O including an Indian company or a branch or unit of such company because it is located in a foreign country would be against the plain meaning of the term and legislative intent.

28. (2006) 6 SCC 530/[2006] 5 STT 67 (SC).

29. *Petron Engineering Construction Private Limited* v. *CBDT* AIR 1989 SC 501.

The plain meaning rule in the interpretation of exemption notification was invoked in DH Brothers. In *DH Brothers*[30], the issue was whether sugarcane crushers fall within the definition of agricultural implements. The notification dated 14th November, 1980 exempted agriculture implements from the levy of sales tax. The court held that a bare reading of the notifications shows that all the implements mentioned by name after the word including are by and large those which are used for cultivation of the land and other operations which foster the growth and preserve the agricultural produce. None of these implements can be worked after the agriculture produce in respect of crop comes to an end. Therefore, the intention of the framers of the notification could only be to limit the general words in the notification to the implements of the same kind as are specified therein.

9.8 Presumption against implied repeal

In a simple repeal there is scarcely any room for expression of contrary opinion. It is now well settled that repeal connotes abrogation or obliteration of one statue by another, from the statute book as completely as if complete, it has never been passed. When an Act is repealed, it must be considered (except as to transactions past and closed) as if it never existed. Effect of repeal has been provided in section 6 of the General Clauses Act, 1897. They read as under:

> "Effect of repeal - Where this Act, or any Central Act or Regulation made after the commencement of this Act, repeals any enactment hitherto made or hereafter to be made, then, unless a different intention appears, the repeal shall not-
>
> (*a*) revive anything not in force or existing at the time at which the repeal takes effect, or
>
> (*b*) affect the previous operation of any enactment so repealed or anything duly done or suffered thereunder ;or
>
> (*c*) affect any right, privilege, obligation or liability acquired, accrued or incurred under any enactment so repealed; or
>
> (*d*) affect any penalty, forfeiture or punishment incurred in respect of any offence committed against any enactment so repealed; or
>
> (*e*) affect any investigation, legal proceeding or remedy in respect of any such right, privilege, obligation, liability, penalty, forfeiture or punishment aforesaid, and any such investigation, legal proceeding or remedy may be instituted, continued or enforced, and any such penalty or forfeiture or punishment may be imposed as if the repealing Act or regulation had not been passed.

On the repeal of the Andhra Pradesh General Sales Tax Act, 1957 by the Andhra Pradesh Value Added Tax which came into force on 1st April, 2005, a question arose regarding initiating and completing penalty proceedings under the APGST Act in the *Gammon India Limited* v. *Special Chief Secretary*[31].

---

30. *DH Brothers Private Limited* v. *CST*, UP AIR 1991 SC 1992.
31. (2006) 3 SCC 354/[2007] 2007 taxmann.com 1787 (SC).

In this case, the appellant while purchasing cement for ready mix concrete had falsely issued from G and claimed a reduced rate of tax from the sellers and obtained the benefit of a lower rate of tax. The court held that in the case of simple repeal, there is scarcely any room for expression of a contrary opinion. But when the repeal is followed by fresh legislation on the same subject, the provisions of the new Act are to be looked into only for the purpose of determining whether they indicate different intention. The line of enquiry would be, not whether the new Act expressly keeps alive old rights and liabilities but whether it manifest an intention to destroy them... It is manifest that every later enactment which supersedes an earlier one or puts an end to earlier state of law is presumed to intend the continuance of rights accrued and liabilities incurred under the superseded enactment unless there was sufficient indication- express or implied- in the later enactment design to completely obliterate the earlier state of law."

In *Southern Petrochemicals Company Limited* v. *Electricity Inspector*[32], the appellant's main contention was that applicable exemption under section 12 and under the notification issued under section 13 of the 1962 Act has remained valid and in force despite the enactment of the 2003 Act.

The Tamilnadu Tax on Consumption or Sale of Electricity Act, 2003 repealed the Tamil Nadu Electricity (Taxation on Consumption) Act, 1962. The court held that a notification issued under the 1962 Act would come within the purview of the words 'anything duly done' as provided in section 20(1) proviso (*a*). it is relevant to note section 20 which is as under:

"20(1) the Tamilnadu Electricity Duty Act, 1939, and the Tamil Nadu Electricity (Taxation and Consumption) Act, 1962 is hereby repealed:

Provided that such repeal shall not affect—

(*a*) the previous operation of any enactment so repealed or anything duly done or suffered thereunder ;

(*b*) any right, privilege, obligation or liability acquired, accrued or incurred under the said Acts;

(*c*) any penalty, forfeiture or punishment incurred in respect of any offence committed against the said Acts;

(*d*) any investigation, legal proceeding or remedy in respect of any such right, privilege, obligation, liability, penalty, forfeiture or punishment aforesaid, and any such investigation, legal proceeding or remedy maybe instituted, continued or enforced, and any such penalty or forfeiture or punishment may be imposed as if the repealing Act or regulation had not been passed.

(2) Notwithstanding such repeal—

(*a*) anything done or any action taken including any Rule, Notification, inspection, order or notice made or issued or any direction given under the repealed laws, shall so far as it is not inconsistent with the provisions of this Act be deemed to have been done or taken under the corresponding provisions of this Act.

(*b*) ** ** **

(*c*) ** ** **

32. (2007) 5 SCC 447.

The effect of repeal seems to have settled in India. The judicial precedent operating in this area include - *State of Punjab* v. *Mohar Singh Pratap Singh*[33]; *Jayantilal Amratlal Lal* v. *Union of India*[34]; *Indian Tobacco Company Limited* v. *CTO*[35]; *TS Baliah* v. *ITO*[36]; *Gajraj Singh* v. *STAT*[37]; *Keshavan Madhava Menon* v. *State of Bombay*[38]; *M.A. Tulloch and Company* v. *State of Orissa*[39]; *Quadrat Ullah* v. *Municipal Board*[40].

9.9 Latin Maxims

Latin maxims denote rules of the language. Ordinarily in statute all words are to be given meaning; same words are to be given same meaning and different words are to be given different meanings. The maxims are as under:—

Noscitur a sociis - When two or more words which are susceptible of analogous meaning are coupled together they are understood to be used in a cognate sense. The meaning of more general words take colour from the less general word. This rule will apply when the intention of the legislature in associating wider words with words of narrow significance is doubtful or is otherwise not clear. Thus, a word will be interpreted in the context of surrounding circumstances.

In a case, the words which were to be interpreted were as follows:

> "All houses kept open at night for public refreshment, resort and entertainment."

It was argued by the defendant that a cafe run by him did not require licence because he did not provide entertainment. The court has held that the entertainment did not mean musical entertainment but the reception and accommodation of the people.

In Rainbow Steel Limited[41] where the words used in entry 15 of a notification under UP Sales Tax Act provided that "old, discarded, unserviceable or obsolete machinery, etc.." will be subjected to Sales Tax at the rate of 5%. The question arose that where the appellant purchased a thermal power plant second hand from the Uttar Pradesh Electricity Board will it be exigible to sales tax under the above entry or not. The principle of *Noscitur a sociis* was invoked and it was pleaded that old which is more general should be restricted to a sense analogous to that of less general expression , namely discarded, unserviceable and obsolete.

The expression old machinery must be old in the sense that it has become non-functional or non-usable. Justice Tulzapurkar observed:

---

33. AIR 1955 SC 84.
34. (1972) 4 SCC174.
35. (1975) 3 SCC 512.
36. AIR 1969 SC 701.
37. (1997) 1 SCC 650.
38. AIR 1951 SC 128 (Seven Judges).
39. AIR 1964 SC 1284.
40. (1974) 1 SCC 202.
41. *Rainbow Steel Limited* v. *STC UP* AIR 1981 SC 2104, see also *State of Bombay* v. *Hind Mazdoor Sabha* AIR 1960 SC 610; *Rohit Pal and Paper Mills Limited* v. *CCE* AIR 1991 SC 754.

The principle of *Noscitur a sociis* is clearly applicable to the construction of the word 'old' occurring in entry 15, and that expression will have to be given a restricted meaning- a sense analogous to that of less general word clubbed with it... the principle is applicable as the general word 'old' is vague, imprecise and ambiguous as there is no indication as to how much old the machinery should be before it could be discarded as old machinery.

Ejusdem generis - General words receive restricted meaning when used in association with other words by application of the rules of *Noscitu a soccis* and *Ejusdem generis*. In *ejusdem generis* a genus or category is created out of words of a class, category or genus. In Powell[41a] the defendant was operating from a place outdoor whereas it was an offence to use a house, office, room or other place for betting. The court held that 'other place' had to refer to 'other indoor places' because the words in the list were indoor places.

In the Indian City Properties Limited[41b], the issue was where on a plot of land their existed a bungalow and also a servant room; a security cabin; a pump room; underground RCC tank with cylinder shaped precast can on the top; an AC plant, whether the municipal commissioner was justified in giving notice for acquiring under section 299 of the Bombay Municipal Corporation Act, 1888.

The question was whether the appellant premises which is sought to be affected by the notice is 'not occupied by any building' or occupied by some other structure external to a building. The court applying the test of independence and permanency held that each item falls in the definition of building and observed as follows:

> "The word 'structure' is used as a generic term so that while all buildings may be structures, all structures are not buildings. That structure which is not a building and is a platform, veranda, step or some other such structure external to a building may be taken over by the Commissioner under section 299 if it is within the regular line of the street. The word 'some other such' must be construed as a structure similar or like platform, veranda or step. The words must be read *ejusdem generis* with the preceding words since the word 'such' means 'of the type previously mentioned'. The underlying characteristics of platforms, verandas and steps is that they are not independent structure but external to building, that is, they are attached to the outside and form inessential part of a building. In our opinion, therefore, in order to be building for the purpose of section 299 the structure would have to be independent and permanent."

This rule will not apply to two-word phrases likewise a single species can never be treated as a reference to a genus. An example of this rule is as under:—

The words 'books, pamphlets, newspaper, and other document' will it include private letters? As the description is 'newspaper and other document' therefore 'private letters' cannot be excluded.

41a. *Powell* v. *Kempton Park Racecourse Co. Ltd.* (1899) AC 143.

41b. *Indian City Properties Ltd.* v. *Municipal Commissioner of Greater Bombay* (2005) 6 SCC 417.

The rule of Ejusdem generis will apply when—

i. The statute contains an enumeration of specific words;

ii. The class is not exhausted by the enumeration;

iii. The general term follows the enumeration; and

There is no indication of a different legislative intent.

Thus, for the rule of *Ejusdem generis* principle to apply, there must be sufficient indication of a category that can be properly described as a class or genus, even though not specified as such in the enactment. If no class can be found, *ejusdem generous* principle is not attracted. If a class can be found, but the specific words exhaust the class, then this principle may not be invoked.[42]

In section 32(1) of the Income-tax Act, 1961, *Explanation* 3 reads as under—

> "For the purposes of this sub-section, the expressions 'assets' and 'block of assets' shall mean—(*a*) tangible assets, being buildings, machinery, plant or furniture; (*b*) intangible assets, being know-how, patents, copyrights, trademarks, licences, franchises or any other business or commercial rights of similar nature."

In SMIFS Securities Limited[42a] it was held that the expression "any other business or commercial rights of similar nature" will include 'goodwill' on the application of the principle of *ejusdem generis*.

Expressio unius est exclusion alterius - Express mention of one or more things of a particular class may be regarded as silently excluding all other members of the class.

In Tempest[43], the statute required that contracts for the sale of 'goods, ware and merchandise' of 10 Pounds or more had to be evidenced in writing. The court had to decide whether this applied to 'stocks and shares'. The court held that the statute did not apply because stocks and shares were not mentioned.

In Parle Biscuit[44], the stand of the state that the entry at serial number 12 relates to 'papers of all kinds' and cardboard boxes being made of paper are also covered by the exclusion is not correct, because serial number 12 of the notification deals with paper of all kinds and Paper Products of the enumerated category. Stand of the state that papers of all kinds are included cannot be correct for the simple reason that had the same been the intention there was no necessity for enumerating various Paper Products.

After analysing the meaning of paper and carton the court held that there cannot be the universal application of any rigid standard for determining the question and has to be decided on the factual background of each case. This has not been done. The type of cardboard box which was used for packing the product of the

42. *Siddheswari Cotton Mills Private Limited* v. *Union of India* AIR 1989 SC 1019; *CWT* v. *SN Kakkar* (1989) 175 ITR 129 (All.).

42a. *Commissioner of Income Tax, Kolkata* v. *SMIFS Securities Limited* (2012) 13 SCC 488.

43. *Tempest* v. *Kilner* (1846) 3 Kings bench 249.

44. *Parle Biscuit Private Limited* v. *State of Bihar* (2005) 9 SCC 669.

appellant has to be seen. Therefore, we think it appropriate to direct the Deputy commissioner of sales tax to consider the question whether the cardboard box used by the appellant fits in with the definition of carton taking into account the product which is packed. For this purpose, the appellant shall be granted an opportunity to substantiate its plea that the cardboard boxes used by it are not factually covered by the entry 'carton'.

Generalia Specialisbus non-derogant - The general rule to be followed in case of conflict between two statute is that later abrogates the earlier one. In other words, a prior special law would yield to a later general law, if either of two conditions is satisfied:

i. The two are inconsistent with each other;

ii. There is some express reference in the later enactment.[45]

Reddento Singula Singulis - Where there are general words of description following an enumeration of particular things, such general words are to be construed as distributivity. Thus, where a complex sentence has more than one subject and more than one object, it may be the right construction to render each to each, by reading the provision distributively and applying each object to its appropriate subject. A similar principle applies to verbs and their subjects, and to other parts of speech. In a recent case[46], it is stated that the principle is clear in its terms. It is when a complex sentence has more than one subject and more than one object that a construction may be required to render each to each by reading the provision distributively.

Ut res valet quam pereat - This principle implies that no provision should be interpreted as superfluous or insensible. However, a word can in some circumstances be omitted if it is absurd or conflicts with another provision.

9.10 Popular meaning

The well-settled principle[47] is that words in a taxing statute must be construed in consonance with their commonly accepted meaning in the trade and their popular meaning. When a word is not explicitly defined, or there is ambiguity as to its meaning, it must be interpreted for the purpose of classification in the popular sense, which is the sense attributed to it by those people who are conversant with the subject matter that the statute is dealing with. This principle should be commended to the authorities as it is a good fiscal policy not to put people in doubt or quandary about their tax liability. The common parlance test is an extension of the general principle of interpretation of statutes for

45. *JK Cotton and Spinning Mills* v. *State of UP* AIR 1961 SC 1170; *UPSEB* v. *Hari Shankar Jain* AIR 1979 SC 65.

46. *Delhi International Airport Ltd.* v. *Airport Economic Regulatory Authority of India* [Civil Appeal No. 8378 of 2018 dated July 11, 2022] see also, *K.V. Kamath* v. *Rangappa Baliga & Co.* AIR 1969 SC 504.

47. *Dunlop India Ltd.* v. *Union of Indian* (1976) 2 SCC 241, and *Commissioner of Central Excise, New Delhi* v. *Connaught Plaza Restaurant (P.) Ltd.*, (2012) 13 SCC 639/[2014] 52 taxmann.com 531 (SC).

deciphering the mind of the lawmaker[48]. However, the above rule is subject to certain exceptions, for example, when there is an artificial definition or special meaning attached to the word in a statute, then the ordinary sense approach would not be applicable[49].

Words in the section of a statute are not to be interpreted by having those words in one and the dictionary in another. In spelling out the meaning of a word in a section, one must take into consideration the setting in which those terms are used and the purpose that they intend to serve.[50]

In the proviso to section 23(1) of the Income-tax Act, 1961 the expressions 'building' and 'residential unit' have not been defined. The High Court in SC Majumdar[51] held that in construing these expressions, we must give meaning to these expressions in the ordinary sense. The building should certainly be one which is habitable and complete and it may either be one-storeyed, two-storeyed or three-storyed.

In the sales tax law, while interpreting item resort should be made not to the scientific or technical meaning of such terms but to their popular meaning or meaning attached to them by those dealing in them, that is to say, their commercial sense.[52] The court while interpreting the word 'coal' in entry one of Part 2 of Schedule II of the Madhya Pradesh Sales Tax Act, 1959 observed that the test that would be applied is what would be the meaning which persons dealing with coal and consumers purchasing it as a fuel would give to that word. A Sales tax statute in levying a tax on goods must in the absence of a technical term or a term of science or art, be presumed to have used an ordinary term as coal according to the meaning ascribed to it in common parlance. Viewed from that angle both a merchant dealing in coal and the consumer wanting to purchase it would regard coal not in a geological sense but in the sense, ordinarily understood and would include charcoal in the term coal.

Their lordship followed the rule of construction echoed by Pollock in *Greenfield* v. *IRC* which is as under:

> '... that if a statute contains language which is capable of being construed in a popular sense such statute is not to be construed according to the strict or technical meaning of the language contained in it, but is to be construed in its popular sense. Popular sense means a sense in which people conversent with the subject matter with which the statute is dealing attribute to it. But if a word in its popular sense and read in an ordinary way is capable of two constructions, it is wise to adopt such a construction as is based on the assumption that Parliament merely intended

48. *Commissioner of Customs and Central Excise, Amritsar (Punjab)* v. *D.l. Steels* [Civil Appeal Nos. 2360-2376 of 2009 decided on 11th July, 2022]/[2022] 140 taxmann.com 253 (SC).

49. *Collector of Central Excise, Kanpur* v. *Krishna Carbon Paper Company* (1989) 1 SCC 150/[1988] 1988 taxmann.com 620 (SC).

50. *CGT* v. *NS Getti Chettiar* (1971) 82 ITR 599 (SC).

51. *S.C. Majumdar* v. *CIT* (1983) 35 CTR 202/13 Taxman 184 (Cal.).

52. *STC* v. *Jaswant Singh* AIR 1967 SC 1454.

> to give so much power as was necessary for carrying out the objects of the Act and not to give any unnecessary powers. In other words, the construction of the words is to be adopted to the fitness of the matter of the statute.
>
> The popular meaning was ascribed by the court by holding that the exemption in respect of 'condensed milk' did not cover 'condensed skimmed milk'.[53]

The word 'minerals' occurring in section 80HHC(2)(*b*)(*ii*) of the Income-tax Act, 1961, whether would include all minerals in all its forms, was the issue that came up before the Supreme Court in *Gem Granites*[54]. Section 80HHC(2) (*b*)(*ii*) provides for deduction in respect of profits retained for export business. However, this deduction initially was not extended to the exporter of minerals. 80HHC(2)(*b*) reads as under:

(*b*) This section does not apply to the following goods or merchandise, namely- (*i*) Mineral oil; and (*ii*) Minerals and ores.

The appellant, who was an exporter of granite claimed for the assessment year 1987-88 that the word 'minerals' does not include granite which has been subjected to cutting and polishing. It is the appellant's case that when granite is so processed it ceases to be mineral. Subsequently, by the amendment of the law in the year 1991 the aforesaid provision was amended as under—

> "Section 80HHC(2)(*b*). This section does not apply to the following goods and merchandise namely - (*i*) Mineral oil, and (*ii*) Minerals and Ores (other than processed minerals and Ores specified in the 12th Schedule."

The court held that there are no words of restrictions which qualify the word mineral and it would be reasonable to assume that in the absence of any such limitation, the word must be read to include all kinds of minerals in all its forms *i.e.* whether subjected to any process or not as long as it continued to retain the characteristics of mineral. To hold that the word 'minerals' never included processed mineral would require our reading words of limitation into an otherwise clear and unambiguous statutory provision.

In another case *i.e.* Shatrusaliya Digvijay Singh Jadeja[55], the interpretation of the word 'pending' occurring in section 95(*i*)(*c*) of the Kar Vivad Samadhan Scheme, 1998, came up before the court as the designated authority held that the appeals and revisions were sham, ineffective or infructuous. According to the department, the revisions filed by the assessees were time-barred, and as such they were not pending in terms of section 95(*i*)(*c*) of the said scheme. The revisions were not pending on September 1998 when the scheme came into force as the revisions were filed in November and December 1998 along with the application for the condonation of delay and consequently such revisions did not come within the meaning of the word 'pending' as mentioned in section 95(*i*)(*c*) of the scheme. It was further pleaded on behalf of the department that there was a difference between appeal and revision under the Income-tax Act

53. *Healthways Dairy Products* v. *Union of India* AIR 1976 SC 2221.
54. *Gem Granite* v. *CIT* (2005) 1 SCC 289.
55. *Commissioner of Income-tax* v. *Shatrusaliya Digvijay Singh Jadeja* [2005] 7 SCC 294.

1961 as an appeal could be filed as a matter of right whereas the remedy of filing revision is a discretionary remedy. On behalf of the assessee it was submitted that the scheme is a code by itself ; that the object of the scheme was to recover the taxes locked in the pending litigation and for the applicability of the scheme, appeals, references, revisions, writ petitions pertaining to the tax cases were all put on a par under section 95 of the scheme. The court held:

> "In our view, the scheme was in substance a recovery scheme though it was nomenclatured as a litigation settlement scheme and was not similar to the earlier voluntary disclosure scheme. The scheme was a complete code by itself. Its object was to put an end to all pending matters in the form of appeals, references, revisions, and writ petitions under the Income-tax Act and the Wealth Tax Act.... the object behind section 95(*i*)(*c*) in putting on par appeals, references and revisions was to put an end to litigation in various forms and various stages under the Income-tax Act and the Wealth Tax Act and, therefore ruling, on the scope of appeals and revisions under the voluntary disclosure scheme will not apply."

After referring to the cases on the interpretation of section 95 wherein it was held that if the appeal or revision is pending on the date of the filing of the declaration, it is not for the designated authority to hold that the appeal/ revision was sham, infective or infructuous. The court quashed the order of the designated authority rejecting the declaration filed by the assessee.

9.11 Ordinary meaning

In the Church of Holy Trinity[56], a statute made it a crime in any manner whatsoever, to prepay the transportation charges of an alien to perform labour or service of any kind in the United States. A church was convicted of violating this statute, having prepaid the transportation of its Rector from England. The Supreme Court of the United States of America reversed the conviction.

Justice Brewer concluded:

> "No one reading such a title would suppose that Congress had in its mind any purpose of staying the coming into this country of ministers of gospel, or, indeed of any class whose task is that of the brain."

Referring to this case in an illuminating article, the New Textualist New Text[57], Lawrence M. Solan has commented:

> "Brewer understood at an intuitive level that while the minister's activities were within the meaning of the statute (labour or service of any kind) they were not within the ordinary meaning of the word. Brewer chose the ordinary meaning approach over the plain meaning approach when the two conflicted."

Another important case is *Smith* v. *The United States*[58]. In this case, John Smith drove from Tennessee to Florida, where he planned to buy cocaine from a contact and offered to trade his unloaded machine gun for the drugs. The federal

56. *Church of Holy Trinity* v. *United States* 143 US 457 (1892).
57. Volume 38 number 5 December 2005 Loyola Law School law review.
58. 508 US 233 (1993).

statute which Smith violated provided an enhanced sentence for anyone who uses or carries a firearm during and in relation to any crime of violence or drug trafficking crime. The statute imposed a minimum of 5 years in prison for those using an ordinary firearm and a minimum of 30 years for those using a machine gun.

The court sentenced Smith to 30 years minimum imprisonment. Supreme Court affirmed the conviction by a vote of 6 to 3. Justice O'Connor writing for the majority said:

> "When a word is not defined by the statute, we construe it normally in accord with its ordinary and natural meaning."

Justice Scalia dissented and wrote:

> "In the search for statutory meaning, we give non-technical words and phrases their ordinary meaning. To use an instrumentality ordinarily means to use it for its intended purpose. When someone asks, do you use a cane? he is not enquiring whether you have your grandfather silver-handled walking stick on display in the hall; he wants to know whether you walk with a cane. Similarly, to speak of using a firearm is to speak of using it for its distinctive purpose *i.e.* as a weapon."

The dissent of Justice Scalia in Chisom[58a] on the use of ordinary meaning is important to note. In Chisom, the question was whether section 2 of the Voting Rights Act applies to judicial elections as well as to legislative elections. Justice Scalia stated:

> "The court, petitioner and petitioner amicus labored mightly to establish that there is a meaning of representatives that would include judges.... and no doubt there is. But our job is not to scavenge the world of English usage to discover whether there is any possible meaning of representatives which suits our preconception that the statute includes judges; Our job is to determine whether the ordinary meaning includes them, and if it does not, to ask whether there is any solid indication in the text or structure of the statute that something other than ordinary meaning was intended."

Nix[59] involved the meaning of the word 'tomato'. Whether a tomato is a fruit or vegetable. At the time, higher tariffs were imposed on the import of vegetables than on imports of fruits. The government maintained that imported tomatoes were subject to a higher duty. The importer said that they should be considered fruits. Botanists call it a fruit and American people call it vegetables. The court observed the ordinary meaning and held tomato vegetables.

On ordinary meaning in an illuminating article, the New Textualist New Text[60], Lawrence M. Solan stated:

> "The key intellectual decision is to focus on the ordinary meaning of statutory words rather than on their plain meaning as found in dictionary definitions. What makes ordinary meaning ordinary? It can only be that in the context in which a word is used, that meaning stands out as the one that was likely intended since

58a. *Chisom* v. *Roemer*, 501 US 380 (1991).

59. *Nix* v. *Hedden* 149 US 304 (1893).

60. Volume 38 number 5 December 2005 Loyola Law School law review.

that is what people generally intend when they use that word. And, if that is the case, the textualist judges and (academics) who rely on ordinary meaning have built context into their analysis without ever looking at anything outside the text.

The shift from focusing on the dictionary to ordinary uses should be seen as an additional step towards reconciling textualist methodology with the goal of providing an interpretation that reflects a Statute's purpose."

9.12 Technical meaning

Words and expressions in taxing statute, unless defined in the statute itself, have to be construed in the sense in which the person dealing with them understands *i.e.*, as per the trade understanding, commercial and technical practice usage.

In the Indicon[61], the core question involved was whether the cement tiles, manufactured by the assessee company, are used for floor coverings in the form of tiles for the purpose of assessment of the rate of excise duty under notification number 59/ 90-CE or the goods are exempted from payment of such duty as claimed by the assessee-company.

The court held that we find that the expression 'floor coverings' in the rolls or in the form of the tiles are not defined in the Central Excises and Salt Act, 1944 or in the Central Excise Tariff Act or in exemption Notification No. 59/90- CE but it has acquired a definite trade and business understanding... floor coverings/ wall coverings which are made out of plastic, coir/textiles have got a distinct identity from the floor materials as the floor covering materials are totally different products which are commonly used as an additional coverage to an existing floor/ wall, only for the purpose of beautification and decoration...

Classification for the purposes of levy of excise duty under the Excise Tariff Act, 1985, also contains rules for interpretation. Rule 1 reads as under:

> "1. The title of sections and chapters are provided for ease of reference only; for legal purposes, classification shall be determined according to the term of the headings and any relative section or chapter notes, and provided such headings or notes do not otherwise require, according to the provisions hereinafter contained."

Following the said rule of interpretation, the Supreme Court in HPL Chemical[62] held the 'denatured salt' fall under the heading of 'minerals' and not 'chemicals' as contended by the revenue. The appellant is engaged in the manufacture of 'hydrazine' falling under chapter heading 28.25 of the Tariff Act. The appellant during the course of manufacture of the final product produces residuary by-products *i.e.*, 'denatured salt'. The appellant filed classification under heading 25.01 carrying Nil rate of duty. The court also relied upon Harmonized System of Nomenclature (HSN) and stated that as per HSN this heading 25.01 relates to sodium chloride, commonly known as salt. Salt is not only used for culinary purposes *i.e.* cooking salt, and table salt, but it also has many other uses and, if necessary, may be denatured to render it unfit for human consumption. The

---

61. *Indocon Structurals (P.) Limited* v. *CCE* (2006) 4 SCC 786/[2006] 2006 taxmann.com 114 (SC).
62. *HPL Chemicals* v. *CCE* (2006) 5 SCC 208.

heading includes ... and also covers residuary sodium chloride, in particular, that is left after chemical processing or obtained as a by-product of the treatment of certain ores.

Another case is *O.K. Play*[63]. In this case, the court observed that the scheme of the Central Excise Tariff is based on the harmonized system of nomenclature and explanatory notes thereto. Therefore, (HSN) along with explanatory notes provides a safe guide for the interpretation of an entry. Further equal importance is required to be given to the rules of interpretation of the Excise Tariff. Under rule 3(*a*) it is provided that the heading having a more specific description shall be preferred to a heading having a more general description. For example, in the case of toys, the description refers to a reduced-size model of an article used by adults. This test helps to understand the difference between toys and furniture. It is also important to note that functional utility, design, shape, and predominant uses have to be taken into account while determining the classification of an item. The above aids assistance are more important than the names in the matter of correct classification.

For proper classification, various tests were laid down. These are "The common parlance test", "marketability test", and "popular meaning test" which are all tools for interpretation to arrive at a decision on the proper classification of a tariff entry. These tests, however, would be required to be applied if a particular tariff entry is capable of being classified in more than one head.[64]

There are other judgments of the Supreme Court on classification. These are Nagaraju Bros,[65] Simplex Mills,[66] Westinghouse Saxby[67]

63. *O.K. Play* v. *CCE* (2005) 2 SCC 460/[2005] 2005 taxmann.com 601 (SC).

64. *CCE* v. *Uni Products India Ltd.* [Civil Appeal Nos. 302-303 of 2009 date of decision 1st May 2020]/[2020] 116 taxmann.com 401 (SC). [The core issue in these appeals is as to whether car mats come under chapter-heading 57.03 or not. In view of the Court the goods were classifiable under chapter heading 570390.90.

65. *A. Nagaraju Bros* v. *State of A.P* 1994 Supp (3) SCC 122.

66. *Central Excise* v. *Simplex Mills Co. Ltd.* (2005) 3 SCC 51.

67. *Westinghouse Saxby Farmer Ltd.* v. *CCE* [Civil Appeal No. 37 of 2009 decided on March 8, 2021 (Three judges)]/[2023] 6 Centax 578 (SC).

10 Simplification and rationalisation of direct taxes

The taxation policy is the most important tool in the hands of the Government to mobilize resources not only to meet its normal expenditure but also to mobilize enough funds for social development, tackle poverty, promote inclusive growth, and take care of growing unemployment.

The working of the Income-tax Act and its administration since independence was reviewed by a number of committees and commissions. These were—

10.1 Committees and Commissions

The Income Tax Investigation Commission 1948

Taxation Enquiry Commission 1953

Nicholas Kaldor India tax report 1956

Tyagi committee 1958

Twelfth report of the law commission of India 1959

Bhoothalingam report on rationalization and simplification of the tax structure 1967

Administrative Reforms Commission 1968

H A Shah Committee 1969

Direct taxes enquiry Committee 1971 (Wanchoo Committee)

Direct taxes laws committee 1977 (Choksi Committee)

Economic Administrative Reforms Commission under the Chairmanship of Shri LK Jha

Kelkar Committee.

10.2 CAG and PAC Reports

In addition to the reports of the committees and commissions mentioned above, there are a number of reports of the CAG and Public Accounts Committee (PAC) on the working of tax administration.

10.3 The Direct Tax Code Bill 2010

The Direct Tax Code, 2010 introduced in Lok Sabha on 27th August, 2010 contained 319 clauses and twenty-second schedules[1]. The statement of the objects and reasons appended to the Bill stated as under-

> "The Income-tax Act, 1961, has been subjected to numerous amendments since its passage fifty years ago. It has been considerably revised, not less than thirty-four times, by amendment Acts besides the amendments carried out through the annual Finance Acts... As a result of all these amendments, the basic structure of the Income-tax Act has been overburdened and its language has become complex. Tax administrators, accountants and taxpayers have raised concerns about the complex structure of the Income-tax Act. In particular, the numerous amendments have rendered the Act difficult to decipher by the average taxpayer...."

The Direct Tax Code sought to consolidate and amend the laws relating to the Direct Taxes. The objectives are as follows: 1. To consolidate and simplify the Direct Tax laws; 2. To strengthen taxation provision for international transactions; 3. To phase out profit-linked incentives and replace them with investment-linked incentives; 4. To rationalize tax incentives and savings; 5. To implement general anti-avoidance rule to curb aggressive tax planning; 6. To tax non-profit making organizations.

The Direct Taxes Code Bill, 2010, introduced in Lok Sabha on 30 August, 2010 was referred to the Standing Committee on 09 September, 2010 for examination and report thereon. The Standing Committee on Finance presented its report on 13 March, 2012. The report contains 17 chapters.

The Direct Tax Code 2010 lapsed on the dissolution of the 14th Lok Sabha.

10.4 Simplification of Tax Laws

Simplification of income -tax has been a continuing exercise in common law countries. A simpler tax system, which is more intuitive and easier to understand, improves public confidence, boosts compliance, and empowers people to make the right decisions for their own circumstances through a better understanding of the consequences of their interaction with the tax system. In the United Kingdom, an independent Office of Tax Simplification was established. Since its creation in 2010, the OTS has offered independent advice and recommendations to the government on making the tax system simpler and easier to interact with taxpayers. The Office of Tax Simplification was established on 20 July, 2010 as an independent adviser to the Chancellor, providing advice on the simplification of the tax system. Finance Act, 2016 placed the OTS on a statutory basis and

1. A draft Direct Taxes Code along with a Discussion Paper was released in August, 2009 for public comments. It proposed to replace the Income-tax Act, 1961 and the Wealth-tax Act, 1957 by a single Act, namely the Direct Taxes Code. Public and stakeholder feedback on the proposals outlined in these documents was analysed and suggestions for amendments received from members of the public, business associations and other bodies were taken into account. Thereafter, a Revised Discussion Paper addressing the major issues was released in June, 2010. The present Bill is the outcome of this process.

set the requirement for HM Treasury to conduct a review of the effectiveness of the OTS every five years, with the first period ending on 28 November, 2021. In its final report[2] on the Review of the Office of Tax Simplification, it is, *inter alia*, stated that the OTS—

- Expose their reasoning behind their recommendations, particularly where there are trade-offs between simplification and other policy objectives that the government must consider;
- More clearly prioritise those recommendations which the OTS considers of most value to taxpayers;
- Maintain and expand the breadth and balance of knowledge, experience, and expertise within the Secretariat, while also seeking professional expertise in how it consults externally;
- Consider the volume and type of output it produces, and focuses more on activities that build its preliminary evidence base and embed its work; and,
- Clarifies its aims and objectives in light of its articulation of how it interprets 'tax simplification', using this to inform which areas it will prioritise over the next five-year period to maximise its impact.

10.5 The tax law rewrites

The tax rewrites in Australia, New Zealand, and the United Kingdom (UK), which occurred from the mid-1990s to the late 2000s, all focused on the legal simplicity (how difficult is a tax law to read and understand) and largely neglected effective simplicity (how easy is it to determine the correct tax liability).[3]

10.6 Seven Key Concepts

Cooper[4] suggests there are atleast seven key concepts that should inform an evaluation of tax simplification:

(1) **Predictability:** In this context, a rule would be simple if that rule and its scope were easily and accurately understood by taxpayers and their advisers.

(2) **Proportionality:** A rule would be simple if the complexity of the solution were no more than reasonably necessary to achieve the intended aim.

2. 2021 Review of the Office of Tax Simplification: Final Report available at https://www.gov.uk/government/publications/2021-review-of-the-office-of-tax-simplification-final-report.
3. B Tran-Nam 'Tax reform and tax simplification: Some conceptual issues and a preliminary assessment' (1999) 21(3) Sydney Law Review 500.
4. GS Cooper 'Themes and issues in tax simplification' (1993) 10(4) Australian Tax Forum 417 quoted in SIMPLIFICATION LESSONS FROM NEW ZEALAND, Chapter 6 accessed on 24th May 2023 available at https://ir.canterbury.ac.nz/bitstream/handle/10092/17764/Pages%20from%202019_Tax_simplification.pdf

(3) **Consistency:** This would apply where a rule deals with similar issues in the same way and without the need to make arbitrary distinctions.

(4) **Compliance:** A rule would be simple if it were easy for taxpayers to comply with without incurring excessive costs.

(5) **Administration:** A rule would be simple if it were easy for a revenue authority to administer.

(6) **Co-ordination:** A rule would be simple if it fitted appropriately with other tax rules; it would be complicated if its relationships with other rules were obscure.

(7) **Expression:** A rule would be simple if it were clearly expressed.

10.7 Road to the Future

Tax policy formulation is a challenging task. Experimentation is inevitable. While a robust architecture of indirect tax (GST) is in place, the re-writing of income tax law in one volume or in more than one volume is keenly awaited.

Subject Index*

*Number(s) after each entry denotes Para No.

APPENDICES

RELEVANT RULES AND FORMS OF INCOME-TAX RULES, 1962

[1][*J. – Indirect transfer prior to 28th May, 2012 of assets situate in India*

Specified conditions under *Explanation* to fifth and sixth provisos to *Explanation 5* to clause (*i*) of sub-section (1) of section 9.

11UE. (1) For the purposes of clauses (*i*), (*ii*) and (*iii*) of the *Explanation* to fifth and sixth provisos to *Explanation 5* to clause (*i*) of sub-section (1) of section 9, the declarant shall furnish an undertaking in Form No. 1 and shall append the undertakings from all the interested parties in Part M of the Annexure to the undertaking in Form No. 1 and furnish all the attachments required to be furnished under any clause or Part thereof.

(2) The conditions for the purposes of clause (*iv*) of the *Explanation* to fifth and sixth provisos to *Explanation 5* to clause (*i*) of sub-section (1) of section 9 shall be the following, namely:—

(*a*) the declarant and all the interested parties shall irrevocably withdraw, terminate or discontinue all the appeals or applications or petitions or proceedings, against the relevant order or orders and furnish evidence thereof and a declaration in the undertaking in Form No. 1 to the effect that it shall not, under any circumstances, reopen or file any such appeal, application, petition or proceeding in future against the relevant order or orders;

(*b*) the declarant and all the interested parties shall irrevocably withdraw, terminate or discontinue all the proceedings for arbitration, conciliation or mediation, or notices thereof against the relevant order or orders and furnish evidence thereof and a declaration in the undertaking in Form No. 1 to the effect that it shall not, under any circumstances, reopen or file any such proceeding or initiate any such arbitration, conciliation or mediation in future against the relevant order or orders;

(*c*) the declarant and all the interested parties shall irrevocably withdraw, terminate or discontinue all the proceedings to enforce or pursue attachments in respect of any award, order or judgment or any other relief against the Republic of India or Indian affiliates with respect to the relevant order or orders and furnish evidence thereof and a declaration in the undertaking in Form No. 1 to the effect that it shall not, under any circumstances, reopen or file any such proceeding in future against the Republic of India or Indian affiliates with respect to the relevant order or orders;

1. Inserted by the IT (Thirty-first Amdt.) Rules, 2021, w.e.f. 1-10-2021.

(*d*) the declarant and all the interested parties shall irrevocably terminate, release, discharge, and forever irrevocably waive all rights, whether direct or indirect, and any claims, demands, liens, actions, suits, causes of action, obligations, controversies, debts, costs, attorneys' fees, court's fees expenses, damages, judgments, orders, declaratory relief, and liabilities of whatever kind or nature at law, in equity, or otherwise, whether now known or unknown previously (or in future discovered), suspected or unsuspected, and whether or not concealed or hidden, which have existed or may have existed, or do exist or which hereafter can, shall or may exist in relation to any award, order, judgment, or any other relief against the Republic of India or Indian affiliates in connection with the relevant order or orders and furnish evidence thereof and a declaration in the undertaking in Form No. 1 to the effect that it shall not, under any circumstances, reopen or file any such proceeding or initiate any such arbitration, conciliation or mediation in future against the relevant order or orders;

(*e*) the declarant and all the interested parties shall irrevocably waive any right to seek or pursue any claim for costs in respect of any proceeding referred to in clause (*a*), (*b*), (*c*) or (*d*), including but not limited to any proceeding initiated by the Republic of India to set aside the award, order or judgment, or any other relief, referred to in clause (*a*), (*b*), (*c*) or (*d*), issued in favour of the declarant or any of the interested parties;

(*f*) the declarant and all the interested parties shall terminate, release, discharge, and forever irrevocably waive any right, whether direct or indirect, any remedies, claims, demands, liens, actions, suits, causes of action, obligations, controversies, debts, costs, attorneys' fees, court's fees, expenses, damages, judgments, orders, compensation, and liabilities of whatever kind or nature at law, in equity, or otherwise, whether now known or unknown, suspected or unsuspected, and whether or not concealed or hidden, which have existed or may have existed, or do exist or which hereafter can, shall or may exist, based on pursuit of any remedy or any and all claims, demands, damages, judgments, awards, costs, expenses, compensation or liabilities of any kind (whether asserted or unasserted), in relation to any facts, events, or omissions occurring at any time in relation to taxation of income referred to in the fifth and sixth provisos to *Explanation* 5 to clause (*i*) of sub-section (1) of section 9 or relevant order or orders, or any related award, judgment or court order, which may otherwise be available to the declarant or any of its interested parties;

(*g*) the declarant and all the interested parties shall indemnify, defend and hold harmless the Republic of India and Indian affiliates from and against any and all costs, expenses (including attorneys' fees and court's fees), interest, damages, and liabilities of any nature arising out of or in any way relating to the assertion or, bringing, filing or maintaining of any claim, at any time after the date of furnishing the undertaking in Form No. 1 by the declarant, by any person and the declarant and all the interested parties shall furnish an indemnity bond to this effect, such that the declarant and the interested parties fully assume the risk of any omission or mistake with respect to identification and procurement of authorisations and undertakings from any related parties or interested parties as provided in the undertaking, and secures the Republic of India and Indian affiliates from any claim related to any relevant order or orders, or in relation to any award, order, judgment, or any other relief against the Republic of India and Indian affiliates in connection with any relevant order or orders;

(*h*) the declarant and all the interested parties shall refrain from facilitating, procuring, encouraging or otherwise assisting any person (including but not limited to any related party or interested party) from bringing any proceeding or claims of any kind related to any relevant order or orders, or in relation to any award, order, judgment, or any other relief against the Republic of India or Indian affiliates in connection with any relevant order or orders; and

(*i*) the declarant and all the interested parties shall notify by a public notice or press release that, by signing the undertaking in Form No. 1 or Part M of the Annexure to the undertaking in Form No. 1, as the case may be, any claims arising out of or relating to the relevant orders or any related award, judgment or court order, no longer subsist, and that such person or entity issuing the public notice has signed the undertaking, and that such undertaking includes an indemnity against any claims brought against the Republic of India or any India affiliate contrary to the undertaking, and that the declarant and all the interested parties shall furnish a copy of such public notice to the Republic of India.

(3) The execution, delivery and performance of the undertaking in Form No. 1 submitted by the declarant, undertakings from all the interested parties in Part M of the Annexure to the undertaking in Form No. 1 and indemnity bond by the declarant and interested parties in Part N of the Annexure to the undertaking in Form No. 1 shall be duly authorised by all necessary corporate action, including but not limited to any board resolution or similar authorisation under applicable law and a copy of such board resolution and legal authorisation shall be furnished by the declarant.]

[2][**Manner of furnishing undertaking under rule 11UE.**

11UF. (1) The undertaking in Form No. 1 under sub-rule (1) of rule 11UE shall be submitted by the declarant to the jurisdictional Principal Commissioner or Commissioner within forty-five days from the date of commencement of the Income-tax (31st Amendment) Rules, 2021.

(2) After the undertaking in Form No. 1 under sub-rule (1) of rule 11UE is furnished by the declarant, the jurisdictional Principal Commissioner or Commissioner shall, within a period of fifteen days from the date of receipt of the said undertaking,—

(*a*) grant a certificate in Form No. 2 accepting such undertaking; or

(*b*) pass an order rejecting such undertaking, where the undertaking in Form No. 1 is incorrect or incomplete or any part thereof or any of the

2. Inserted by the IT (Thirty-first Amdt.) Rules, 2021, w.e.f. 1-10-2021.

attachments or evidences or the indemnity bonds provided therein or any of the authorisations, as referred to in sub-rule (3) of rule 11UE is incorrect or incomplete or not furnished, after giving an opportunity of being heard to the declarant.

(3) After the grant of certificate in Form No. 2, the conditions under sub-rule (2) of rule 11UE shall be fulfilled by the declarant and interested parties and an intimation to this effect shall be filed by the declarant in Form No. 3 within sixty days of the date of receipt of certificate in Form No. 2 under sub-rule (2) with the jurisdictional Principal Commissioner or Commissioner.

(4) The jurisdictional Principal Commissioner or Commissioner may, on an application made by the declarant, extend the period of sixty days under sub-rule (3) by a further period not exceeding sixty days.

(5) Where the intimation in Form No. 3 is filed after the period of sixty days under sub-rule (3) or further period extended under sub-rule (4), as the case may be, then, notwithstanding anything contained in any other provision of rule 11UE and this rule, such intimation in Form No. 3 shall be treated as invalid and the provisions of this rule shall apply as if such person had never furnished the intimation in Form No. 3.

(6) No intimation in Form No. 3 under sub-rule (3) shall be required to be furnished by the declarant if the following conditions are satisfied, namely:—

(*a*) the declarant or any of the interested parties has not filed, with respect to all the relevant order or orders, any—

(*i*) appeal or application or petition or proceeding;

(*ii*) arbitration, conciliation or mediation and no notices have been given thereof; or

(*iii*) proceeding to enforce or pursue attachments in respect of any award, order or judgment or any other relief against the Republic of India or Indian affiliates; and

(*b*) where, with respect to the relevant order or orders, any—

(*i*) appeals or applications or petitions or proceeding;

(*ii*) arbitration, conciliation or mediation; or

(*iii*) proceeding to enforce or pursue attachments in respect of any award, order or judgment or any other relief against the Republic of India or Indian affiliates,

has been filed or notice thereof has been given by the declarant or any interested parties, the declarant and all such interested parties have irrevocably withdrawn all such appeals, applications, petitions, proceeding, arbitration, conciliation and mediation and no further appeal or application or petition or proceeding or arbitration or conciliation or mediation has been filed by the declarant or any such interested party against the Republic of India or any of the Indian Affiliates before the withdrawal of such arbitration, conciliation or mediation and evidence thereof has been furnished at the time of furnishing the undertaking in Form No. 1 referred to in sub-rule (1) of rule 11UE; and (*c*) where with respect to the relevant order or orders, any,—

(*i*) appeals or applications or petitions or proceeding;

(*ii*) the arbitration, conciliation or mediation;

(*iii*) the proceeding to enforce or pursue attachments in respect of any award, order or judgment or any other relief against the Republic of India or Indian affiliates;

had been filed by the declarant or any of the interested parties and have been disposed of, no further appeal or application or petition or proceeding or arbitration or conciliation or mediation has been filed by the declarant or any such interested party against the Republic of India or any of the Indian Affiliates on or before the disposal of such arbitration, conciliation or mediation and evidence thereof has been furnished at the time of furnishing the undertaking in Form No. 1 referred to in sub-rule (1) of rule 11UE.

(7) After the receipt of intimation in Form No. 3 under sub-rule (3) or grant of certificate in Form No. 2 under sub-rule (2) in cases covered under sub-rule (6), the jurisdictional Principal Commissioner or Commissioner shall pass an order granting relief in Form No. 4 or decline to grant relief in accordance with the procedure specified in sub-rule (8).

(8) The jurisdictional Principal Commissioner or Commissioner may, after giving an opportunity of being heard to the declarant, decline to grant relief under sub-rule (7) where,—

(*a*) the declarant has not fulfilled any of the conditions stipulated under sub-rule (2) of rule 11UE;

(*b*) the intimation in Form No. 3 or any part thereof is incorrect or incomplete;

(*c*) the intimation in Form No. 3 has not been filed in a case other than that covered under sub-rule (6);

(*d*) any of the attachments provided in Form No. 3 is incorrect or incomplete or has not been furnished;

(*e*) any of the evidences required to be furnished along with Form No. 3 is incorrect or incomplete or has not been furnished; or

(*f*) the intimation in Form No. 3 submitted by the declarant is not duly authorised by all necessary corporate action, including but not limited to any board resolution or similar authorisation under applicable law or a copy of such board resolution or legal authorisation is incorrect or incomplete or not furnished by the declarant.

(9) The order granting the relief under sub-rule (7) or declining to grant relief under sub-rule (8) shall be passed,—

(*a*) within a period of thirty days from the date of receipt of Form No. 3 by the Principal Commissioner or Commissioner, in cases where intimation in Form 3 has been furnished to the Principal Commissioner or Commissioner under sub-rule (3);

(*b*) within thirty days of the issue of Form No. 2, in cases covered under sub-rule (6).

(10) No order rejecting the undertaking in Form No. 1 under clause (*b*) of sub-rule (2) or declining relief under sub-rule (8), shall be passed by the Principal Commissioner or Commissioner without the approval of the Chief Commissioner.

(11) For the purpose of rejecting the undertaking under clause (*b*) of sub-rule (2) or declining to grant relief under sub-rule (8), the Principal Commissioner or Commissioner shall intimate the reasons thereof to the declarant and give him an opportunity of submitting a renewed undertaking in Form No. 1 or renewed intimation in Form No. 3, as the case may be, within a further period not exceeding thirty days.

(12) Where the renewed undertaking or renewed intimation is not filed within such further period under sub-rule (11), then, notwithstanding anything contained in any other provision of the rule 11UE and this rule, such undertaking or intimation shall be treated as invalid and the provisions of this rule shall apply as if such person had never furnished the undertaking in Form No. 1 or intimation in Form No. 3, as the case may be.

(13) The extended period allowed under sub-rule (11) for submitting a renewed undertaking in Form No. 1 or a renewed intimation in Form No. 3 shall be excluded from,—

(*a*) the period of fifteen days under sub-rule (2) for granting a certificate in Form No. 2 or passing an order rejecting such undertaking, as the case may be, by the jurisdictional Principal Commissioner or Commissioner; or

(*b*) thirty days under clauses (*a*) and (*b*) of sub-rule (9) for passing an order granting relief under sub-rule (7) or declining relief under sub-rule (8), as the case may be, by the jurisdictional Principal Commissioner or Commissioner.

(14) For the purposes of computing the period of limitation under sub-rule (2) or (9), where immediately after the exclusion of the period or extended period allowed to the declarant, the period of limitation available to the Principal Commissioner or Commissioner, for granting certificate or passing or issuing an order under sub-rule (2) or (9), is less than fifteen days, such remaining period shall be extended to fifteen days and the period of limitation under said sub-rules shall be deemed to be extended accordingly.

(15) The undertaking in Form No. 1 shall be deemed to have never been filed if the Principal Commissioner or Commissioner has passed an order rejecting the undertaking in Form No. 1 under clause (*b*) of sub-rule (2) or declined to grant relief to the declarant under sub-rule (8).

(16) The directions of the jurisdictional Principal Commissioner or Commissioner, in Form No. 4, shall be binding on the Assessing Officer who shall,—

(*a*) give effect to such directions and pass an order and issue the refund, if any, and revoke attachments, if any, within a period of fifteen days from the date of the receipt of such directions; and (*b*) file an application to withdraw any appeal or application or petition or proceeding filed by any income-tax authority or intimate the concerned person, where appeals or applications or petitions or proceeding has been filed by any other person representing the Republic of India, with respect to the specified orders covered under Form No. 4, within sixty days from the date of receipt of such directions.

(17) Any dispute with respect to the undertaking or part of the undertaking or indemnity bond specified Forms prescribed under these rules or in respect of any direction or order issued thereunder shall be governed by the relevant Indian laws and be decided in accordance with the procedures specified under the Act, under the exclusive jurisdiction of the relevant income-tax authorities, tribunals or courts in India, as the case may be, which are empowered to decide disputes under the Act.

(18) The Form Nos. 1, 2, 3 and 4 of Appendix IV shall be the Forms for the purposes of this rule and rule 11UE.

Explanation.—For the purposes of this rule and rule 11UE, unless the context otherwise requires,—

(*a*) "declarant" means the person in whose case a specified order has been passed or made, as the case may be;

(*b*) "Indian affiliate" means any of departments, agencies, instrumentalities, public sector companies, and other entities of the Republic of India, owned or controlled, directly or indirectly, allegedly or in fact, by any thereof, as well as any officials, officers, directors, employees, attorneys, representatives, those providing financing, and agents of any of these persons, whether in India or in any other country or territory outside India;

(*c*) "interested party" means the following, namely:—

(*i*) all the companies or entities in the entire chain of holding of the declarant till the ultimate holding company or entity;

(*ii*) any person to whom the declarant has transferred any of its claims under any award, judgment, or court order pertaining to the relevant orders or under the relevant orders or granted any rights;

(*iii*) any person other than the person mentioned in sub-clauses (*i*) and (*ii*), in whose favour any interest has been created or assigned by the declarant or under any law or rules made thereunder with respect to any of the relevant order; and

(*iv*) any person who has initiated any proceedings with respect to any of the relevant orders;

(*d*) "related party" means affiliates, predecessors, successors, all the companies or entities in the entire chain of holding till the ultimate holding company or entity, subsidiaries (whether direct or indirect), assignees, agents, shareholders (present and future), owners, directors, officers, those providing financing, and employees of the declarant;

(*e*) "relevant order" means any specified order passed or made in respect of income accruing or arising through or from the transfer of an asset or a capital asset situate in India in consequence of the transfer of a share or interest in a company or entity registered or incorporated outside India made before the 28th day of May, 2012, particulars whereof are provided in Part A of the Annexure to the undertaking in Form No. 1;

(*f*) "specified order" means,—

(*i*) an assessment or reassessment order under section 143, section 144, section 147 or section 153A or section 153C; or

(*ii*) an order passed for enhancing the assessment or reducing a refund already made or otherwise increasing the liability of the assessee under section 154; or

(*iii*) an order passed deeming a person to be an assessee in default under sub-section (1) of section 201; or

(*iv*) an order passed imposing a penalty under Chapter XXI or under section 221;

(*g*) "ultimate holding company or entity" means a company or an entity that has ultimate control of the declarant directly or indirectly and such company or entity is not itself controlled by, or is subsidiary of, any other company or entity.]

[1]*APPENDIX IV*

FORM NO. 1

[*See* rule 11UE (1)]

Undertaking under sub-rule (1) of rule 11UE

To,

Principal Commissioner/Commissioner

....

Sir/Madam,

I...(name in block letters) son/daughter of .... designation ....and nationality ....and related passport number.................. (hereinafter referred to as "signatory") having Permanent Account Number/Aadhaar Number (*see* Note 1)................. on behalf of .... (name of the declarant) having Permanent Account Number/Aadhaar number/Tax Deduction Account Number (*see* Note 2) ....and being duly authorised and competent to represent the declarant in this regard pursuant to Board Resolution and legal authorisation (*see* Note 3), as the case may be, hereby declare as follows:

(*a*) That specified orders have been passed or made in respect of income accruing or arising through or from the transfer of an asset or a capital asset situate in India in consequence of the transfer of a share or interest in a company or entity registered or incorporated outside India made before the 28th day of May, 2012 and particulars of such specified orders are provided in Part A of the Annexure.

(*b*) The declarant has (strike off the options that are not applicable),

(*i*) not filed any appeal or application or petition or proceeding before any income-tax authority or Authority for Advance Rulings constituted under section 245-O of the Act or the Board for Advance Rulings constituted under section 245-OB or Income-tax Settlement Commission constituted under section 245B or the Interim Board for Settlement constituted under section 245AA or any tribunal or court against the relevant orders, and hereby undertakes that it shall not file any appeal, application, petition or proceeding in future against the relevant order or orders. Particulars of such relevant order or orders are provided in Part B of the Annexure;

(*ii*) filed one or more appeals or applications or petitions or proceeding before any income-tax authority or Authority for Advance Rulings constituted under section 245-O of the Act or the Board for Advance Rulings under section 245-OB or Income-tax Settlement Commission constituted under section 245B or the Interim Board for Settlement constituted under section 245AA or any tribunal or court against the relevant orders and has irrevocably withdrawn, on a with prejudice basis, all such appeals or applications or petitions or proceeding and evidence thereof is furnished herewith and hereby undertakes that it shall not file any appeal, application, petition or proceeding in future against the

1. Inserted by the IT (Thirty-first Amdt.) Rules, 2021, w.e.f. 1-10-2021.

relevant order or orders. Particulars of such appeals or applications or petitions or proceeding filed and irrevocably withdrawn with prejudice by the declarant, are provided in Part C of the Annexure;

(*iii*) filed one or more appeals or applications or petitions or proceeding before any income-tax authority or Authority for Advance Rulings constituted under section 245-O of the Act or the Board for Advance Rulings under section 245-OB or income-tax Settlement Commission constituted under section 245B or the Interim Board for Settlement constituted under section 245AA or any tribunal or court against the relevant order or orders and all the appeals or applications or petitions or proceeding filed by the declarant have been disposed of and no further appeal or application or petition or proceeding has been filed by the declarant and evidence thereof is furnished herewith and hereby undertake that it shall not file any appeal, application, petition or proceeding in future against the relevant order or orders. Particulars of such appeals or applications or petitions or proceeding filed and disposed of, are provided in Part C of the Annexure;

(*iv*) filed appeals or applications or petitions or proceeding before any income-tax authority or Authority for Advance Rulings constituted under section 245-O of the Act or the Board for Advance Rulings under section 245-OB or Income-tax Settlement Commission constituted under section 245B or the Interim Board for Settlement constituted under section 245AA or any tribunal or court against the relevant orders and one or more of such appeals or applications or petitions or proceeding are pending as on the date of this undertaking and hereby undertakes to irrevocably withdraw, terminate and discontinue any and all such appeals or applications or petitions or proceeding that are pending as on the date of signing this undertaking, on a with prejudice basis, in accordance with clause (*e*) below. The declarant further undertakes that it shall not file any such appeal, application, petition or proceeding in future against the relevant order or orders. Particulars of such pending appeals or applications or petitions or proceeding filed by the declarant and their status as on the date of this undertaking, are provided in Part D of the Annexure;

(*c*) The declarant has (strike off the options that are not applicable),

(*i*) not initiated any proceeding for arbitration, conciliation or mediation, and no notice has been given thereof under any law for the time being in force or under any agreement entered into by India with any other country or territory outside India, whether for protection of investment or otherwise against the relevant orders, and hereby undertakes that it shall not initiate any such arbitration, conciliation or mediation in future. Particulars of such relevant order or orders are provided in Part B of the Annexure;

(*ii*) initiated proceeding for arbitration, conciliation or mediation, or notices thereof has been given, under any law for the time being in force or under any agreement entered into by India with any other country or territory outside India, whether for protection of investment or otherwise against the relevant order or orders and has irrevocably, on a with prejudice basis, withdrawn any such proceeding for arbitration, conciliation or mediation, and notices given thereof and evidence thereof is furnished herewith. The declarant hereby undertakes that it shall not reopen in future any such proceeding or initiate or file any such arbitration, conciliation or mediation in future arising out of or in connection with the relevant order or orders. Particulars of such proceeding for arbitration, conciliation or mediation and notices given thereof, initiated and irrevocably withdrawn with prejudice by the declarant, are provided in Part E of the Annexure;

(*iii*) initiated proceeding for arbitration, conciliation or mediation, or notices thereof has been given, under any law for the time being in force or under any agreement entered into by India with any other country or territory outside India, whether for protection of investment or otherwise against the relevant order or orders and all the arbitration, conciliation or mediation filed by the declarant have been disposed of and no further proceeding has been initiated by the declarant and evidence thereof is furnished herewith. The declarant hereby undertakes that it shall not reopen in future any such proceeding or initiate or file any such arbitration, conciliation or mediation in future arising out of or in connection with the relevant order or orders. Particulars of such proceeding for arbitration, conciliation or mediation and notices given thereof, initiated and disposed of, are provided in Part E of the Annexure;

(*iv*) initiated proceeding for arbitration, conciliation or mediation, or notices thereof has been given, under any law for the time being in force or under any agreement entered into by India with any other country or territory outside India, whether for protection of investment or otherwise against the relevant order or orders and one or more of such proceeding or notices are pending on the date of undertaking and hereby undertakes to irrevocably withdraw, terminate and discontinue any and all such proceeding or notices for arbitration, conciliation or mediation that are pending as on the date of signing this undertaking, on a with prejudice basis, in accordance with clause (*e*) below. Particulars of such pending proceeding and notices filed by the declarant are provided in Part F of the Annexure. The declarant hereby further undertakes that it shall not initiate any such arbitration, conciliation or mediation in future arising out of or in connection with the relevant order or orders;

(*v*) received or got any awards, orders, judgments or any other reliefs issued in favour of the declarant, arising out of or in any way relating to the imposition of tax, interest and penalty based on the relevant order or orders, under any agreement entered into by India with any other country or territory outside India, whether for protection of investment or otherwise and hereby undertakes to irrevocably waive any right to seek or pursue any claim or costs or declaratory relief in relation to or arising out of such awards, orders or judgments or any other relief that may have been ordered, issued or passed against India and any Indian affiliate, whether it is in proceeding initiated by the declarant or by India and any Indian affiliate. The declarant also undertakes to irrevocably waive any right to seek or pursue any claim for costs or relief in respect of any proceeding initiated by the Republic of India to set aside such award, order or judgment or any other relief issued in favour of the declarant. The declarant hereby undertakes that it shall not initiate or file any such arbitration, conciliation or mediation in future. Particulars of such awards, orders, judgment or any other relief are provided in Part G of the Annexure;

(*d*) The declarant has (strike off the options that are not applicable),

(*i*) not initiated any proceeding to enforce or pursue attachments in connection with any awards, orders, judgments, any other relief that may have been ordered, issued or passed by any tribunal or court or other judicial, *quasi-judicial* or administrative authority in relation to the said arbitration, conciliation or mediation proceeding in favour of the declarant as referred to in clause (*c*) of this undertaking either against the Republic of India and any Indian affiliate, and hereby undertakes that it shall not initiate any such proceeding in future. Particulars of such award, order or judgment are provided in Part B of the Annexure;

(*ii*) initiated proceeding to enforce or pursue attachments in connection with any awards, orders, judgments or any other relief that may have been ordered, issued or passed by any tribunal or court or other judicial, *quasi-judicial* or administrative authority in relation to the said arbitration, conciliation or mediation proceeding in favour of the declarant, as referred to in clause (*c*) of this undertaking against the Republic of India and any Indian affiliate. The declarant has irrevocably and with prejudice withdrawn or discontinued any such proceeding and hereby undertakes that it shall not reopen any such proceeding in future or file or initiate fresh proceeding to enforce or pursue attachments and evidence thereof is furnished herewith. Particulars of such proceeding, initiated and withdrawn or discontinued by the declarant, are provided in Part H of the Annexure;

(*iii*) initiated proceeding to enforce or pursue attachments in connection with any awards, orders, judgments or any other relief that may have been ordered, issued or passed by any tribunal or court or other judicial, *quasi-judicial* or administrative authority in relation to the said arbitration, conciliation or mediation proceeding in favour of the declarant, as referred to in clause (*c*) of this undertaking against the Republic of India and any Indian affiliate. All such proceeding filed by the declarant have been disposed of and no further proceeding has been filed by the declarant and evidence is herewith furnished and hereby undertakes that it shall not reopen any such proceeding in future or file or initiate fresh proceeding to enforce or pursue attachments. Particulars of such proceeding, initiated and disposed of, are provided in Part H of the Annexure;

(*iv*) initiated proceeding to enforce or pursue attachments in connection with any awards, orders, judgments, or any other relief that may have been ordered, issued or passed by any tribunal or court or other judicial, *quasi-judicial* or administrative authority in relation to the said arbitration, conciliation or mediation proceeding in favour of the declarant as referred to in clause (*c*) of this undertaking, either against the Republic of India and any Indian affiliate and one or more of such proceeding are pending on the date of undertaking and, the declarant has obtained one or more orders from any court or other authority which remain outstanding against India and any Indian Affiliate. The declarant hereby undertakes that it shall not file in future any such proceeding to enforce or pursue attachments regarding any awards, orders, judgments, or any other relief that may have been ordered, issued or passed by any tribunal or court or other judicial, *quasi-judicial* or administrative authority in relation to the said arbitration, conciliation or mediation proceeding in favour of the declarant as referenced in clause (*c*) of this undertaking or to enforce the orders from any court or other authority which remain outstanding against Republic of India and any Indian Affiliate. The declarant further undertakes to fully cooperate with the Republic of India or any Indian affiliate which is subject to such outstanding order, in order to set-aside or otherwise nullify any such outstanding order, and irrevocably and with prejudice waives any rights or remedies arising from such outstanding order. Particulars of such proceeding are provided in Part I of the Annexure. The declarant also undertakes to irrevocably withdraw, terminate and discontinue with prejudice any and all such proceeding to enforce or pursue attachments in accordance with clause (*e*).

(*e*) The declarant hereby undertakes as follows:

(*i*) to irrevocably and with prejudice withdraw, discontinue, terminate and take all necessary steps to irrevocably and with prejudice close the pending proceeding referred in sub-clause (*iv*) of clause (*b*), sub-clause (*iv*) of clause (*c*), sub-clause (*v*) of clause (*c*) and sub-clause (*iv*) of clause (*d*) of this undertaking, as well as any other pending proceeding against India or Indian affiliates relating to the relevant order or orders and not referenced in clauses (*b*), (*c*) and (*d*) above, and not to pursue in any way and by any means in future the pending proceeding as referenced in clauses (*b*), (*c*), and (*d*) above, and any other pending proceeding relating to the relevant order or orders not referred in the above clauses and any other fresh proceeding relating to the relevant order or orders. In so acting, declarant shall act in accordance with this undertaking and in full cooperation with the Republic of India;

(*ii*) to irrevocably terminate, release, discharge, and forever irrevocably waive any right, whether direct or indirect, and any claims, demands, liens, actions, suits, causes of action, obligations, controversies, debts, costs, attorneys' fees, court's fees, expenses, damages, judgments, orders, declaratory reliefs and liabilities of whatever kind or nature at law, in equity, or otherwise, whether now known or unknown previously (or in future discovered), suspected or unsuspected, and whether or not concealed or hidden, which have existed or may have existed, or do exist or which hereafter can, shall or may exist, in relation to any award, order, judgment, or any other relief as referred in clauses (*b*), (*c*) and (*d*) of this undertaking, against the Republic of India and all Indian affiliates, ordered, issued or passed in connection with the relevant order or orders, whether it is in proceeding initiated by the declarant or by Republic of India and any Indian Affiliate. The declarant further undertakes to fully cooperate with the Republic of India or any Indian affiliate which is subject to any outstanding order referenced in clause (*d*), in order to set-aside or otherwise nullify any such outstanding order, and irrevocably and with prejudice waives any rights or remedies arising from such outstanding order. For the avoidance of doubt, the declarant's irrevocable waiver includes irrevocable waiver of any right provided by any existing *ex parte*, provisional, or other kind of court order permitting enforcement or attachment against the Republic of India and any Indian affiliate, in furtherance of any award, order judgment, or any other relief that may have been ordered or issued or passed by any arbitral tribunal as referred in clauses (*b*), (*c*) and (*d*) above. For further avoidance of doubt, the declarant also undertakes to irrevocably waive any right to seek or pursue any claim for costs in respect of any proceeding initiated by Republic of India and any Indian affiliate to set aside such award, order or judgment ordered, issued or passed in favour of the declarant. Such irrevocable waiver includes, but is not limited to, any right under any relevant *ex parte* order;

(*iii*) to irrevocably waive any right to seek or pursue any claim for costs in respect of any proceeding initiated by the Republic of India to set aside such award, order or judgment, or any other relief issued in favour of the declarant.

(*f*) The declarant specifically represents that all Parts of the Annexure as described in this undertaking are full and complete to the best of its knowledge.

(*g*) The declarant hereby undertakes to irrevocably terminate, release, discharge, and forever irrevocably waive any right, whether direct or indirect, and any remedies, claims, demands, liens, actions, suits, causes of action, obligations, controversies, debts, costs, attorneys' fees, court's fees, expenses, damages, judgments, orders, compensation, and liabilities of whatever kind or nature at law, in equity, or otherwise, whether now known or unknown, suspected or unsuspected, and whether or not concealed or hidden, which have existed or may have existed, or do exist or which hereafter can, shall or may exist, based on pursuit of any remedy or any and all claims, demands, damages, judgments, awards, costs, expenses, compensation or liabilities of any kind (whether asserted or unasserted) in relation to any facts, events, or omissions occurring from the beginning of time to the date of this undertaking and thereafter in future in relation to taxation of said income or relevant order or orders, or any related award, judgment or court order, which may otherwise be available to the declarant under any law for the time being in force, in equity, under any statute or under any agreement entered into by Republic of India with any country or territory outside Republic of India, whether for protection of investment or otherwise, whether it is in proceeding initiated by the declarant or by Republic of India and any Indian affiliate. For the avoidance of doubt, the declarant's above waiver includes an irrevocable waiver of any claim against India and any Indian Affiliate to costs incurred or interest accrued in relation to the relevant order or orders, or any related ongoing or completed litigation, arbitration, conciliation or mediation. Moreover, for the avoidance of any doubt, the declarant hereby undertakes (for itself and on behalf of all related parties) to forgo any reliance on any right under any award, judgment, or court order pertaining to the relevant order or orders or under the relevant order or orders.

(*h*) The declarant further represents that as of the date of this undertaking, it has not transferred any of its claims under any award, judgment, or court order pertaining to the relevant order or orders or under the relevant order or orders, or granted any rights, to third parties, and further undertakes to not transfer any of its claims to third parties after entering this undertaking. Where any such claim or right is transferred, the declarant confirms that it has provided the particulars of all the interested parties in Part L, and the undertakings from each of such interested parties is attached with this undertaking in accordance with Part M of the Annexure.

(*i*) In the event that, notwithstanding the foregoing, any person asserts, brings, files or maintains any claim against the Republic of India or Indian affiliates (hereinafter collectively referred to as "releasees")at any time on or after the date of furnishing this undertaking, the declarant shall indemnify, defend and hold harmless such releases from and against any and all costs, expenses (including attorney's fees and court's fees), interest, damages, and liabilities of any nature arising out of or in any way relating to the assertion or, bringing, filing or maintaining of such claim. The declarant specifically represents that, to the best of its knowledge, after —

(*i*) the execution of this undertaking;

(*ii*) the execution of any separate related undertaking by any other party in connection with the relevant order or orders; and

(*iii*) irrevocable withdrawal of all pending proceeding as outlined in this undertaking,

no other claim regarding the said relevant order or orders referenced above, or any related award, judgment, or court order, shall remain outstanding against the Republic of India or any Indian affiliates. To avoid any doubt, the declarant's indemnity of releases under this clause shall include any claim brought by any third party alleging that it has obtained the declarant's claims under an award, judgment or court order or the relevant order or orders. An indemnity bond to this effect is attached in Part N of the undertaking.

(*j*) For the removal of any doubt, the declarant fully assumes the risk through the indemnity in clause (*i*) of any omission or mistake with respect to securing releases against any related claim by any person. If the declarant fails to obtain any release from such person, the declarant warrants that it will indemnify the Republic of India or any Indian affiliates from any defence costs, court costs, and damages. An indemnity bond to the effect of clauses (*i*) and (*j*) is annexed to the undertaking.

(*k*) The declarant further undertakes to refrain from facilitating, procuring, encouraging or otherwise assisting any person (including but not limited to any related party or interested party) from bringing any proceeding or claims of any kind referred to in the above clauses, or any proceeding or claim of any kind related to any relevant order or orders referred to above (whether in respect of tax, interest or penalty). The declarant shall notify by a public notice or press release, at any time before furnishing intimation in Form No. 3 where this Form is required to be furnished under rule 11UF and before furnishing this undertaking in other cases, that by signing this undertaking any claims arising out of or relating to the relevant order or orders or any related award, judgment or court order, no longer subsist. Such public notice or press release shall include, among other things, confirmation that,—

(*i*) the declarant (and its related parties) forever irrevocably forgo any reliance on any right and provisions under any award, judgment, or court order pertaining to the relevant order or orders or under the relevant order or orders;

(*ii*) the declarant has provided this undertaking, which includes a complete release of the Republic of India and any Indian Affiliates with respect to any award, judgment, or court order pertaining to the relevant order or orders or under the relevant order or orders, and with respect to any claim pertaining to the relevant order or orders;

(*iii*) the undertaking also includes an indemnity against any claims brought against the Republic of India or any Indian affiliate, including by related parties or interested parties, contrary to the release; and

(*iv*) the declarant confirms it will treat any such award, judgment, or court order as null and void and without legal effect to the same extent as if it had been set aside by a competent court and will not take any action or initiate any proceeding or bring any claim based on that.

(*l*) The declarant confirms that the undertakings given herein are intended to be enforceable by the Republic of India, including so as to secure the irrevocable waiver, withdrawal or discontinuance (as appropriate) of all the proceeding and claims referred to in any of the clauses of this undertaking.

(*m*) The declarant represents and warrants that:

(*i*) it has full legal power and authority to execute and deliver this undertaking(including but not limited to the issuance of the indemnity described in clauses (*i*) and (*j*) under applicable law;

(*ii*) the execution, delivery and performance of this undertaking(including but not limited to the issuance of the indemnity described in clauses (*i*) and (*j*) has been duly authorised by all necessary corporate action, including but not limited to any board resolution or similar authorisation under applicable law (*see* Note 3);

(*iii*) this undertaking constitutes the legal, valid and binding obligation of the declarant, enforceable against the declarant in accordance with its terms;

(*iv*) such authorisations described in the above sub-clauses (*i*), (*ii*) and (*iii*) are effective under applicable law, and to this end, letters from local counsel in the relevant jurisdictions are attached to this undertaking which confirm the legality of such authorisations under applicable law.

(*n*) The declarant confirms that by submitting the present undertaking, it fulfils the conditions specified in the *Explanation* below the sixth proviso to *Explanation 5* to clause (*i*) of sub-section (1) of section 9.

(*o*) The details of the bank account in which the refund may be credited are provided in Part J of the Annexure.

(*p*) The details of all the interested parties are provided in Part K and Part L of the Annexure. The undertaking in Part M of the Annexure by each of such persons is attached with this undertaking. The declarant represents and warrants that:

(*i*) all such undertakings have been executed and delivered by the person who has full legal power and authority to execute and deliver such undertakings;

(*ii*) the execution, delivery and performance of this undertaking has been duly authorised by all necessary corporate action; and

(*iii*) this undertaking constitutes the legal, valid and binding obligation of the declarant, enforceable against such person in accordance with its terms. Such separate, related undertakings may take the same form as this undertaking.

(*q*) The declarant is or is not covered under sub-rule (6) of rule 11UF and in case if the declarant is not covered under said sub-rule all the conditions provided under sub-rule (2) of rule 11UE have been fulfilled.

(*r*) This undertaking is governed by relevant Indian law and any dispute with respect to this undertaking shall be subject to Indian laws and be decided in accordance with the procedures specified in the Act under the exclusive jurisdiction of the relevant income-tax authorities, tribunals or courts in Republic of India, as the case may be, which are empowered to decide disputes under the Act.

I also confirm that I am aware of all the consequences and implications of this undertaking.

Place: ....

Date: ....

Signature

....

Attachments:

1. The Board Resolution or legal authorisation, as the case may be, as referred to in clause (*m*) of the undertaking.
2. An indemnity bond to the effect of clause (*i*) and clause (*j*) of the undertaking attached in Part N of the undertaking.
3. Copy of the public notice referred to in clause (*k*) of the undertaking, where Form No. 3 is not required to be furnished under sub-rule (6) of rule 11UF.
4. Attachments as required in different parts of the Annexure to this undertaking.

Notes:

1. This information is required to be furnished where the Permanent Account Number or Aadhaar Number of the signatory is available.
2. Company Identification Number and Taxpayer Identification Number are to be provided where Permanent Account Number or Aadhaar Number or Tax Deduction Account Number of the declarant are not available.
3. The Board Resolution or legal authorisation, as referred to in clause (*m*) of the undertaking shall, among other things:
   (*a*) record the signatory's power and authority to give the undertaking on behalf of the declarant; and
   (*b*) record the declarant's power and authority to indemnify defend and hold harmless the Republic of India and the Indian affiliates in accordance with clause (*i*) of the undertaking.

Verification

Verified that the contents of this undertaking are true to the best of my knowledge and belief. No part of the undertaking is false and nothing has been concealed or misstated therein.

Verified at .... place .... on this the .... day .... of .... month .... year ....

Place: ....

Date: ....

Signature

....

Annexure

Part A– Particulars of the relevant order or orders:

Sr. No.	*Assessment Year or Financial year*	*Income-tax authority passing the order*	*Details of the order under consideration*		*Taxes or penalty determined*	*Interest*	*Total demand*	*Relief, provided in any appeal proceeding, if any*	*Demand recovered from the declarant*	*Pending demand or refund due as on date*	*Details of the attachments made by any income-tax authority*
			Section and sub-section of the Income-tax Act, 1961	*Date of order*							
(1)	*(2)*	*(3)*	*(4)*	*(5)*	*(6)*	*(7)*	*(8)*	*(9)*	*(10)*	*(11)*	*(12)*

Part B - Particulars of the relevant order or orders covered by sub-clause (*i*) of clauses (*b*), (*c*) and (*d*) of the undertaking:

Sl. No.	*Sl. No. in Part A where the relevant order is mentioned*	*No appeal or application or petition or proceeding before any income-tax authority or Authority for Advance Rulings constituted under section 245-O of the Act or the Board for Advance Rulings under section 245-OB or Income-tax Settlement Commission constituted under section 245B or the Interim Board for Settlement constituted under section 245AA or any tribunal or court has been filed (refer clause (b)(i) of the undertaking).*	*No proceeding has been initiated for arbitration, conciliation or mediation, and no notice has been given thereof under any law for the time being in force or under any agreement entered into by India with any other country or territory outside India, whether for protection of investment or otherwise (refer clause (c)(i) of the undertaking).*	*No proceeding initiated to enforce or pursue attachments in connection with any award, order or judgment, any other relief that may have been ordered or issued or passed by any tribunal or court or other judicial or administrative authority in relation to the said arbitration, conciliation or mediation proceeding in favour of the declarant against the Republic of India and Indian affiliates (refer clause (d)(i) of the undertaking)*
(1)	*(2)*	*(3)*	*(4)*	*(5)*
-	-	Applicable or Not applicable	Applicable or Not applicable	Applicable or Not applicable

Part C - Particulars of the appeals or applications or petitions or proceeding under sub-clauses (*ii*) and (*iii*) of clause (*b*) of the undertaking :

Sr. No.	*Sl. No. in Part A where the relevant order is mentioned*	*Nature of appeals or applications or petitions or proceeding*	*Income-tax authority or Authority for Advance Rulings constituted under section 245-O of the Act or the Board for Advance Rulings under section 245-OB or Income-tax Settlement Commission constituted under section 245B or the Interim Board for Settlement constituted under section 245AA or any tribunal or court before whom such appeals or applications or petitions or proceeding has been filed*	*Date of filing the appeals or applications or petitions or proceeding*	*Date of disposing of or withdrawal such appeals or applications or petitions or proceeding (Please attach a copy of order by the income-tax authority or Authority for Advance Rulings constituted under section 245-O of the Act or the Board for Advance Rulings under section 245-OB or Income-tax Settlement Commission constituted under section 245B or the Interim Board for Settlement constituted under section 245AA or any tribunal or court accepting the withdrawal or disposing of)*
(1)	*(2)*	*(3)*	*(4)*	*(5)*	*(6)*

Part D - Particulars of the appeals or applications or petitions or proceeding under sub-clause (*iv*) of clause (*b*) of the undertaking :

Sr. No.	*Sl. No. in Part A where the relevant order is mentioned*	*Nature of appeals or applications or petitions or proceeding*	*Income-tax authority or Authority for Advance Rulings constituted under section 245-O of the Act or the Board for Advance Rulings under section 245-OB or Income-tax Settlement Commission constituted under section 245B or the Interim Board for Settlement constituted under section 245AA or any tribunal or court before whom such appeals or applications or petitions or proceeding has been filed*	*Date of filing the appeals or applications or petitions or proceeding*
(1)	*(2)*	*(3)*	*(4)*	*(5)*

Part E - Particulars of the proceeding for arbitration, conciliation or mediation, or notices under sub-clauses (*ii*) and (*iii*) of clause (*c*) of the undertaking:

Sr. No.	*Sl. No in Part A where the relevant order is mentioned*	*Nature of proceeding for arbitration, conciliation or mediation, or notices thereof with case number or Notice given*	*Particulars (including the name of the country) where such proceeding for arbitration, conciliation or mediation are pending or notices thereof have been issued*	*Date of initiating the proceeding for arbitration, conciliation or mediation/issue of notice*	*Name of the agreement entered into by India under which the proceeding for arbitration, conciliation or mediation are pending*	*Status of the proceeding for arbitration, conciliation or mediation*	*Date of disposing of or withdrawal of such proceeding for arbitration, conciliation or mediation, or notices [Please attach evidence of such disposing of or withdrawal, including order of the Tribunal or court or other judicial or quasi-judicial or administrative authority]*
(1)	*(2)*	*(3)*	*(4)*	*(5)*	*(6)*	*(7)*	*(8)*

Part F - Particulars of the proceeding for arbitration, conciliation or mediation, or notices under sub-clause (*iv*) of clause (*c*) of the undertaking:

Sr. No.	*Sl. No. in Part A where the relevant order is mentioned*	*Nature of proceeding for arbitration, conciliation or mediation, or notices thereof with case number or Notice given*	*Particulars (including the name of the country) where such proceeding for arbitration, conciliation or mediation are pending of notices thereof have been issued*	*Date of initiating the proceeding for arbitration, conciliation or mediation/ issue of notice*	*Name of the agreement entered into by India under which the proceeding for arbitration, conciliation or mediation are pending*	*Status of the proceeding for arbitration, conciliation or mediation*
(1)	*(2)*	*(3)*	*(4)*	*(5)*	*(6)*	*(7)*

Part G - Particulars of the award, order or judgment or any other relief under sub-clause (*v*) of clause (*c*) of the undertaking :

Sr. No.	*Sl. No. in Part A where the relevant order is mentioned*	*Nature of such award, order or judgment or any other relief*	*Particulars (including the name of the country) where proceeding related to such award, order, judgment or any other relief were held*	*Date of such award, order, judgment or any other relief along with reference number*	*Status of the award, order, judgment or any other relief*
(1)	*(2)*	*(3)*	*(4)*	*(5)*	*(6)*

Part H - Particulars of the proceeding to enforce any award, order or judgment or any other relief under sub-clauses (*ii*) and (*iii*) of clause (*d*) of the undertaking:

Sr. No.	*Sl. No. in Part A where the relevant order is men-tioned*	*Nature of proceeding to enforce such award, order or judgment or any other relief*	*Particulars (includ-ing the name of the country) where such proceeding to enforce any award, order or judgment or any other relief are taking place*	*Date of filing proceeding to enforce any award, order or judgment or any other relief*	*Nature of such award, order or judgment or any other relief (Attach copy thereof)*	*Status of the proceeding to enforce such award, order or judgment or any other relief*	*Date of disposing of or with-drawal of proceeding to enforce such award, order or judgment or any other relief [Please attach a copy of evidence of such disposing of/withdrawal, including order of the Court or other judicial authority)]*
(1)	*(2)*	*(3)*	*(4)*	*(5)*	*(6)*	*(7)*	*(8)*

Part I - Particulars of the proceeding to enforce any award, order or judgment or any other relief under sub-clause (*iv*) of clause (*d*) of the undertaking:

Sr. No.	*Sl. No. in Part A where the relevant order is mentioned*	*Nature of proceed-ing to enforce such award, order or judgment or any other relief*	*Particulars (including the name of the country) where such pro-ceeding to enforce any award, order or judgment or any other relief are taking place*	*Date of filing pro-ceeding to enforce any award, order or judgment or any other relief*	*Nature of such award, order or judgment or any other relief (Attach copy thereof)*	*Status of the pro-ceeding to enforce such award, order or judgment or any other relief*
(1)	*(2)*	*(3)*	*(4)*	*(5)*	*(6)*	*(7)*

Part J - Details of bank account in Republic of India to which the refund is to be remitted

Sr. No.	*Bank Name and Address*	*Account Number and other required details for remittance*
(1)	*(2)*	*(3)*

Part K - Details of all the companies or entities in the entire chain of holding of the declarant till the ultimate holding company or entity of the declarant:

Sl. No.	*Name of holding company*	*Percentage of the ownership by such holding company in the declarant as on the date of undertaking*	*If the ownership in the declarant is not held directly by such holding company, the chain of ownership with the names of all the companies in the chain of ownership*
(1)	*(2)*	*(3)*	*(4)*

Part L - Details of all the interested parties other than the interested parties covered under Part K

Sl. No.	*Name of such persons whose interest may be affected directly or indirectly by this undertaking*	*Nature of interest of such person*	*Amount of interest of such person (Rs.), if available*
(1)	*(2)*	*(3)*	*(4)*

Part M- Undertaking by person(s) declared in Part K and Part L of the Undertaking

To,

Principal Commissioner/Commissioner

....

Sir/Madam,

I......................................(name in block letters) son/daughter of .... designation ....and nationality ....and related passport number.................. (hereinafter referred to as signatory) having Permanent Account Number/Aadhaar Number (*see* Note 1)..........................on behalf of .... (name of the interested party) having Permanent Account Number/Aadhaar number/Tax Deduction Account Number (*see* Note 2) .... and being duly authorised and competent to represent the interested party in this regard pursuant to Board Resolution and legal authorisation (*see* Note 3), as the case may be, hereby declare as follows:

(*a*) The particulars of specified orders that have been passed or made in respect of income accruing or arising through or from the transfer of an asset or a capital asset situate in India in consequence of the transfer of a share or interest in a company or entity registered or incorporated outside Republic of India made before the 28th day of May, 2012 in the case of declarant and the nature of interest of the interested party in such specified orders are provided in Part MA of the Annexure.

(*b*) The interested party has (strike off options that are not applicable),

(*i*) not filed any appeal or application or petition or proceeding before any income-tax authority or Authority for Advance Rulings constituted under section 245-O of the Act or the Board for Advance Rulings under section 245-OB or Income-tax Settlement Commission constituted under section 245B or the Interim Board for Settlement constituted under section 245AA or any tribunal or court against the relevant order or orders, and hereby undertakes that it shall not file any appeal, application, petition or proceeding in future against the relevant order or orders. Particulars of such relevant order or orders are provided in Part MB of the Annexure;

(*ii*) filed one or more appeals or applications or petitions or proceeding before any income-tax authority or Authority for Advance Rulings constituted under section 245-O of the Act or the Board for Advance Rulings under section 245-OB or Income-tax Settlement Commission constituted under section 245B or the Interim Board for Settlement constituted under section 245AA or any tribunal or court against the relevant order or orders and has irrevocably, on a with prejudice basis, withdrawn all such appeals or applications or petitions or proceeding or such appeals or applications or petitions or proceeding have been disposed at any time before the date of filing Form No. 1, and hereby undertake that it shall not file any appeal, application, petition or proceeding in future against the relevant order or orders. Particulars of such appeals or applications or petitions or proceeding filed and irrevocably withdrawn with prejudice by the interested party, are provided in Part MC of the Annexure;

(*iii*) filed one or more appeals or applications or petitions or proceeding before any income-tax authority or Authority for Advance Rulings constituted under section 245-O of the Act or the Board for Advance Rulings under section 245-OB or Income-tax Settlement Commission constituted under section 245B or the Interim Board for Settlement constituted under section 245AA or any tribunal or court against the relevant order or orders and all the appeals or applications or petitions or proceeding filed by the interested party have been disposed of and no further appeal or application or petition or proceeding has been filed by the interested party and evidence thereof is furnished herewith and hereby undertake that it shall not file any appeal, application, petition or proceeding in future against the relevant order or orders. Particulars of such appeals or applications or petitions or proceeding filed and disposed of, are provided in Part MC of the Annexure;

(*iv*) filed appeals or applications or petitions or proceeding before any income-tax authority or Authority for Advance Rulings constituted under section 245-O of the Act or the Board for Advance Rulings under section 245-OB or Income-tax Settlement Commission constituted under section 245B or the Interim Board for Settlement constituted under section 245AA or any tribunal or court against the relevant order or orders and one or more of such appeals or applications or petitions or proceeding are pending as on the date of this undertaking and hereby undertakes to irrevocably withdraw, terminate and discontinue any and all such appeals or applications or petitions or proceeding that are pending as on the date of signing this undertaking, on a with prejudice basis, in accordance with clause (*e*) below. The interested party further undertakes that it shall not file any such appeal, application, petition or proceeding in future against the relevant order or orders. Particulars of such pending appeals or applications or petitions or proceeding filed by the interested party and their status as on the date of this undertaking, are provided in Part D of the Annexure. Particulars of any appeals or applications or petitions or proceeding as described in this clause (*b*) which are not covered by the sub-clauses (*i*) and (*ii*) are also provided in Part MD of the Annexure;

(*c*) The interested party has (strike off options that are not applicable),

(*i*) not initiated any proceeding for arbitration, conciliation or mediation, and no notice has been given thereof under any law for the time being in force or under any agreement entered into by Republic of India with any other country or territory outside India, whether for protection of investment or otherwise against the relevant order or orders, and hereby undertakes that it shall not initiate any such arbitration, conciliation or mediation in future. Particulars of such relevant order or orders are provided in Part MB of the Annexure;

(*ii*) initiated proceeding for arbitration, conciliation or mediation, or notices thereof has been given, under any law for the time being in force or under any agreement entered into by India with any other country or territory outside India, whether for protection of investment or otherwise against the relevant order or orders and has irrevocably, on a with prejudice basis, withdrawn any such proceeding for arbitration, conciliation or mediation, and notices given thereof. The interested party hereby undertakes that it shall not reopen in future any such proceeding or initiate or file any such arbitration, conciliation or mediation in future arising out of or in connection with the relevant order or orders. Particulars of such proceeding for arbitration, conciliation or mediation and notices given thereof, initiated and irrevocably withdrawn with prejudice by the interested party, are provided in Part ME of the Annexure;

(*iii*) initiated proceeding for arbitration, conciliation or mediation, or notices thereof has been given, under any law for the time being in force or under any agreement entered into by Republic of India with any other country or territory outside India, whether for protection of investment or otherwise against the relevant order or orders and all the arbitration, conciliation or mediation filed by the interested party have been disposed of and no further proceeding has been initiated by the interested party and evidence thereof is furnished herewith. The interested party hereby undertakes that it shall not reopen in future any such proceeding or initiate or file any such arbitration, conciliation or mediation in future arising out of or in connection with the relevant order or orders. Particulars of such proceeding for arbitration, conciliation or mediation and notices given thereof, initiated and disposed of, are provided in Part ME of the Annexure;

(*iv*) has initiated proceeding for arbitration, conciliation or mediation, or notices thereof has been given, under any law for the time being in force or under any agreement entered into by Republic of India with any other country or territory outside Republic of India, whether for protection of investment or otherwise against the relevant order or orders and one or more of such proceeding or notices are pending on the date of undertaking and hereby undertakes to irrevocably withdraw, terminate and discontinue any and all such proceeding or notices for arbitration, conciliation or mediation that are pending as on the date of signing this undertaking, on a with prejudice basis, in accordance with clause (*e*). Particulars of such pending proceeding and notices filed by the interested party are provided in Part F of the Annexure. The interested party hereby further undertakes that it shall not initiate any such arbitration, conciliation or mediation in future arising out of or in connection with the relevant order or orders. Particulars of any proceeding for arbitration, conciliation or mediation, or notices thereof, which are not covered by the sub-clause (*i*) and sub- clause (*ii*), are also provided in Part MF of the Annexure;

(*v*) received or got any awards, orders, judgments or any other reliefs issued in favour of the interested party, arising out of or in any way relating to the imposition of tax, interest and penalty based on the relevant order or orders, under any agreement entered into by India with any other country or territory outside India, whether for protection of investment or otherwise and hereby undertakes to irrevocably waive any right to seek or pursue any claim or costs or declaratory relief in relation to or arising out of such awards, orders or judgments or any other relief that may have been ordered, issued or passed against India and any Indian affiliate, whether it is in proceeding initiated by the interested party or by India and any Indian affiliate. The interested party also undertakes to irrevocably waive any right to seek or pursue any claim for costs in respect of any proceeding initiated by the Republic to set aside such award, order or judgment issued in favour of the interested party. The interested party hereby undertakes that it shall not initiate or file any such arbitration, conciliation or mediation in future. Particulars of such awards, orders, judgment or any other relief are provided in Part MG of the Annexure;

(*d*) The interested party has (strike off options that are not applicable),

(*i*) not initiated any proceeding to enforce or pursue attachments in connection with any awards, orders, judgments, or any other relief that may have been ordered, issued or passed by any tribunal or court or other judicial, quasi-judicial or administrative authority in relation to the said arbitration, conciliation or mediation proceeding in favour of the interested party as referred to in clause (*c*) of this undertaking either against the Republic of India and any Indian affiliate, and hereby undertakes that it shall not initiate any such proceeding in future. Particulars of such award, order or judgment are provided in Part MB of the Annexure;

(*ii*) initiated proceeding to enforce or pursue attachments in connection with any awards, orders, judgments or any other relief that may have been ordered, issued or passed by any tribunal or court or other judicial, quasi-judicial or administrative authority in relation to the said arbitration, conciliation or mediation proceeding in favour of the interested party, as referred to in clause (*c*) of this undertaking against the Republic of India and any Indian affiliate. The interested party has irrevocably and with prejudice withdrawn or discontinued any such proceeding and hereby undertakes that it shall not reopen any such proceeding in future or file fresh proceeding to enforce or pursue attachments. Particulars of such proceeding, initiated and withdrawn or discontinued by the interested party, are provided in Part MH of the Annexure;

(*iii*) initiated proceeding to enforce or pursue attachments in connection with any awards, orders, judgments or any other relief that may have been ordered, issued or passed by any tribunal or court or other judicial, quasi-judicial or administrative authority in relation to the said arbitration, conciliation or mediation proceeding in favour of the interested party, as referred to in clause (*c*) of this undertaking against the Republic of India and any Indian affiliate. All such proceeding filed by the interested party have been disposed of and no further proceeding has been filed by the interested party and evidence is herewith furnished and hereby undertakes that it shall not reopen any such proceeding in future or file or initiate fresh proceeding to enforce or pursue attachments. Particulars of such proceeding, initiated and disposed of, are provided in Part MH of the Annexure;

(*iv*) initiated proceeding to enforce or pursue attachments in respect of any awards, orders, judgments, or any other relief that may have been ordered, issued or passed by any tribunal or court or other judicial, quasi-judicial or administrative authority in relation to the said arbitration, conciliation or mediation proceeding in favour of the interested party as referred to in clause (*c*) of this undertaking, either against the Republic of India and any Indian affiliate and one or more of such proceeding are pending on the date of undertaking and, interested party has obtained one or more orders from any court or other authority which remain outstanding against India and any Indian affiliate. The interested party hereby undertakes that it shall not file in future any such proceeding to enforce or pursue attachments regarding any awards, orders, judgments, or any other relief that may have been ordered, issued or passed by any tribunal or court or other judicial, quasi-judicial or administrative authority in relation to the said arbitration, conciliation or mediation proceeding in favour of the interested party as referenced in clause (*c*) of this undertaking or to enforce the orders from any court or other authority which remain outstanding against India and any Indian affiliate. The interested party further undertakes to fully cooperate with the Republic of India or any Indian affiliate which is subject to such outstanding order, in order to set-aside or otherwise nullify any such outstanding order, and irrevocably and with prejudice waives any rights or remedies arising from such outstanding order. Particulars of such proceeding, are provided in Part MI of the Annexure. Particulars of any such proceeding, to enforce or pursue attachments in connection with any awards, orders, judgments, or any other relief, which are not covered by the sub-clauses (*i*) and (*ii*), are also provided in Part MI of the Annexure. The interested party also undertakes to irrevocably withdraw, terminate and discontinue with prejudice any and all such proceeding to enforce or pursue attachments in accordance with clause (*e*) below;

(*e*) The interested party hereby undertakes as follows:—

(*i*) to irrevocably and with prejudice withdraw, discontinue, terminate and take all necessary steps to irrevocably and with prejudice close the pending proceeding referred in sub-clause (*iv*) of clause (*b*), sub-clause (*iv*) of clause (*c*), sub-clause (*v*) of clause (*c*) and sub-clause (*iv*) of clause (*d*) of this undertaking, as well as any other pending proceeding against Republic of India or Indian affiliates relating to the relevant order or orders and not referenced in clauses (*b*), (*c*) and (*d*) above, and not to pursue in any way and by any means in future the pending proceeding as referenced in clauses (*b*), (*c*) and (*d*), and any other pending proceeding relating to the relevant order or orders not referred in the above clauses and any other fresh proceeding relating to the relevant order or orders. In so acting, interested party shall act in accordance with this undertaking and in full cooperation with the Republic of India;

(*ii*) to irrevocably terminate, release, discharge, and forever irrevocably waive any right, whether direct or indirect, and any claims, demands, liens, actions, suits, causes of action, obligations, controversies, debts, costs, attorneys' fees, court's fees, expenses, damages, judgments, orders, declaratory reliefs, and liabilities of whatever kind or nature at law, in equity, or otherwise, whether now known or unknown previously (or in future discovered), suspected or unsuspected, and whether or not concealed or hidden, which have existed or may have existed, or do exist or which hereafter can, shall or may exist, in relation to any award, order, judgment, or any other relief as referred in clauses (*b*), (*c*) and (*d*) of this undertaking, against the Republic of India and all Indian affiliates, ordered, issued or passed in connection with the relevant order or orders, whether it is in proceeding initiated by the interested party or by India and any Indian affiliate. For the avoidance of doubt, the interested party's irrevocable waiver includes irrevocable waiver of any right provided by any existing *ex parte*, provisional, or other kind of court order permitting enforcement or attachment against the Republic of India and any Indian affiliate, in furtherance of any award, order judgment, or any other relief that may have been ordered or issued or passed by any arbitral tribunal as referred in clauses (*b*), (*c*) and (*d*). The interested party further undertakes to fully cooperate with the Republic of India or any Indian affiliate which is subject to any outstanding order referenced in clause (*d*), in order to set-aside or otherwise nullify any such outstanding order, and irrevocably and with prejudice waives any rights or remedies arising from such outstanding order. For further avoidance of doubt, the interested party also undertakes to irrevocably waive any right to seek or pursue any claim for costs in respect of any proceeding initiated by Republic of India and any Indian Affiliate to set aside such award, order or judgment ordered, issued or passed in favour of the interested party. Such irrevocable waiver includes, but is not limited to, any right under any relevant *ex parte* order;

(*iii*) to irrevocably waive any right to seek or pursue any claim for costs in respect of any proceeding initiated by the Republic of India to set aside such award, order or judgment, or any other relief issued in favour of the interested party.

(*f*) The interested party specifically represents that all Parts of the Annexure as described in this undertaking are full and complete to the best of its knowledge.

(g) The interested party hereby undertakes to irrevocably terminate, release, discharge, and forever irrevocably waive any right, whether direct or indirect, and any remedies, claims, demands, liens, actions, suits, causes of action, obligations, controversies, debts, costs, attorneys' fees, court's fees, expenses, damages, judgments, orders, compensation, and liabilities of whatever kind or nature at law, in equity, or otherwise, whether now known or unknown, suspected or unsuspected, and whether or not concealed or hidden, which have existed or may have existed, or do exist or which hereafter can, shall or may exist, based on pursuit of any remedy or any and all claims, demands, damages, judgments, awards, costs, expenses, compensation or liabilities of any kind (whether asserted or unasserted) in relation to any facts, events, or omissions occurring from the beginning of time to the date of this undertaking and thereafter in future in relation to taxation of said income or relevant order or orders, or any related award, judgment or court order, which may otherwise be available to the interested party under any law for the time being in force, in equity, under any statute or under any agreement entered into by India with any country or territory outside India, whether for protection of investment or otherwise, whether it is in proceeding initiated by the interested party or by India and any Indian affiliate. For the avoidance of doubt, the interested party's above waiver includes an irrevocable waiver of any claim against India and any Indian affiliate to costs incurred or interest accrued in relation to the relevant order or orders, or any related ongoing or completed litigation, arbitration, conciliation or mediation. Moreover, for the avoidance of any doubt, the interested party hereby undertakes to forgo any reliance on any right under any award, judgment, or court order pertaining to the relevant order or orders or under the relevant order or orders.

(*h*) The interested party further represents that as of the date of this undertaking, it has not transferred any of its claims under any award, judgment, or court order pertaining to the relevant order or orders or under the relevant order or orders, or granted any rights, to third parties, and further undertakes to not transfer any of its claims to third parties after entering this undertaking.

(*i*) In the event that, notwithstanding the foregoing, any person asserts, brings, files or maintains any claim against the Republic of India or Indian affiliates (hereinafter collectively referred to as releases) at any time on or after the date of furnishing this undertaking, the interested party shall indemnify, defend and hold harmless such release from and against any and all costs, expenses (including attorneys' fees and court's fees), interest, damages and liabilities of any nature arising out of or in any way relating to the assertion or, bringing, filing or maintaining of such claim. The interested party specifically represents that, to the best of its knowledge, after—

(*i*) the execution of this undertaking;

(*ii*) the execution of any separate related undertaking by any other party in connection with the relevant order or orders; and

(*iii*) irrevocable withdrawal of all pending proceeding as outlined in this undertaking,

no other claim regarding the said relevant order or orders referenced above, or any related award, judgment, or court order, shall remain outstanding against the Republic of India or any Indian affiliate. To avoid any doubt, the interested party's indemnity of releases shall include any claim brought by any third party alleging that it has obtained the interested party's claims under an award, judgment or court order or the relevant order or orders. An indemnity bond to this effect is attached in Part N of the undertaking.

(*j*) For the avoidance of any doubt, the interested party fully assumes the risk through the indemnity in clause (*i*) of any omission or mistake with respect to securing releases against any related claim by any person. If the interested party fails to obtain any release from such person, the interested party warrants that it will indemnify the Republic of India or any Indian affiliates from any defense costs, court costs, and damages. An indemnity bond to the effect of clauses (*i*) and (*j*) is annexed to the undertaking.

(*k*) The interested party further undertakes to refrain from facilitating, procuring, encouraging or otherwise assisting any party (including but not limited to any related party) from bringing any proceeding or claims of any kind referred to in the above clauses, or any proceeding or claim of any kind related to any relevant order or orders referred to above (whether in respect of tax, interest or penalty). The interested party shall notify by a public notice or press release, at any time before furnishing intimation in Form No. 3 where Form No.3 is required to be furnished under rule 11UF and before furnishing this undertaking in other cases, that by signing this undertaking any claims arising out of or relating to the relevant order or orders or any related award, judgment or court order, no longer subsist. Such public notice shall include, among other things, confirmation that,—

(*i*) the interested party forever irrevocably forgoes any reliance on any right and provisions under any award, judgment, or court order pertaining to the relevant order or orders or under the relevant order or orders;

(*ii*) the interested party has provided this undertaking, which includes a complete release of the Republic of India and any Indian Affiliate with respect to any award, judgment, or court order pertaining to the relevant order or orders or under the relevant order or orders, and with respect to any claim pertaining to the relevant order or orders;

(*iii*) the undertaking also includes an indemnity against any claims brought against the Republic of India or any Indian affiliate contrary to the release; and

(*iv*) the interested party confirms it will treat any such award, judgment, or court order as null and void and without legal effect to the same extent as if it had been set aside by a competent court and will not take any action or initiate any proceeding or bring any claim based on that.

(*l*) The interested party confirms that the undertakings given herein are intended to be enforceable by the Republic of India, including so as to secure the irrevocable waiver, withdrawal or discontinuance (as appropriate) of all the proceeding and claims referred to in any of the clauses of this undertaking.

(*m*) The interested party represents and warrants that:

(*i*) it has full legal power and authority to execute and deliver this undertaking (including but not limited to the issuance of the indemnity described in clauses (*i*) and (*j*) under applicable law;

(*ii*) the execution, delivery and performance of this undertaking (including but not limited to the issuance of the indemnity described in clauses (*i*) and (*j*) has been duly authorised by all necessary corporate action, including but not limited to any board resolution or similar authorisation under applicable law (*see* Note 3);

(*iii*) this undertaking constitutes the legal, valid and binding obligation of the interested party, enforceable against the interested party in accordance with its terms;

(*iv*) such authorisations described in the above sub-clauses (*i*), (*ii*) and (*iii*) are effective under applicable law, and to this end, letters from local counsel in the relevant jurisdictions are attached to this undertaking which confirm the legality of such authorisations under applicable law; and (*n*) This undertaking is governed by relevant Indian law and any dispute with respect to this undertaking shall be subject to Indian laws and be decided in accordance with the procedures specified in the Act under the exclusive jurisdiction of the relevant income-tax authorities, tribunals or courts in India, as the case may be, which are empowered to decide disputes under the Act.

I also confirm that, I am aware of all the consequences and implications of this undertaking.

Place: ....

Date: ....

Signature

....

Attachments:

1. The Board Resolution and legal authorisation, as referred to in clause (*m*) of Part M.
2. An indemnity bond to the effect of clauses (*i*) and (*j*) of Part M in Part N of the undertaking in Form No. 1.
3. Copy of the public notice referred to in clause (*k*) of Part M, where Form No. 3 is not required to be furnished under sub-rule (6) of rule 11UF.
4. Attachments as required in different parts of the Annexure to Part M of this undertaking.

Notes:

1. This information is required to be furnished where the Permanent Account Number or Aadhaar Number of the signatory is available.
2. Company Identification Number and Taxpayer Identification Number are to be provided where Permanent Account Number/Aadhaar Number or Tax Deduction Account Number of the interested party are not available.
3. The Board Resolution or legal authorisation, as referred to in clause (*m*) of the undertaking shall, among other things:
   (*a*) record the Signatory's power and authority to give the undertaking on behalf of the interested party; and
   (*b*) record the interested party's power and authority to indemnify defend and hold harmless the Republic of India and the Indian affiliates in accordance with clause (*i*) of the undertaking.

Verification

Verified that the contents of this undertaking are true to the best of my knowledge and belief. No part of the undertaking is false and nothing has been concealed or misstated therein.

Verified at .... place .... on this the .... day .... of.................... month .... year ....

Place: ....

Date: ....

Signature

....

Annexure

Part MA- Particulars of the relevant order or orders:

Sl. No.	*Assessment Year or Financial year*	*Income-tax Authority passing the order*	*Details of the order under consideration*		*Nature of interest of the interested party*
			Section and sub-section of the Income-tax Act, 1961	*Date of order*	
(1)	*(2)*	*(3)*	*(4)*	*(5)*	*(6)*

Part MB- Particulars of the relevant order or orders covered by sub-clause (*i*) of clauses (*b*), (*c*) and (*d*) of the undertaking :

Sl. No.	*Sl. No. in Part MA where the relevant order is mentioned*	*No appeal or application or petition or proceeding before any Income-tax authority or Authority for Advance Rulings constituted under section 245-O of the Act or the Board for Advance Rulings under section 245-OB or Income-tax Settlement Commission constituted under section 245B or the Interim Board for Settlement constituted under section 245AA or any tribunal or court has been filed (refer clause (b)(i) of the undertaking)*	*No proceeding has been initiated for arbitration, conciliation or mediation, and no notice has been given thereof under any law for the time being in force or under any agreement entered into by India with any other country or territory outside India, whether for protection of investment or otherwise (refer clause (c)(i) of the undertaking)*	*No proceeding initiated to enforce or pursue attachments in connection with any award, order or judgment, any other relief that may have been ordered or issued or passed by any tribunal or court or other judicial or administrative authority in relation to the said arbitration, conciliation or mediation proceeding in favour of the interested party against the Republic of India and Indian affiliates (refer clause (d)(i) of the undertaking)*
(1)	*(2)*	*(3)*	*(4)*	*(5)*
		Applicable or Not applicable	*Applicable or Not applicable*	*Applicable or Not applicable*

Part MC- Particulars of the appeals or applications or petitions or proceeding under sub-clauses (*ii*) and (*iii*) of clause (*b*) of the undertaking :

Sl. No.	*Sl. No. in Part MA where the relevant order is mentioned*	*Nature of appeals or applications or petitions or proceeding*	*Income-tax authority or Authority for Advance Rulings constituted under section 245-O of the Act or the Board for Advance Rulings under section 245-OB or Income-tax Settlement Commission constituted under section 245B or the Interim Board for Settlement constituted under section 245AA or any tribunal or court before whom such appeals or applications or petitions or proceeding has been filed*	*Date of filing the appeals or applications or petitions or proceeding*	*Date of disposing of or withdrawal such appeals or applications or petitions or proceeding (Please attach a copy of order by the income-tax authority or Authority for Advance Rulings constituted under section 245-O of the Act or the Board for Advance Rulings under section 245-OB or Income-tax Settlement Commission constituted under section 245B or the Interim Board for Settlement constituted under section 245AA or any tribunal or court accepting the withdrawal or disposing of)*
(1)	*(2)*	*(3)*	*(4)*	*(5)*	*(6)*

Part MD- Particulars of the appeals or applications or petitions or proceeding under sub-clause (*iv*) of clause (*b*) of the undertaking :

Sl. No.	*Sl. No. in Part MA where the relevant order is mentioned*	*Nature of appeals or applications or petitions or proceeding*	*Income-tax authority or Authority for Advance Rulings constituted under section 245-O of the Act or the Board for Advance Rulings under section 245-OB or Income-tax Settlement Commission constituted under section 245B or the Interim Board for Settlement constituted under section 245AA or any tribunal or court before whom such appeals or applications or petitions or proceeding has been filed*	*Date of filing the appeals or applications or petitions or proceeding*
(1)	*(2)*	*(3)*	*(4)*	*(5)*

Part ME- Particulars of the proceeding for arbitration, conciliation or mediation, or notices under sub-clauses (*ii*) and (*iii*) of clause (*c*) of the undertaking :

Sl. No.	*Sl. No Part MA where the relevant order is mentioned*	*Nature of proceeding for arbitration, conciliation or mediation, or notices thereof with case number or notice given*	*Particulars (including the name of the country) where such proceeding for arbitration, conciliation or mediation are pending or notices thereof have been issued*	*Date of initiating the proceeding for arbitration, conciliation or mediation/issue of notice*	*Name of the agreement entered into by India under which the proceeding for arbitration, conciliation or mediation are pending*	*Status of the proceeding for arbitration, conciliation or mediation*	*Date of disposing of or withdrawal of such proceeding for arbitration, conciliation or mediation, or notices [Please attach evidence of such disposing of or withdrawal, including order of the Tribunal or court or other judicial or quasi-judicial or administrative authority]*
(1)	*(2)*	*(3)*	*(4)*	*(5)*	*(6)*	*(7)*	*(8)*

Part MF – Particulars of the proceeding for arbitration, conciliation or mediation, or notices under sub-clause (*iv*) of clause (*c*) of the undertaking:

Sl. No.	*Sl. No. in Part MA where the relevant order is mentioned*	*Nature of proceeding for arbitration, conciliation or mediation, or notices thereof with case number or notice given*	*Particulars (Including the name of the country) where such proceeding for arbitration, conciliation or mediation are pending of notices thereof have been issued*	*Date of initiating the proceeding for arbitration, conciliation or mediation or issue of notice*	*Name of the agreement entered into by India under which the proceeding for arbitration, conciliation or mediation are pending*	*Status of the proceeding for arbitration, conciliation or mediation*
(1)	*(2)*	*(3)*	*(4)*	*(5)*	*(6)*	*(7)*

Part MG- Particulars of the award, order or judgment or any other relief under sub-clause (*v*) of clause (*c*) of the undertaking :

Sl. No.	*Sl. No. in Part MA where the relevant order is mentioned*	*Nature of such award, order or judgment or any other relief*	*Particulars (including the name of the country) where proceeding related to such award, order, judgment or any other relief were held*	*Date of such award, order, judgment or any other relief along with reference number*	*Status of the award, order, judgment or any other relief*
(1)	*(2)*	*(3)*	*(4)*	*(5)*	*(6)*

Part MH- Particulars of the proceeding to enforce any award, order or judgment or any other relief under sub-clauses (*ii*) and (*iii*) of clause (*d*) of the undertaking:

Sl. No.	*Sl. No. in Part MA where the relevant order is mentioned*	*Nature of proceeding to enforce such award, order or judgment or any other relief*	*Particulars (Including the name of the country)where such proceeding to enforce any award, order or judgment or any other relief are taking place*	*Date of filing proceeding to enforce any award, order or judgment or any other relief*	*Nature of such award, order or judgment or any other relief (Attach copy thereof)*	*Status of the proceeding to enforce such award, order or judgment or any other relief*	*Date of disposing of/withdrawal of proceeding to enforce such award, order or judgment or any other relief (Please attach a copy of evidence of such disposing of or withdrawal, including order of the Court or other judicial authority)*
(1)	*(2)*	*(3)*	*(4)*	*(5)*	*(6)*	*(7)*	*(8)*

Part MI- Particulars of the proceeding under sub-clause (*iv*) of clause (*d*) of the undertaking :

Sl. No.	*Sl. No. in Part MA where the relevant order is mentioned*	*Nature of proceeding to enforce such award, order or judgment or any other relief*	*Particulars (including the name of the country)where such proceeding to enforce any award, order or judgment or any other relief are taking place*	*Date of filing proceeding to enforce any award, order or judgment or any other relief*	*Nature of such award, order or judgment or any other relief (Attach copy thereof)*	*Status of the proceeding to enforce such award, order or judgment or any other relief*
(1)	*(2)*	*(3)*	*(4)*	*(5)*	*(6)*	*(7)*

Part N - Indemnity Bond

This Indemnity Bond ("**Bond**") is made on this .... day of ...., 2021 by .... (name in block letters) son/daughter of .... designation and nationality .... and related passport number .... (hereinafter referred to as "**Signatory**") having Permanent Account Number/Aadhaar Number/Tax Deduction Account Number (*See* Note 1)__________on behalf of .... (name of the declarant or interested party, as the case may be) having Permanent Account Number/Aadhaar number/Tax Deduction Account Number .... (*See* Note 2) and being duly authorised and competent to represent the declarant or interested party, as the case may be, in this regard pursuant to Board Resolution or legal authorisation (*See* Note 3), of the **FIRST PART**.

And

The Republic of India and any Indian affiliate (hereinafter collectively referred to as "**releasees**") of the **OTHER PART**.

WHEREAS :

A. The Income-tax Rules, 1962 have been amended and the Income-tax (31st Amendment) Rules, 2021 have come into force from the date of their publication in the Official Gazette.

B. The declarant or interested party, as the case may be, has filed an undertaking under sub-rule (1) of rule 11UE of the Income-tax Rules, 1962, to which this indemnity bond is annexed. Any defined terms not defined herein shall have the same meaning as the definitions given under rule 11UE and the undertaking.

C. Pursuant to the above, the declarant or interested party, as the case may be, has agreed to indemnify, defend and hold harmless the Republic of India and Indian affiliates from and against any and all costs, expenses (including attorney fees and court fees), interest, damages, and liabilities of any nature arising out of or in any way relating to the assertion or, bringing, filing or maintaining of any claim at any time after the date of furnishing the undertaking in Form No.1 by any person, related to any relevant order or orders, or in relation to any award, order, judgment, or any other relief, or to any dispute underlying the award, and the declarant or interested party, as the case may be, has agreed to furnish an indemnity bond to this effect, such that the declarant or interested party, as the case may be, fully assumes the risk of any omission or mistake with respect to identification and procurement of authorisations and undertakings from any related parties or interested parties as provided in the undertaking, and securing the Republic of India and Indian affiliates from any claim related to any relevant order or orders, or in relation to any award, order, judgment, or any other relief or to the dispute underlying the award against the Republic of India or Indian affiliates in connection with the relevant order or orders.

D. Accordingly the declarant or interested party, as the case may be, is executing this Indemnity Bond in favour of the Republic of India on the terms appearing hereunder.

NOW THIS INDEMNITY BOND WITNESSETH AS FOLLOWS:

1. In the event that any person or entity asserts, brings, files or maintains any claim against any release at any time on or after the date of furnishing this undertaking, related to any relevant order or orders or in relation to any award, order, judgment, or any other relief, or to any dispute underlying the award, against the Republic of India or Indian affiliates in connection with

the relevant order or orders, the declarant or interested party, as the case may be, shall indemnify, defend and hold harmless such releases from and against any and all costs, expenses (including attorney fees and court fees), interest, damages, and liabilities of any nature arising out of or in any way relating to the assertion or, bringing, filing or maintaining of such claim.

2. The declarant or interested party, as the case may be, specifically represents that, to the best of its knowledge, after —

   (*i*) the execution of this undertaking;

   (*ii*) the execution of any separate related undertaking by any other party in connection with the relevant order or orders; and

   (*iii*) withdrawal of all pending proceeding as outlined in this undertaking,

   that no other claim regarding the said relevant order or orders referenced above, or any related award, judgment, or court order, or any aspect of the dispute underlying the award shall remain outstanding against the Republic of India or other release.

   Explanation I.—For the removal of any doubt, the declarant's or interested party's indemnity of releases under this clause shall include any claim brought by any third party alleging that it has obtained declarant's or interested party's, as the case may be, claims under an award, judgment or court order or the relevant order or orders.

   Explanation II.—The declarant or interested party, as the case may be, fully assumes the risk through this indemnity of any omission or mistake with respect to securing releases against any related claim by any person. If the declarant or interested party, as the case may be, fails to obtain any release from such person, the declarant or interested party, as the case may be, indemnifies through this document the releases from any defence costs, court costs, and damages.

3. This Indemnity Bond shall be governed by the relevant laws of India and the Delhi High Court shall have sole jurisdiction to entertain and try any dispute or difference arising out of or in connection with the terms of this Bond.

IN WITNESS WHEREOF the undersigned herein has signed and set his hands on this .... day of ...., 2021.

For and on behalf of the declarant or interested party, as the case may be,

....

Name and address of Witness   *Signature of the Witness*

1.

2.

Place: ....

Date: ....

Notes:

1. This information is required to be furnished where the Permanent Account Number or Aadhaar Number of the signatory is available.

2. Company Identification Number and Taxpayer Identification Number are to be provided where Permanent Account Number or Aadhaar Number or Tax

Deduction Account Number of the declarant or interested party, as the case may be, are not available.

3. The Board Resolution or legal authorisation, as referred to in clause (*m*) of the undertaking shall, among other things:
   (*a*) record the signatory's power and authority to give the undertaking on behalf of the declarant or interested party, as the case may be; and
   (*b*) record the declarant or interested party's power and authority, as the case may be, to indemnify defend and hold harmless the Republic of India and the Indian affiliates in accordance with clause (*i*) of the undertaking

FORM NO. 2

[*See* rule 11UF]

Form for Certificate under sub-rule (2) of rule 11UF

<Name of the declarant>

Address of the declarant

Sir/Madam

1. The .... (name of the declarant) (hereinafter referred to as the declarant) with Permanent Account Number/Aadhaar number/Tax Deduction Account Number/Company Identification Number and Taxpayer Identification Number...................................has filed an undertaking in Form No. 1 dated .... under .... sub-rule (1) of the rule 11UE of the rules.
2. Pursuant to the undertaking filed by the declarant in Form No. 1 under sub-rule (1) of rule 11UE, the provisions of fifth proviso to *Explanation* 5 to clause (*i*) of sub-section (1) of section 9 of the Act shall be applicable to the orders mentioned below, subject to the fulfilment of the conditions specified in said proviso read with relevant rules and fulfilment of the undertakings by the declarant in Form No.1:

TABLE

Sl. No.	*Sl. No. of the Table in Part A of Form No. 1 where the relevant order is mentioned*	*Assessment year or Financial year*	*Income-tax authority passing the order*	*Details of the order under consideration*		*Taxes or penalty determined*	*Interest*	*Total demand*	*Relief, provided in any appeal proceeding, if any*	*Demand recovered from the declarant*	*Pending demand or refund due as on date*	*Details of the attachments made by any income-tax authority*
				Section and sub-section of the Income-tax Act, 1961	*Date of order*							
(1)	*(2)*	*(3)*	*(4)*	*(5)*	*(6)*	*(7)*	*(8)*	*(9)*	*(10)*	*(11)*	*(12)*	*(13)*

3. Demand recovered, as per the column (11) of the Table above, shall be refunded to the declarant, subject to the conditions under sub-rule (2) of the rule 11UE and the provisions of the Act, without any interest as per the provisions of the sixth proviso to *Explanation* 5 to clause (*i*) of sub-section (1) of section 9 of the Act, attachments, if any, the details whereof are provided in column (13) of the Table, shall be revoked and appeals or applications or petitions or proceeding, if any, filed by any income-tax authority or any other person representing the Republic of India with respect to the specified orders, as per column (2) of the Table, shall be withdrawn or intimation shall be sent to the concerned person, on the issue of Form No. 4, as per the procedure provided in sub- rule (16) of rule 11UF. Further, no interest under section 244A of the Act will be payable to the declarant as per the provisions of sixth proviso to *Explanation 5* to clause (*i*) of sub-section (1) of section 9 of the Act.

Certificate No. ....

Place: ....

Date: ....

(Principal Commissioner/Commissioner of Income-tax)

FORM NO. 3

[*See* rule 11UF]

Intimation for withdrawal under sub-rule (3) of rule 11UF

To,

The Principal Commissioner/Commissioner

....

Sir/Madam,

I.. (name in block letters) son/daughter of .... designation ....and nationality ....and related passport number.................. (hereinafter referred to as signatory) having Permanent Account Number/ Aadhaar Number ....(*see* Note 1) on behalf of ....(name of the declarant) having Permanent Account Number/Aadhaar number/Tax Deduction Account Number (*see* Note 2) .... and being duly authorised and competent to represent the declarant in this regard pursuant to Board Resolution and legal authorisation (*see* Note 3), as the case may be, hereby confirm that the declarant has received an order in Form No. 2 dated ....

Pursuant thereto, I confirm that the pending appeals or applications or petitions, arbitration, conciliation, mediation, claims or other proceeding, if any, as referred in Part D, Part F, Part G, Part I and Part M of the undertaking in Form No.1 dated...... have been irrevocably, on a with prejudice basis, withdrawn or discontinued and are not being pursued. The evidence of action taken in this regard are enclosed herewith.

Place: ....

Date: .... *Signature/Verification*

Attachments:

1. Attach the Board Resolution or legal authorisation, as the case may be, as referred to in clause (*m*) of the undertaking.

2. Attach the evidence of action taken as referred above.

Verification

Verified that the contents of this intimation are true to the best of my knowledge and belief. No part of the intimation is false and nothing has been concealed or misstated therein.

Verified at .... place .... on this the .... day .... of .... month .... year ....

Place: ....

Date: ....

Signature

....

Notes:

1. This information is required to be furnished where the Permanent Account Number or Aadhaar Number of the signatory is available.

2. Company Identification Number and Taxpayer Identification Number are to be provided where Permanent Account Number or Aadhaar Number or Tax Deduction Account Number of the interested party are not available.

3. The Board Resolution or legal authorisation, as referred to in clause (*m*) of the undertaking and such Board resolution or legal authorisation shall, among other things :

(*a*) record the signatory's power and authority to give the undertaking on behalf of the interested party; and

(*b*) record the interested party's power and authority to indemnify defend and hold harmless the Republic of India and the Indian affiliates in accordance with clause (*i*) of the undertaking).

FORM NO. 4

[*See* rule 11UF]

Order by Principal Commissioner or Commissioner under sub-rule (7) of rule 11UF

Whereas..(Name and Permanent Account Number/ Aadhaar number/Tax Deduction Account Number/Company Identification Number and Taxpayer Identification Number of the declarant) (hereinafter referred to as declarant) had furnished undertaking under clause (*a*) of the rule 11UE, which was received on ....(Date);

and whereas Form No. 2 dated .... was issued to the declarant as per sub-rule (2) of rule 11UF.

The declarant has filed the intimation in Form No. 3 dated .... as per sub-rule (3) of the rule 11UF or the case of the declarant is covered under sub-rule (6) of rule 11UF.

Now, therefore, in exercise of the powers conferred by sub-rule (7) of rule 11UF, it is hereby certified that the following specified orders shall be deemed to have never been passed and refund determined as per column (12) of the Table shall be issued to the declarant, and the attachments, if any, as per column (13) of the Table shall be revoked, to the extent they relate to the specified orders mentioned in the Table below :

TABLE

Sl. No.	*Sl. No. of the Table in Form No.2*	*Assessment year/or Financial year*	*Income-tax authority passing the order*	*Details of the order under consideration*		*Taxes or Penalty determined*	*Interest*	*Total demand**	*Relief, provided in any appeal proceeding, if any*	*Demand recovered from the declarant*	*Refund determined in pursuance of this order*	*Attachments made by any income-tax authority to be revoked in pursuance of this order*
				Section and sub-section of the Income-tax Act, 1961	*Date of order*							
(1)	*(2)*	*(3)*	*(4)*	*(5)*	*(6)*	*(7)*	*(8)*	*(9)*	*(10)*	*(11)*	*(12)*	*(13)*

Further, no interest under section 244A of the Act will be payable to the declarant as per the provisions of sixth proviso to *Explanation 5* to clause (*i*) of sub-section (1) of section 9 of the Act.

The Assessing Officer is directed to give effect to above and pass an order and issue the refund, if any, and revoke attachments, if any, and withdraw any appeals or applications or petitions or proceeding, filed by any income-tax authority or intimate the concerned person, where appeals or applications or petitions or proceeding has been filed by any other person representing the Republic of India, with respect to the specified orders mentioned in column (2) of the Table, within a period of fifteen days from the date of the receipt of such order.

Place: ....

Date: ....

(Principal Commissioner/Commissioner of Income-tax)

To

(1) The declarant

(2) Assessing Officer

(3) Concerned Appellate Forum.

APPENDIX 2

PROVISIONAL COLLECTION OF TAXES ACT, 2023

[NO. 50 OF 2023]

An Act to provide for the immediate effect for a limited period of provisions in Bills relating to the imposition or increase of duties of customs or excise.

BE it enacted by Parliament in the Seventy-fourth Year of the Republic of India as follows:—

Short title.

1. This Act may be called the Provisional Collection of Taxes Act, 2023.

Definition.

2. In this Act, a "declared provision" means a provision in a Bill in respect of which a declaration has been made under section 3.

Power of Central Government to make declaration.

3. Where a Bill to be introduced in Parliament on behalf of the Government provides for the imposition or increase of a duty of customs or excise with or without change in tariff classification, the Central Government may cause to be inserted in the Bill a declaration that it is expedient in the public interest that any provision of the Bill relating to such imposition or increase shall have immediate effect under this Act.

Effect of declarations under this Act, and duration thereof.

4. (1) A declared provision shall have the force of law immediately on the expiry of the day on which the Bill containing it is introduced.

(2) A declared provision shall cease to have the force of law under the provisions of this Act—

(*a*) when it comes into operation as an enactment, with or without amendment;

(*b*) when the Central Government, in pursuance of a motion passed by Parliament, directs, by notification in the Official Gazette, that it shall cease to have the force of law; or

(*c*) if it has not already ceased to have the force of law under clause (*a*) or clause (*b*), then on the expiry of the seventy-fifth day after the day on which the Bill containing it was introduced.

Refunds to be made in certain cases.

5. (1) Where a declared provision comes into operation as an enactment in an amended form before the expiry of the seventy-fifth day after the day on which the Bill containing it was introduced, refunds shall be made of all duties collected which would not have been collected if the provision adopted in the enactment had been the declared provision:

Provided that the rate at which refunds of any duty may be made under this sub-section shall not exceed the difference between the rate of such duty proposed in the declared provision and the rate of such duty in force when the Bill was introduced.

(2) Where a declared provision ceases to have the force of law under clause (*b*) or clause (*c*) of sub-section (2) of section 4, refunds shall be made of all duties collected which would not have been collected if the declaration in respect of it had not been made.

Repeal.

6. The Provisional Collection of Taxes Act, 1931 (16 of 1931) is hereby repealed.